EDUCATION AND TEACHER PROFESSIONALISM

EDUCATION AND TEACHER PROFESSIONALISM

Study of Teachers and Classroom Processes

STHABIR KHORA

RAWAT PUBLICATIONS
Jaipur • New Delhi • Bangalore • Hyderabad • Guwahati

ISBN 978-81-316-0421-2

Published by
Prem Rawat for **Rawat Publications**
Satyam Apts, Sector 3, Jawahar Nagar, Jaipur 302 004 (India)
Phone: 0141 265 1748 / 7006 Fax: 0141 265 1748
E-mail: info@rawatbooks.com
Website: www.rawatbooks.com

New Delhi Office
4858/24, Ansari Road, Daryaganj, New Delhi 110 002
Phone: 011 2326 3290

Also at *Bangalore, Hyderabad* and *Guwahati*

Typeset by Sangnee Media Solutions Pvt. Ltd., Noida

Printed at Chaman Enterprises, New Delhi

CONTENTS

List of Tables and Figures ix
List of Appendices xi
Glossary xiii
Acknowledgements xv

1

WHAT IS EDUCATION? **1**
Introduction 1
Philosophical Perspectives: The Aims of Education 1
  Liberal or Technical Education 1
  Humanism 3
  Indigenous Orientation 5
Philosophical Perspectives: Important Factors in the Process of Education 6
  Importance of Environment in Education 6
  Education and Freedom 9
  Education and Experience 10
  Learning in Stages 11
Sociological Perspectives 13
  The Functional Paradigm 13
  Bourdieu's Theory of Cultural Capital 14
  Bernstein's Theory of Invisible Pedagogy 15
  Althusser's Ideological State Apparatus 16
  Illich's Deschooling Society 16
  Archer's Centralized and Decentralized School Systems 17
  Freire's Critical Consciousness 18
  Apple's Hidden Curriculum 18
  Giroux's Critical Pedagogy 19
Education: Towards a Definition 21

2

WHAT IS TEACHER PROFESSIONALISM? 26
The Taxonomic Approach to Professions 26
The Criticism of the Taxonomic Approach 32
The Power Approach 33
Professionalism and the Contemporary Society: Lack of Trust and Consequent Hybrid Professionalism 34
Teaching as a Profession: The Taxonomic Approach 36
Difference between Teaching and Other Professions: The Debate within the Taxonomic Approach 37
Outright Rejection of the Taxonomy Approach with Regard to Teaching as a Profession 38
Teacher Professionalism 40
Teacher Professionalism: Difference between the Indian and the Western Context 42

3

THE STATE AND TEACHER PROFESSIONALISM 46
Introduction 46
A Brief History of Teacher Education 47
- Teacher Education in India: A Historical Overview 50
- Teacher Education in Post-Independent India 52
- National Policy on Education, 1986 54
- National Council for Teacher Education 56
- Model Teacher Education Curriculum 57

The State and Teacher Education 60
- Pre-Service Education 60
- Teacher Professional Development 62
- Teaching Standards: What to Teach 68
- Workload of Teachers 69
- Salary 71
- Status 72

The State and Teachers' Organizations 76
- Teachers' Organizations in India 77
- The State and Teacher Unions in Other Countries of the World 83

Conclusion 85

4

DEVELOPMENT OF EDUCATION IN ORISSA **86**
The Historical Legacy 86
Growth of Schooling 87
The Pre-independence Period 87
The Post-independence Period: Till 1960 90
Education between 1960 and 1980 92
School Education in the 1990s 93
Education after 2000 95
Elementary Education in Contemporary Orissa 96
Education of Scheduled Castes (SCs) and Scheduled Tribes (STs) 98
Literacy Programmes 100
Teacher Education 103
Pre-independence Period 103
Post-independence Period 104
Teacher Education in Contemporary Orissa 107
The Financial Support to Primary Education: Walking the Tightrope 108
The Educational Backwardness of the Koraput and Western Districts: The Issue of Poverty 110
Conclusion: The Continuing Concern 112

5

TEACHER PROFESSIONALISM IN RURAL AREAS: A CASE OF LAXMIPUR IN ORISSA **114**
The Problem: Teacher Professionalism—Much Needed But Unexplored Area 114
The Methodology of the Study 116
Tools of Data Collection 118
The Selection Procedure of Teachers 118
The Field Site: Introduction to Laxmipur 119
The Categorization of Teachers 124

6

FACETS OF TEACHER PROFESSIONALISM: SUBJECT KNOWLEDGE, TEACHING SKILLS AND DISCIPLINE STYLE **130**
Subject Knowledge 130
Teaching Skills 133
Teaching in the Classroom: Voice and Language 137
Discipline Style 139
Conclusion 144

7

TEACHER PROFESSIONALISM IN SCHOOL AND LOCAL CONTEXTS **145**
Introduction 145
Teacher Professionalism and the School Infrastructure 146
Teacher Professionalism and the School Sub-culture 150
Teacher Professionalism and the Sub-cultures amongst the Teachers 152
The Attitude Towards the Tribals 155
Facets of Teacher Professionalism in the Locality 157
Various Degrees of Professionalism 157
Regularity as an End in Itself 159
The Culture of Excuse 159
The Issue of Local and Non-local Teachers 160
The Importance of Location 160
The View about Dedication and Teaching 161
Conclusion 162

8

THE TEACHER AND THE EXTERNAL CONTEXT **166**
Views on Authority 166
Views on Teacher Organization 168
Views on Award 170
Views on Salary 171

9

CONCLUSION
Emerging Contours 177

Appendices 181
Bibliography 220
Index 241

LIST OF TABLES AND FIGURES

Tables

2.1	Teacher autonomy and collaboration with the public to increase professionalism	29
2.2	Different reactions to pressured professionalism	35
2.3	Ingredients of hybridized professionalism in public domains	35
3.1	Progress on teacher education schemes	55
3.2	Pre-service training of teachers for different levels of education	58
3.3	The five models of staff development: their assumptions	63
3.4	Teacher professional development model	64
3.5	Chronology of the oldest teacher's organizations in India	79
4.1	Growth of schools in Orissa in pre-independence period	90
4.2	Access to pre-primary education in Orissa	97
4.3	Literacy rates of some of the primitive tribes of Orissa	99
4.4	Progress of hostel facilities for tribal children in Orissa	99
4.5	Districtwise distribution of schools for tribal children	100
4.6	Progress of total literacy campaign till October 1992	103
5.1	Indicators related to population, education and teachers in Laxmipur	121
5.2	Profile of teachers in the study	122
5.3	Categorization of teachers in this study	128
6.1	Subject knowledge, Teaching style, Discipline style and Teacher-child relationship	141
7.1	Professionalism amongst head teachers	154
7.2	Teachers and their attitudes towards the tribals	158
7.3	Teachers and dominant themes of their lives	163
8.1	Teachers' views on salary, authority, teacher organization and award	174

Figures

3.1	Relationship between the state and teacher professionalism	47
3.2	Hypothetical determinants of the occupational prestige of teaching	73

4.1 Administrative set up of school education in Orissa 96

5.1 Teacher professionalism 125

5.2 Teachers along a continuum of regularity and making an effort to teach 127

7.1 Teacher professionalism, the school and the local context 146

LIST OF APPENDICES

3.1	Development of teacher education institutions in India	181
3.2	Comparison of salary in different countries	182
3.2.1	Teachers' salaries in US dollars (PPP) at starting salary, after 15 years of experience and at the top of the salary scale, with minimum level of training, by level of education	182
3.2.2	Teachers' salaries in relative terms/Teachers' salaries in US dollars (PPP) as a percentage of GDP per capita, at starting salary, after 15 years of experience and at the top of the salary scale, with minimum level of training, by level of education	184
3.3	Pre-service teacher education requirements for primary education, 2001	186
3.4	Professional development for teachers, public schools-2004	188
3.5	Pupil–teacher ratio/pupils to teaching staff ratios by level of education, calculations based on full time equivalents	193
3.6	Average class size in primary education by type of institutions	195
3.7	Workload of teachers in primary education	197
3.8	Age distribution of teachers	198
3.9	Percentage of women among teachers in public and private institutions, by level of education (based on headcounts)	200
4.1	The structure of administration of education in Orissa in 1872	202
4.2	The structure of administration of education in Orissa in 1875	202
4.3	Number of new primary school and EGS centres opened and enrollment in DPEP Phase I and II	202
4.4	Ratio of upper primary schools to primary schools and primary and upper primary schools (Schools per DI)	203
4.5	SSS (Swechchasevi Siksa Sahayaka) position as on 20-03-2002	204
4.6	Number of teachers according to educational qualification	205
4.7	Achievement of primary school teachers in language	205
4.8	Achievement of primary school teachers in mathematics	206
4.9	Regionwise and social groupwise incidence of poverty, rural Orissa, 1999–2000	206
4.10	NSS regionwise trend in poverty ratio, rural Orissa	207
4.11	Districtwise poverty ratio	207
4.12	Development ranking of districts in Orissa in 1990	208

4.13	Poverty in Orissa, 1999–2000, NSSO 55th round	208
4.14	Growth of literacy in Orissa	209
4.15	Natural calamities in Orissa	209
4.16	Growth of education in Orissa	209
4.17	Growth of education in Orissa 1991–92 to 1997–98	210
4.18	Compound rate of growth (%)	211
4.19	Distribution of primary school by management	211
4.20	Access of schooling facilities in Orissa	212
4.21	Financial support to primary education in Orissa (in crore)	213
4.22	Financial support to primary education in Orissa (in crore)	216
4.23	Financial support to primary education in Orissa (in crore)	217
7.1	Infrastructure of schools	218

GLOSSARY

Activity Method	The method which emphasizes translating learning tasks into activities
Amin	A job in the revenue department
APL	Above Poverty Line
BDO	Block Development Officer
BPL	Below Poverty Line
Brahmin	The upper caste
BRC	Block Resource Centre
BRCC	Block Resource Centre Coordinator
CI	Circle Inspector
CL	Casual Leave
CRC	Cluster Resource Centre
CT	Certified Teacher
DA	Dearness Allowance
DI	District Inspector of Schools
DIET	District Institute of Education and Training
DPEP	District Primary Education Programme
DWO	District Welfare Officer
ECCE	Early Childhood Care and Education
EGS	Education Guarantee Scheme
ET	Elementary Teacher
Ex-Board	The government upper primary school located in Laxmipur
HBCSE	Homi Bhaba Centre for Science and Education
Head Pundit	Head Master
HSC	High School Certificate
IAS	Indian Administrative Service
ICSE	Indian Council of Secondary Education
IGNOU	Indira Gandhi National Open University

ITI	Industrial Training Institute
Karan	A middle caste, equivalent to Kayastha of North India
Kuvi	The language spoken by the Kondh tribe
MDM	Mid-day Meal
ME	Middle English
MIL	Mother Indian Language
MTA	Mother-Teacher Association
NCERT	National Council for Educational Research and Training
NCTE	National Council for Teacher Education
NGO	Non-Government Organization
NPEGL	National Programme for Education of the Girl Child
Paraja	A tribe of Orissa
PG	Post Graduate
PHC	Primary Health Centre
PTA	Parent Teacher Association
PWD	Public Works Department
RI	Revenue Inspector
SC	Scheduled Caste
SCERT	State Institute of Education Research and Training
SHG	Self-Help Group
SI	School Inspector
SSA	Sarva Siksa Abhiyan
SSS	Swechchasevi Shiksa Sahayaka (Contract Teacher)
ST	Scheduled Tribe
Sundhi	A backward caste lower in rank than Brahmin and Karan
TRW	Tribal and Rural Welfare (Department)
TLM	Teaching Learning Material
Unmesha	The awareness campaign by the SSA programme
UP	Upper primary
VEC	Village Education Committee
VLW	Village Level Worker

ACKNOWLEDGEMENTS

This book grew out of my Ph.D. thesis 'Teacher Professionalism: A Study of Teachers and Classroom Processes'. My foremost gratitude goes to Prof. Denzil Saldanha who not only guided me during the Ph.D. but even afterwards in making it see the light of the day. My colleagues Jacob Aikara, Wankhede, Padma, Ranu and Leena were always my sources of inspiration.

I am thankful to all the teachers who cooperated with me during my fieldwork. My wife Laxmi and daughter Amanda bore with my lesser attention to them during the fieldwork. My father Balabhadra Khora, who retired as a primary teacher, and mother Ratnamani have faced every hardship so that I live well. I dedicate this book to them.

Sthabir Khora

1

WHAT IS EDUCATION?

Introduction

Derived from a Latin word *educare* (meaning 'to bring up'), education is understood in many ways. This is more so when we survey different theoretical perspectives on education that deal with it differently. They dwell on the aims of education, which are the important factors in the process of education and the relation between education and society. Underlying all these are the notions about what is education. For example, the prime focus of the sociology of education is the relation between the society and education. But most of the sociological perspectives have focused primarily on schooling and that too the formal one. Thus, what they have done is to analyze the relationship between schooling and society. On the other hand, the philosophical perspectives see education as broader than schooling. Their concerns are also different. While sociology of education predominantly concerns itself with education as a medium of domination, the philosophical perspectives dwell on the aims of education. Thus, the underlying notion of education and the concerns among different perspectives are not the same. They deal with different facets of education. Taking any single class of perspectives gives a partial view of education, whereas taking them together gives a more wholesome picture.

Philosophical Perspectives: The Aims of Education

Liberal or Technical Education

The aim of education, broadly, could be either liberal or technical. It means whether education should be pursued for its own sake or for the sake of livelihood. Pursuing education for its own sake entails pursuing it for some ideals.

Plato envisages education only for the guardians and not for others in the society. Plato's scheme of education, which can go up to forty years of age, initially starts with music and gymnastics. The arduous physical training is up to the age of thirty. Even the music is with a martial rhyme and not to awaken the sensuous or the effeminate. The stories that children hear are about the past heroes. Thus, the emphasis is on a tough body. It is only after the age of thirty that the guardians are fit to study the dialectics. Dialectics is the responsible discussion of men of reason. The aim of dialectics and gymnastics implies the coordination of body, mind and soul. Underlying the scheme is the superiority of intellectual pursuit and the inferiority of bodily exercise. The aim of education for Plato is *goodness* in a transcendental sense from which emanates all good on this earth. What happens in the world is imperfect imitation of ideas which exist independently of their manifestation. The most important idea, from which all other ideas emanate, is goodness. That's why goodness should be the aim of education. His notion was a transcendental idealism of education to realize the idea of goodness (Curtis and Boultwood, 1953). The duality of intellectual–practical remains with Aristotle also. Aristotle prescribes a liberal education for citizens and technical education for the slaves. By liberal education, he means disinterested intellectual pursuit. It is pursued for its own sake and not for money, nor under any influence or with a narrow specialization (Chambliss, 1996; Curtis and Boultwood, 1953). Both Plato and Aristotle did not visualize an inclusive education and their conception of education was elitist.

Gandhi (1962) emphasized the utilitarian and the vocational aspect of education to a greater extent than the intellectual aspect. Education should be related to the existing economy. Thus, for example, weaving should be a necessary aspect of education in India. Education should involve the coordination of body, mind and soul. In contrast to him, Tagore considers that narrow utilitarianism can never be the ultimate aim of education (Mukherjee, 1962). He was not against books per se, but was against the bookish approach to education. The pupils should read a wide variety of books but should not be bookish. Vivekananda also did not believe in an uncritical approach to books. According to him, one has more education than any man who has got a whole library by heart if one has assimilated five ideas and made them one's life and character. He also emphasized the vocational aspect of education. He said, 'Sit at their (Westerners) feet and learn from them the arts, industries and the practicality necessary for the struggle for existence' (Mani, 1965, p. 370). Probably only Tagore did not bother much of education and livelihood as he had a notion of education which can be considered romantic. For others, the link between education and livelihood is an important concern. For example, Radhakrishnan was of the view that 'it is relatively inexpensive to train students in arts, law and commerce, but it costs a great deal to train them in science, engineering and technology which are essential for the development of our natural resources' (ibid.). This does not mean that liberal education is not important. Thomas Huxley, who spent his life promoting science education in England, opined that science teaching will be imperfect until social science is made one of the great topics of instructions (Curtis and Boultwood, 1953).

Dewey (1916) sees the issue in an entirely different way. He holds that divisions like practical–intellectual and culture–vocation are not immanent, but reflect the division in the society. What is needed is a basic liberal and technical education for all. This gives a new and useful perspective on this issue. The issue is not dead even today. But the way out is that society needs both appropriate skills and values. Therefore, what is needed is both liberal and technical/vocational education.

Humanism

Another aim which is evident among different philosophical perspectives is humanism. This follows from the debate on liberal versus technical education. If liberal education entails inculcation of certain values, then what are those values? What kind of values and orientations education should develop?

The aims of education, according to Comnious, are faith and reverence, uprightness in morals and knowledge of language and arts in that order. He aimed at developing a grand method of teaching all things to all men. Locke considered *balanced vision* as the goal of education. Education should develop 'large-sound-roundabout sense'. This means rising above tradition (the slavery of precedence) and enthusiasm (passion as contrasted to reason) (ibid). Herbart, a pioneer educationist, emphasized *interest* as the aim of education. Education should develop interest as many-sided as life. This interest includes following five moral ideas:

(i) Inner freedom: when will and convictions are in accord, i.e., one wills what one is convinced of;

(ii) Perfection: when different strivings of the will are in accord, i.e., the will is concentrated and not scattered;

(iii) Goodwill: this implies the sense of benevolence;

(iv) Idea of rights: when the will of the individual is superseded by the will of the group; and

(v) Idea of equality: when intentional acts of good and evil are recompensed, i.e., there is balance of actions and individuals recompense their bad actions and reciprocate other's good actions (Curtis and Boultwood, 1953).

These values are relevant even in the present era. They may be the official goals of education in many countries.

Zakir Hussain, who was responsible for the formulation of Basic Education at Wardha Congress, 1937, gave the following features as the qualifications of an educated person:

(a) He has no blinkers;

(b) He is no philistine;

(c) He is not conceited and never imagines he has reached the destination;

(d) He is not a hard boiled egg, i.e., he is willing to learn always; and

(e) He is no internally dissipated busy body (Mani, 1965).

This underscores the value of inquisitiveness and humility in education. Education has no end. One has to approach education in an unbiased way. Only then one's education will progress.

The aim of education, according to Tagore, is the pursuit of *bhuma* or the infinite. The pool of knowledge, which belongs to the humanity, transcending the boundaries of countries, is the goal of education. His notion of *bodher sadhana* (inculcation of empathy), which should be the aim of education, implies the development of a humane human being. *Bodher sadhana* is constantly expanding the boundary and sphere of one's empathy to include the whole humanity. For Radhakrishnan, education must be humane to be complete. It must include not only the training of the intellect but also the refinement of the heart and the spirit (Mani, 1965). For Vivekananda, the aim of education is to understand human suffering and not to be away from them. He questions, 'What is the goal of your education? Either a clerkship or a roguish lawyer, or at the most a deputy magistrate, which is another form of clerkship—isn't that all? What good it will do to you or the country at large? Open eyes and what a piteous cry for food is rising in the land of Bharat, proverbial for its wealth! Will your education fulfill this want?' (ibid., p. 379) … 'Well you consider a man educated if he can pass some examinations and deliver good lectures. The education which does not help the common mass of people to equip themselves for the struggle for life, which does not bring out the strength of character, a spirit of philanthropy, and the courage of a lion—is it worth the name?' (ibid., pp. 369–70). We can readily grasp the importance of it if we place it in the context of education in colonial India according to the scheme of Macaulay. For Vivekananda, religion is the most vital aspect of India. An education sans spirituality cannot revive India. He wanted Western sciences along with *Vedanta*.

The above discussion underscores the importance of inculcation of certain values by education. The important values, which can be deduced from the above discussion, are equality, sympathy and an open mind to learn. These values make education complete along with the skills that are necessary for livelihood. Often a great deal of effort and thinking goes on the paedagogical aspect of education. But the aims of education are equally important in the present era when communalism, religious fundamentalism and the likes are posing a threat to the society.

Indigenous Orientation

Most Indian thinkers like Gandhi, Aurobindo and Vivekananda had experienced colonialism. Therefore, one of the aims of education for them was that it should have an indigenous orientation. Gandhi held that we should keep the windows open so that all kinds of ideas flow in, but should not be swept off our feet. That's why he emphasized on vocational education symbolized in khadi. Tagore also believed that any education that is not based on the masses is going to fail. The main weak point of the national movement was precisely this. Educational swaraj means education rooted in people's history, economy, society and needs. This kind of education should be provided to all so that there should be equality to all (Mukherjee, 1962).

What was meant by educational swaraj by Tagore? The national movement in education was becoming narrow in an unwarranted glorification of India to the exclusion of important elements from other countries. This chauvinism could not have impressed Tagore who had travelled widely and whose friends from abroad were supporting Shantiniketan to the point of staying there. Vivekananda, who got his recognition first in America, said, 'we shall add to our stock what others have to teach, but we must always be careful to keep intact what is essentially our own' (Mani, 1965, p. 376). What is important is a critical mentality. It is not useful to blindly copy others and not having a critical mentality. 'We should not merely give what the public want, but educate them to want the true and beautiful' (Radhakrishnan, as cited in ibid., p. 195). This reminds us to be free from a slavish attitude towards education. Zakir Hussain, who helped formulate the concept of Basic Education in 1937, had the urgency for indigenous orientation of education. He said, 'Fellow teachers! I do sincerely feel, I belong to the fraternity... let us not always wait till others think out things for us and we set out mechanically and soullessly to execute them. Let's evolve a healthy professional opinion, a high professional sense of national duty… we are not just wage earners… we have to breathe the spirit of the intellect, of objective morality and social responsibility into the work of the hand and to give to intellectual work a firm foundation of concrete, purposeful activity' (ibid., p. 315).

The above discussion underscores the importance of contextualizing education. India started with an education which was not meant to arouse the critical faculty. Though during the British period there was not much scope for manoeuvre, it is sad that the legacy did not go after attaining independence. The biggest proof of a lack of indigenous orientation of education was the decline of Basic Education in post-independence India. This is a serious issue. The so-called liberal education has precluded the vocational. But it has not generated the required critical consciousness which it was supposed to do.

Philosophical Perspectives: Important Factors in the Process of Education

Importance of Environment in Education

Education is a process of learning. The individual acquires the capacity to survive in the society through this process. This process is influenced by many factors. The most important among these is environment. The importance of environment has been emphasized since early times. Pestalozzi and Montessori emphasized a home-like environment as a precondition for the cognitive development of the child. Pestalozzi experimented it in a school in a village, Nuehof in Switzerland, where he taught destitute children. He established a sort of paternal relation with them. Soon the children developed good personalities, if not academic soundness. He later experimented this approach in another school in Burgdorf where children, made destitute by war, were taught (Curtis and Boultwood, 1953). His conception of object lesson involves the understanding of the objects or the environment around oneself through the method of number, form and name. What he propounds is that one learns the immediate environment first and then expands further. Thus, the cycle of knowledge also expands further. He also propounded *simultaneous instruction* or learning in groups rather than alone. Pestalozzi influenced Froebel, the founder of kindergarten, who had spent time with Pestalozzi in the latter's school (ibid). For Froebel, the immediate environment of gifts is important for the children to realize their potential. Children are to be taken to the garden around the school. Though they are allowed to play, the overall situation remains under the supervision of the teacher. Thus, the environment is a prepared one.

For Montessori (1984), the environment is important even when the child is in the womb. The child has astounding sensory power. Whatever impression is made during childhood influences the child throughout his/her life. Her experimental school 'Casa dei Bambini' (home of children) in Rome was made as homely as possible. All children of both sexes did the cleaning and prepared food. Her conception of school was that it should be a home away from home. For Montessori, the sensitivity of even a two-year-old child cannot be ignored. The child learns indirectly through his/her mind's eyes. He/she also learns indirectly through environment. Therefore, the child should be exposed sufficiently to the environment, for example, to different social situations like marriage, dinner, community gatherings and the like. The child in this case is not a big child but as small as one or two years' old. We should not underestimate his/her learning capability. Montessori provides the example that any child can learn any language if brought up in that environment. But it is difficult in a later period. According to her, the child is full of *elan vital* or *horme*. This can be called life force. Education should develop this potential. She does not hold the doctrine of pre-formation. All the capacities are in an abstract form initially, which she calls *nebulae*. Education is a development from nothingness to fullness. The job of a teacher is to provide a little bit of guidance initially. All these underscore the individuality of the child and freedom in learning.

Montessori focussed more on home as environment. Tagore and Rousseau emphasized environment in a larger sense as well as in a different sense. For both, the school should exist amidst the greenery of nature. Tagore had nostalgia for the ancient *tapovan* type of environment away from the crowd of city life. He held that the ideal institution has to be established away from the turmoil of the human habitation, in solitude, under the open sky, amidst wide fields, trees and plants. There, the tutors will be occupied in quiet studies and teaching and the pupils will grow up in the sacred and profound atmosphere of learning. Learning should be through and in nature. For him, the atmosphere prevailing in the institution is as much important as the curriculum (Mukherjee, 1962).

Rousseau too portrays the early education of Emile in a picturesque landscape away from city life. Emile is the hero of the book by the same name by Rousseau which contains his educational ideas. The reason for seclusion is that if the child is placed in the usual environment of city and amidst his parents, he will be corrupted by existing corrupt ideas. He gives an example that two city children, when left alone, would create more mayhem than a whole group of rural children (Sri Aurobindo International Institution of Educational Research, 1988). Krishnamurti, who has established many schools in picturesque locations, holds similar belief. Here is a quote from him: 'That's what education is. You have been sent here, or you have come here (school) contaminated by an insane world. Do not fool yourself. You have been conditioned by that insane world, shaped by past generations—including your parents—and you come here and you have to uncondition yourself, you have to undergo a tremendous change. Does that change take place? Or are we just saying: well, we are doing a bit of good work here and there day after day, and by the time you are in two or four years time off you go with a little patchwork done?' (Krishnamurti, 1978, p. 177)

Dewey (1916) defines environment in a different sense. For him, environment is that with which the individual varies. Thus, the environment for a child may contain certain elements from past and may not contain certain elements of the present. In this sense, the subjects like history and geography provide the imaginary environment for the child. For Dewey, method cannot be separated from mind and situation. The situation does not exist outside the mind. Therefore, he prefers to use *to mind* instead of *mind*. His conception of environment as 'that with which one varies' implies that situation outside the mind has no meaning to the subject.

Thus, it can be said that as is the environment so is the child. But there is hardly anybody like Rousseau who wants the environment to be uncontrolled. Once it is agreed that the environment is to be controlled to some extent, the role of teacher comes into being. Her-bart said that it is mere folly to leave man to nature. In the Froebelian scheme, the environment is a 'prepared' one and the occupations like weaving, playing with clay and the like have to be directed. For Tagore, the mere pill of a method cannot deliver the goods. True education can be delivered only by a teacher and not by a method. All these point out that the best of environments does not obviate the role of a teacher.

Education and Freedom

The importance of the freedom and individuality is a point which hardly anybody can disagree. Zakir Hussain says that education is not pressing into shape but a letting loose and setting free which respects the unique and specific individuality of the educand. He emphasized the point by Schleiermacher—a German philosopher—that all preparations must at the same time be a satisfying experience and all satisfying experience must also be a preparation. His contemporary and another educationist, Radhakrishnan said, 'Unfortunately in our schools we look upon children as mere raw stuff on which we can impose our unjust views through our powerful wills. We inject them with our views and make them as corrupt as we are'... 'true education needs conversation and debate, exchange of opinion and thoughts with friends with whom one can speak and listen easily, sympathetically and without fear, but are the opportunities for these adequate? (Mani, 1965, p. 188). This resonates very well with the ideas of Paulo Freire who belonged to another continent.

For Aurobindo, the first principle of teaching is that nothing can be taught. The teacher is not an instructor or taskmaster. He is a helper and a guide. His business is to suggest and not to impose. He does not actually train the pupil's mind. He only shows him how to perfect his instruments of knowledge and helps him and encourages him in this process. He does not impart knowledge to him. He shows to him how to acquire knowledge for himself. He does not call forth the knowledge that is within; he only shows where it lies and how it can be habituated to rise to the surface (Mani, 1965, pp. 328–29).

Montessori expresses the relation between teacher and child in the phrase *I–Thou* of Martin Buber, which underscores the individuality of the child in contrast to the *I–It* relation. Individuality and freedom is the hallmark of Montessori method. It is also reflected in her opinion that the child teaches himself/herself. The child should not be helped unnecessarily but should be allowed to do things independently.

Freedom in education means that the individuality of the child should be respected during the process of education. For example, an *I–Thou* relation underscores a dialogical relation where the child has the space for dialogue with the teacher. But an *I–It* relation implies a command and objective relation. Educationists are against such relation. This is a burning issue in contemporary Indian education.

Education and Experience

Everybody learns from experience. A child also gradually builds up on the experience which aids him/her in his/her learning. But there are different kinds of experiences. Pestalozzi, Froebel and Montessori have construed experience in the sense of sensory experience. On the other hand, Dewey and Tagore have interpreted it in the broad sense of life.

The importance of experience is manifested in the concept of *anschauung* by Pestalozzi. The Pestalozzian way of learning involves learning the number, the form and the name through the *anschauung* way. For example, when one sees a camel, he/she sees its form, its number (one) and the name (camel). This is the *anschauung*. Tomorrow, if a being comes in a different way, one will hesitate to call it a camel. Number, form and name also signify the study of mathematics, art and painting, and literature (Chambliss, 1996).

The *kindergarten* method, propounded by Froebel, also emphasized experience to realize the potential of children. *Kinder* means children and *garten* means garden. The Froebelian philosophy suggests that the children already have the seed of what they will become in future (doctrine of pre-formation). Since god is the ultimate source, there is interconnection among things. The purpose of education is to make children realize the unity and the potential. The occupations—like weaving, interlacing, games like parquetry, playing manipulable toys like small cubes making larger cubes, cylinders—are to realize the unity and the potential within them. Froebel's concept of *darstellung* also points to this. *Darstellung* means realizing the potential through communicating—in clay or some other malleable material, in playing with the cubes, in making a circle and singing a song. In short, it is a *creative self-expression* (Hugen, Neville, Posthelwaite, 1985).

Normalization is as important to Montessori as the *anschauung* is to Pestalozzi and *darstellung* to Froebel. *Normalization* happens when a child completes a piece of work by exercising his/her body and mind. For example, 'walk nicely' cannot be taught effectively unless the child does it practically. Thus, the experience is essential for understanding walking. For Montessori, the movement of hand and the body are not only important in themselves but also for mental development. Mental concentration is also required in playing (Montessori, 1984). Tagore also had the notion of learning while walking, which he thought would go well, though he did not give any technical reason for so.

Dewey (1916) emphasized the importance of experience not in the narrow sense of mere sensory perception. He rather underlined it in the broader sense of experience of life. Education is renewal of life with all its varied experience. It means that when one moves from experience to experience, he/she develops the capability to master as well as predict situations. This is probably the most important contribution of Dewey to educational thought. Education in this sense cannot have a stoppage at any point of time in one's life. Therefore, the goal of education can only be further education.

Tagore wants the children to learn from life. Curriculum should not only be related to everyday life, but it should also be interesting to the children. For him, we know the people of the books, not those of the world; the former are interesting to us, but the latter tiresome. Happiness educates. Sorrow also educates. We cannot do without discipline nor can we live without freedom. On the one hand, we have a ready access to the world of readymade things; and on the other hand, we have the freedom of getting things through our own independent efforts (Mukherjee, 1962).

The above discussion on the varied views on experience underscores the importance of freedom in education. Unless the freedom is there, the child can neither have a meaningful experience nor can he/she build on this experience. Without the freedom, the child would not be allowed to use his/her experience to learn. This is a major issue in curriculum development in India. Often children read in the textbooks something that they cannot relate to their experience. Matching curriculum to the contextual experience of children is a challenge, which has not been met successfully in India so far.

Learning in Stages

The cognitive process of learning has always been a bit of mystery to teachers and educationists. By now, there are many theories on learning. Some of them have delineated stages in learning. Following is the discussion on some of the earliest attempts.

According to Herbart, children learn through *apperception*, i.e., linking a new presentation to an earlier presentation. The self is a collection of presentations. When a child comes across a red rose, it is a presentation. When he/she comes across a white rose, it is again a presentation. The earlier presentation of the red rose is subdued now. It will surface again when the child sees a red rose. Thus, the child may have a conception of a red rose after some time. Originally, the Herbartian scheme had the aim of preserving among children the desired presentations to the point of mathematical precision (Chambliss, 1996). It may be mentioned that Herbart was a mathematician. Taking together his conception of self as a collection of presentations and learning through apperception, he prescribes the method of teaching as follows:

- Preparation: Revision of old knowledge.
- Presentation: Presenting the new knowledge.
- Association: Pointing the link between the new and old knowledge.
- Systematization: Trying to show the broader unity among the presentations.
- Application: Applying it practically to some situation (Curtis and Boultwood, 1953). The above method points to the stages of *interest-desire-volition-action.*

Dewey proceeds in a similar manner. For Dewey, thinking is *trying to find out the connection*, which has resemblance with apperception of Herbart. The right steps of learning for him, which are like that of Herbart, are the following:

(a) The situation should be interesting.

(b) If any problem, it should be genuine.

(c) The pupil should have access to necessary information.

(d) The pupil should be let to think of possible solutions.

(e) The pupil should have opportunity to exercise those solutions (Dewey, 1916).

It has been discussed earlier that Dewey emphasized the freedom of the child inlearning. Capability to master situations and predict situations are the principal goals of learning for him. Progress means this. That's why Dewey's conception of education is called *progressive* because all the while, the child is mastering situations and acquiring the capability to predict situations.

The four stages of *educative work* laid down by Zakir Hussain echo similar stages of learning. They are:

(i) Consciousness of the problem.

(ii) Formation of a plan of work.

(iii) Execution of the work.

(iv) Self-criticism.

In short, educative work is that in which mind and body work together. The stages *play-sport-casual occupation-work* basically show the progressive working of body and mind. The job of education is to lead pupils from one stage to the next (Mani, 1965).

Knowledge of the stages of learning is probably the cornerstone of what makes teaching a profession. This is what the general public is ignorant about and a professional teacher is knowledgeable about. But it seems that a stage is yet to come when we will be able to agree on the right stages of learning.

Sociological Perspectives

While the philosophical perspectives pursue the ideals of education, sociological perspectives unravel existing education. As has been stated earlier, the sociological perspectives explore the relation between education and society. There are two major contributions of sociology of education. First, it brings out the various ways in which education perpetuates the reproduction of existing society due to the existing stratification and domination of one class over another. Second, it explores the possibility of education as an aid to resist domination. Some of the important sociological perspectives on education are discussed below.

The Functional Paradigm

The functional paradigm looks at the society through an organic analogy—a system where each part contributes to the functioning of the whole system. Thus, function means an action on part of a sub-system that contributes to the maintenance of the whole system. Durkheim is considered as one of the founding fathers of sociology. He employed the functional paradigm in his analysis of religion. Talcott Parsons developed the functional paradigm later. Both have conceived education as something contributing to the integration of society.

Durkheim views education as a means of socialization. Education inculcates the sentiments, ideas and tendencies that sustain the group life. It promotes the homogeneity that is necessary for group life. Education operates in particular socio-historical contexts. Thus, its functions will differ from context to context. Each society has its own ideal and this ideal gets inculcated through education. The state and the teacher have an important role to play in this endeavour. The state acts through the teacher. The teacher imparts the sentiments and values that are necessary for the child to adjust to the milieu. The teacher symbolizes the great moral ideas of his times which are transmitted to the children.

Durkheim's views can be considered as essentially focussing on the stabilizing function of education. Parsons too concentrated on the stabilizing function of education. Education plays a role in the formation of consensus. This starts at the school level itself. For Parsons, the important function of education is the inculcation of necessary skills and values among pupils, which are necessary to function in the society. He says, 'Our main problem then is a dual problem: first of how the school-class functions to internalize in its pupils both the commitment and capacities for successful performance for their future adult roles and second of how it functions to allocate these human resources within the role structure of adult society' (Parsons, 1964, as cited in Demaine, 1981, pp. 20–21). Robert Dreben elaborates the values that are necessary in the society and which the school inculcates among children: 'Thus, although the school provides opportunities for pupils to gain experience in cooperative situations, in the last analysis it is the *individual* assessment that counts…schooling then assures most pupils the experience of both winning and losing, and to the extent that they gain some modicum of gratification from academic activities it teaches them to approach their work in a frame of mind conducive to *achievement*' (Dreben as cited in Karabel and Halsey, 1977, p. 546). Thus, the school inculcates the values of individualism and achievement among children, which are necessary to survive in a society like the American society. However, both these values are by no means universally valued. There were and still are societies that promote collectivism through the schools. The functional paradigm makes the following two assumptions:

(1) It sees the school as an inherently neutral institution.

(2) It sees the school as devoid of any dynamics reproducing whatever is expected of it. Thus, it does not take into account the powers of human beings to change the existing social structure.

The functional paradigm portrays education in a positive light. However, there are also some other theories, which may be regarded as advancements over the functional paradigm. They bring out the various ways in which education reproduces existing society and, thus, reproduces existing domination in the society. Though the theories of cultural capital and invisible paedagogy do not mention class domination, the implication is that education perpetrates the domination of one class over others.

Bourdieu's Theory of Cultural Capital

The theory of cultural capital propounded by Pierre Bourdieu challenges the inherent neutrality of the school (Bourdieu, 1997). Functionalism portrays the school as a neutral institution and remains silent about the reproduction of domination. The cultural capital theory shows how the school helps in the reproduction of domination through the mechanism of cultural capital. There are three kinds of cultural capital. These are:

(i) The embodied: This is the ingrained ability, which masquerades as hereditary; for example, the business skill of a person coming from a family of business background for generations.

(ii) The objectified: These are the cultural goods and by implication the bads; for example, paintings and wine.

(iii) The institutionalized: These are the institutional credentials; for example, the degree that says that a particular person has mastered cookery which differentiates him from a person who may be a better cook but does not have a certificate.

Embodied cultural capital like social interaction skills is more dependent on family background than school. But it helps one in the school. Similarly, cultural goods like television helps in the school. Thus, the curriculum and teaching of school favours the pupils from the dominant class who have a smooth sailing in contrast to their working-class counterparts because of their cultural background. Thus, the school is not inherently neutral but is slanted in favour of the dominant class.

Bernstein's Theory of Invisible Pedagogy

The theory of invisible pedagogy propounded by Basil Bernstein points to yet another way in which domination is perpetrated. The four assumptions of invisible pedagogy are:

(i) Women in their mother aspect are the transmitter of cultural reproduction.

(ii) Implicit time sequence: The control is implicit and not explicit. Though there is no hard and fast rule as to when one is going to finish mathematics and when geography, one has to finish overall by certain time limit.

(iii) Possible open space: This is the blurring of the boundary between the classroom and the playground.

(iv) Control through interpersonal communication: This is different from the usual explicit way of control through reward and punishment. If a child does not behave properly, then, the teacher will try to control him/her by not paying attention rather than by giving some explicit punishment.

The invisible pedagogy relies on *weak classification* and *weak frames*. Weak classification means that the invisible pedagogy does not emphasize the clear-cut division like science, literature, etc. It also means that pupils are allowed to play, to do whatever they want, but only apparently. The teacher is in firm control of the context all the while. This is the *strong frame* behind the weak frame. Bernstein relates invisible pedagogy to the manipulation of frames as the new way of domination by the new middle class.

The theory of invisible pedagogy brings out the subtle ways in which control is exercised in a capitalist society. This is especially true in private schools in India where there is a lot of freedom on the surface but a lot of control beneath.

Althusser's Ideological State Apparatus

Althusser points to another way in which the school helps in the perpetration of domination by the concept of *ideological state apparatus* (Althusser, 1972). Education builds consent for the dominant class. Thus, the state, which is an agent of the dominant class, does not rule through force (the *repressive state apparatus*, i.e., the army, police, etc.) but through consent, which is manufactured through ideological state apparatus like the school. The church, which was the predominant ideological state apparatus in the pre-capitalist era, is now replaced with the school as the dominant ideological state apparatus. *Education-family* couple now replaces the erstwhile *church-family* couple as the predominant ideological state apparatus. Children do notjust know the know-how through education but they also know the rules of good behaviour and submission to rules. The function of the ideological state apparatus is to inculcate the dominant ideology among the subjects. For Althusser, the ideology does not exist outside the subject. He defines ideology as the imaginary relation of men to their real conditions of production. For example, no capitalist system will project the picture of an enterprise where the workers are not happy. The question thus arises: if ideology does not stay outside the subject, how will the liberation come? Paulo Freire, Michael Apple and Henry Giroux deal with this issue, which will be taken up later on.

Illich's Deschooling Society

There are many scholars, who have analyzed the oppressive character of education in the society. But none has voiced the abolition of formal schooling itself as the solution. Ivan Illich stands out as one of the few scholars, who has advocated the abolition of formal schooling as a means towards educational liberation.

In the book *Deschooling Society* (1971), Illich argued that 'by monopolizing schooling, the state vastly extends the control over all aspects of life including work, leisure, politics and family'. He visualizes school as a sort of factory where vast numbers of pupils are churned out according to the demands of the urban society. This is almost like a factory churning out mass-standardized products for the market. The consumer pupils only desire the marketable knowledge and skills. They are not liberated but indoctrinated. Their learning is determined by others, especially the teachers, who exercise control over them.

Contemporary schooling system generates attitude of submission and prevents critical thinking. Therefore, deschooling is not only abolishing the state school system but also uncritical thinking and submissiveness. Emancipation is not possible within the framework of the state school system. Illich's alternative suggestion was to distribute among parents financial vouchers by which they can fund the type of education they want. In this scheme, the pupils would not be exploited by the teachers.

Archer's Centralized and Decentralized School Systems

Margaret Archer's analysis is an improvement on earlier theories dealing with the role of education in perpetration of domination. According to Archer, centralized and decentralized school systems exercise different degrees of domination.

Any educational system is closely linked to the political system. The form an educational system takes depends on struggles for political power, involve concession to allies and compromises with the opponents. In the centralized school system, there is one educationally dominant group, which exercises the control over the school system. Thus, the voices of other groups are suppressed. But it is not necessary that the educationally dominant group is also the politically and socially dominant group. Sometimes it can be one of the dominant groups.

In the decentralized school system, there are more than one actor in the field of education. Therefore, there is a greater scope of autonomy to different actors in such a system. The striking features of the system are alternative curricula, texts and teaching methods.

However, Archer believes that resistance is possible even in a centralized system. This can be done by rejecting the ideology of the dominant system and building up an alternative system of curricula and teaching methods (Archer, 1984).

Freire's Critical Consciousness

Paulo Freire (1973) sees the existing education as a *banking system of education*. In this system, knowledge is deposited into pupils like money in a bank account. As the capital gives returns in due course, so also the accumulated knowledge is supposed to gain to oneself material privileges. This results in *Assistentialism*. As the name suggests, it means people become just the adjuncts to the system by such education. It perpetuates a *culture of silence*.

According to Freire, the role of education is to develop *critical consciousness*. Critical consciousness in turn develops a scientific temper, to find out the causality of situations and events. It makes people question their existing situation. Thus, education has the potential of being an instrument of liberation. Freire says that critical consciousness is not about the oppressed taking the role of a new oppressor, rather the oppressed should demolish the structure which allows oppression. It is not a tenant becoming a landlord and oppressing some other tenant, but equal distribution of land.

Apple's Hidden Curriculum

Michael Apple (1995) initially refines the theory of cultural reproduction. For him, in the present age, technical/administrative knowledge is the cultural capital par excellence. Schools are not merely sites of reproduction but they are also the reservoirs of the cultural capital by appropriating it from their students and the society. Thus, the school is also a site of production of domination.

Capitalism in the present age is trying to control the schools through management techniques like standardization and pre-packaging of curriculum reducing the teachers to mere executors. It is also separating conception from execution. Experts are used to make the curricula. They also provide a sort of legitimacy to the system. But how many teachers are consulted on preparation of the curriculum?

After pointing out how domination happens in the present age through education, Apple brings out signs of hope. He quotes different studies which point out that workers do not accept whatever the management prescribes. Similarly, though in principle teachers are expected to execute predetermined package material, actually it need not be so.

He also hints at a broader coalition of teachers with other workers since teachers are also the largest workforce of the state.

Apart from teachers, Apple also points out how students are resisting the force of capitalism. He quotes Paul Willis' study *Learning to Labor* (1977) where working class students are divided into *ear'oles* (ear holes) and lads. The *ear'oles* lend too much ear to what the teacher says and the lads do not care what the teacher says. In this case, the lads are resisting. But they are helping in the reproduction of inequality. If they do not study well, they are going to be the future workers. But what is significant is that the role models are neither the lads nor the *ear'oles* but those who manage both— those who could manage their studies without sacrificing the fun. The same happens to the girls also. Since working class girls cannot dream of higher studies because of financial reasons, the realistic possibility for them is marriage and house. Therefore, they project sexuality instead of intellectuality. This again reproduces gender inequality. In both the cases, the lads and the working class girls do not reject the dominant culture for nothing. They know that getting middle classjobs are not easy. Thus, Apple cautions that we should not underestimate the power of structure.

Giroux's Critical Pedagogy

Henry Giroux(1983)tries to show how education can serve as an instrument of liberation instead of domination. He derives some of the elements which are salient in critical theory, for example, the concept of relative autonomy from Gramsci and applies it to education to show that education has an inherent potential to become an instrument of human emancipation.

Giroux levels some criticisms to the existing theories before proceeding to the above task. He says that orthodox Marxist theory, the functionalist theory, the theory of invisible pedagogy, hidden curriculum and cultural reproduction have the following drawbacks:

(a) These theories, though point out the various insightful ways in which domination is perpetrated, do not offer a ray of hope. They portray 'domination through education' as a sort of fait accompli. They do not retrieve the subject from the dominance of structure. Since they do not define culture as 'lived experience', they also expose the subject to the dominance of culture.

(b) They do not take into account the factors of race and gender sufficiently.

There is some strength in these two criticisms. Giroux has not criticized thinkers like Michael Apple and Paul Willis who have tried to avoid the pessimistic approach in their writings. Giroux points out, after this, the three elements that constitute the spirit of critical theory, which is going to be useful for the theory and practice of education. They are:

(i) The principle of negativity.

(ii) The principle of contradiction.

(iii) The principle of mediation.

(i) *The principle of negativity*: It implies that the subjects should develop critical consciousness. The role of education should be to develop critical consciousness in the sense used by Freire. This means a capacity to question the existing situation and try to find out the causality and by implication the cause of the domination. It also implies the resistance by the subject to domination. What Giroux really wants is *immanent negativity* (my phraseology). He gives an example why this has to be responsible. Teachers, not preparing for classroom, and not going to the classroom, may claim that they are resisting domination. Actually, it is just an act of unprofessionalism rather than an act of resistance. It has to be immanent because there is a need to be constantly aware of the capitalist domination in many forms. Today, it may be the managerial techniques; tomorrow it may be something else. Capitalism sometimes fools people by apparently giving some choice but limiting the list of choices itself. Today, one can propagate bohemian ethics in the United States of America, but not communism.

(ii) *The principle of contradiction*: It implies that there is a gap between what the state professes and what it actually does. Often a lot of regimentation happens in the name of quality and standard. One should be always alert to such deeds by the state.

(iii) *The principle of mediation*: It implies that the subject has the power to mediate between the structure and the outcome. Teachers and students are not entirely powerless before the capitalist state. They can do their act of resistance in the classroom and the school. It also qualifies the Marxist notion of correspondence between the base and the superstructure. It gives power to culture in the sense of 'lived experience'. Traditional Marxist theory reduces culture to a part of superstructure that ultimately gives in to the economic base.

The Gramscian principle of relative autonomy points out to the possibility of mediation. Althusser also agrees on this. What they say is that the superstructure is determined by the base/sub-structure in the *last instance* and not immediately. The phrase *last instance* implies relative autonomy and reciprocity.

Education: Towards a Definition

Education has transformed itself from the exclusive preserve of a few to a human right of all. There are many theoretical perspectives on education. They are psychological, sociological and philosophical. Broadly, I identify three most important questions that preoccupy thinking on education. These are: what to educate, how to educate and why to educate. Out of these three questions, what to educate implies the 'content' of education, the question of how implies the 'method' and the question of why implies the 'aim' of education. These three questions are interrelated. For example, the question of why depends on the question of what to educate. To make it more clear, the making of a good citizen (the aim) depends on whether the curriculum includes the rights, duties and values (the content) of a good citizen. Moreover, the question of future makes it imperative to dwell on the state of the present and the stock taking of present gives hint to the scenario about the future. Thus, the question of 'why to educate' is not very helpful unless there is an awareness of 'what is the present state'. The question 'what to educate' is important on this ground. Similarly, the question 'why to educate' is also dependent on 'how to educate'. You cannot teach the values of democracy by a method that is undemocratic.

I start with the assumption that education is a process that involves three agencies, i.e., the learner, the teacher or some facilitating agency and the society. It is a process that entails the interaction of these three agencies in various forms. For example, society can act through the state or the community or the family, learners range from children to olds and there are, at present, non-human facilitating agencies like the computer and the internet. Theories on education can be said to be those, which say something *about* the interaction of these agencies or *on* these agencies. Thus, it involves why to educate (what this interaction should aim at), how to educate (how should they interact) and what to educate (what this interaction is, in its manifest and latent sense). Thinkers have dealt at length on these particular questions. But most of them have traversed normative, sociological or cognitive directions. Moreover, though they have contributed to education without any doubt, in many cases, they have refrained from defining education or defined it normatively, sociologically or cognitively. The conception of education, which many thinkers have, is difficult to be implemented in the present society. For example, the 'freedom'[1], implicit in Tagore, the natural method[2] of Rousseau, is difficult to be implemented on a large scale in the present society. Vivekananda and Aurobindo (Sri

Aurobindo International Institute of Educational Research, 1988) had a nativist[3] conception of education, which will not give importance to our state-prescribed curriculum. Some of the concepts propounded by Montessori (1984) like 'elan vital' and 'horme'[4] are very abstract and difficult to be verified empirically.

If we contrast the philosophical thinking and the sociological thinking on education, we can see that the philosophical thinking has taken a very broad view of education. For example, when Tagore (Mukherjee, 1962) and Dewey (1916) wants, the pupil to learn from life, they are not making education coterminous with school. The 'transcendental goodness'[5] of Plato, the 'interest' that is as many-sided as life of Herbart (Curtis and Boultwood, 1953), the 'humane human being' of Tagore (Mukherjee, 1962)—all these certainly cannot be attained in the limited precincts of a school. On the other hand, the role of 'cultural capital' of Bourdieu (1997), the 'invisible pedagogy' of Bernstein (1997), 'the school class function' of the functionalist paradigm (Dreben; 1977, Demaine, 1981)—all these have their explicit reference point as the school. They have also not made education as coterminous with school. They have only focussed on school with the underlying assumption that this is the site which matters most in the process of education.

There has not been any attempt so far to define education to combine the philosophical, sociological and cognitive traditions. We do not have a definition which has a space for the three important questions related to education, i.e., what, why and how to educate? I will try to define education that includes important elements from different thinkers and that

(a) is as much applicable to formal, informal, nonformal, distance education,
(b) is a blend between empirical and ideal notion of education,
(c) can be operationalized, and
(d) can be viewed abstractiy and can be applied to empirical contexts as well.

Education can thus be defined as a *dialectical process between the learner/s and a predefined subject matter mediated by manifest agent/s and latent environment.*

Education is not a one-way-process. The dialectical nature of education has been emphasized by many thinkers. Dialectics has many different meanings (Hall, 1967). But I am using it here broadly as a process where there is a space for questioning and individuality. The only exception could be the 'sruti' tradition of learning 'Vedas', which was counted as education. In the 'sruti' tradition, the learner was supposed to exactly memorize 'Vedas' and chant without the permission to make any change whether he/she understood or not. But this approach is criticized by none other than Vivekananda who opined that 'I take as much from Vedas as reason permits' (Mani, 1965, p. 380). Dialectics, whether in the sense of between the learner and the subject matter, between the learner and the teacher—the *I–thou*[6] relation of Buber (Nash, Kazamias, Perkonson, 1965) which is supported by Montessori (1984)—or between the school and the state (Apple, 1995), does happen and should happen in education.

Here is an example of dialectics between the learner and the subject matter. Tagore says that he wants pupils to read a wide variety of books but not to be bookish (Mukherjee, 1962). I interpret this that reading should not be uncritical. The report of the Secondary Education Commission, 1972 holds similar opinion. To quote, 'It seems to be presumed that anyone who can read a book, in the sense of passing his eyes over words or pronouncing them with his lips, has studied it. This is an untenable presumption. Study implies several mental processes: interpretation of words into their appropriate meanings, the art of building up ideas and sifting the significant from unimportant details of illustration or from incompetent padding' (Government of India, 1972, p. 105).

The above discussion was about the dialectics between the learner and the subject matters but some dialectics is happening now between the state and the school. The culture of teaching manuals, readymade self-instructable materials for pupils, etc. are more concerned with making the teacher an educational worker than a professional. Apple (1995) has pointed out this factor of standardization, which he calls managerial techniques. The adoption of these methods by the state would not improve the teacher professionally. There is always the necessity of interpretation of the 'curriculum' in the context of the local variations in its meaning to the pupils. Many textbooks might write 'walk *on* the left' while it should be 'walk *to* your left'. It is not easy for the state to entirely control the school. There are, in reality, very large and critical areas of classroom life that are not amenable to outside control. According to Berliner (1987), teachers make up to 30 non-trivial work-related decisions every hour in a classroom context where an estimated 1,500 interactions may take place between teachers and pupils each day (as cited in Burke, 1998).

Thus, what is useful about calling education as a dialectical process is that it gives agency to subjects and brings out the complexities of the process. If we do not accept education as a dialectical process, we will fall into a theoretical trap where education (whether in the narrow sense of school or in a broader sense) is 'an instrument of domination' without the scope for the subjects to get out of it. Emancipation as a goal of education is the concern of some of the leading educational thinkers (Freire, 1972; Apple, 1995; Giroux, 1983) though their immediate focus is on school. The phrase 'manifest agent' implies the role of the teachers, and also points to the broader mediating role of the state. The phrase 'latent environment' implies mediating agencies like 'invisible pedagogy' and 'cultural capital'. The subject to be learned by the pupil is usually predefined. To give a mundane example, how much control a 5th class child has over the curriculum, which he/she has to learn? Or, how much control many of us have about the kind of movies we would like to watch? By calling subject matter 'predefined', the significant role of society in the process of education is recognized. For example, the subject matter will vary from society to society, from democracy to authoritarian. What 'education' is in an authoritarian society is not the same in a democratic society. This does not make it an out-and-out instrument of domination because of the dialectical nature of the process.

It is useful to see education as a dialectical process between the *learner* and *a predefined subject matter* rather than between the *learner* and the *teacher.* Today, teachers are seen as facilitators rather than direct imparters of knowledge. The learner learns himself/herself. The teacher, the computer, the local self-government or the state can only facilitate this manifestly or latently.

Taken together, this definition points some direction towards answering the questions what to educate, how to educate and why to educate. It emanates from this definition that these questions will be dealt with differently by different societies, but there is a limit to which the definition of education can accommodate diverse leanings. For example, can we think about an education process that is not dialectical, and does not recognize the individuality of the learner? We better call it indoctrination. Education cannot be for enslavement of either body or mind. The phrase 'predefined subject matter' in this definition gives a lot of latitude to the society and the state to decide the questions—what to educate and why to educate—but the term 'dialectical' places a limit to the state and the society.

Notes

1. Tagore always wanted education in a free atmosphere in ample space with trees, not a rigid curriculum or uniform. It is vague but one can get a feel of it from some of his statements like 'our wearing shoes are our protest to god for not providing us hoof' or 'till the age of seven let the child know nothing of dress and shame'.

2. Natural method: It is the method suggested in Rousseau's writings. It implies that the individuals should be left free without much guidance. Intervention should be when the individual is likely to harm or injure himself/herself.
3. Nativism: Vivekananda and Aurobindo considered that knowledge is already within us (preformation) and education is unfolding of that. It is opposed to the social conception of knowledge.
4. élan vital and horme: Basically, it means the abstract potential within the child. It borders on spirituality.
5. For Plato, earthly ideas are partial representations of ideal ideas. *Goodness* in the transcendental sense is the source of all earthly ideas of goodness.
6. 'I–thou' relation is the relation between 'subject–subject' as contrasted to 'I–it' which is 'subject–object'. Basically, the 'I–thou' relation emphasizes the individuality of the learner.

2

WHAT IS TEACHER PROFESSIONALISM?

The Taxonomic Approach to Profession

Professionalism today is a much talked about word in education. As compared to professionalization and profession, professionalism as a concept is of recent origin. But since it is linked to the concept of profession, it will be useful to understand first the concept of profession.

The early approach to the concept of profession was the taxonomic approach. The taxonomic approach took medicine and the law as their referents (Evetts, 2003; Sciulli, 2005). Taking a historical analysis of these two professions, the taxonomic approach defined a profession in terms of certain characteristics which were applicable to the three classical professions—medicine, law and divinity. Though there have been various criticisms about these characteristics—that how these will be applicable to others, or whether these are absolute or relative—nonetheless these characteristics exercise considerable influence now in visualizing about a profession. So, it will be useful to discuss these characteristics:

(a) *A profession has an abstract theoretical knowledge base.*
Andrew Abbott underscores the significance of abstract knowledge in making a profession (Wueste, 1991). A profession has or should have a theoretical abstract knowledge base from which it draws and applies to particular cases. Professional skills cannot be purely based on hands on experience (Carr, 2000). One cannot be a doctor by curing somebody by trial and error method. An act can be

professional only if it is based on some theoretical knowledge base. This is not to say that a profession is not based on some trial and error. What differentiates the *professional* from the *technician* and a *profession* from a *vocation* is that in the case of a technician, the trials and errors are individual affairs while in the case of a profession it is a collective affair. The trials and errors by individuals are constantly fed back to the common pool of theoretical knowledge. This is how a profession can profess *to know better*.

No doubt, a profession should have an *abstract theoretical knowledge* base, but the knowledge should not be such that it is not *educationally communicable*. This is emphasized by Abraham Flexner and Myron Lieberman (Singh, 1984). The inference one can draw here is that individual members come and go, but the profession stays on. If the knowledge pool upon which a profession is based is entirely made up of 'intuitions' and 'insights', then the profession can hardly proceed in time. Thus, an educationally communicable technique is essential for a profession to survive and prosper.

(b) *A profession is responsible for the decision that is made in the name of the profession.*

If a profession is based on an abstract theoretical knowledge base, then it involves studying in an academic setting for some time. It is somewhat easier to learn the practices and skills but it is not so easy to understand the theoretical bases upon which these skills are based. A technician learns things by *doing*. A professional *understands* and is supposed to comprehend the theoretical bases upon which every act of skill is based.

Likewise, a profession is based on a theoretical knowledge base, then the members of that profession are supposed to know better than the laymen on certain matters. The word 'profession' originates from the word *profess*, which originally conveyed the sense of knowing better.

'According to the Oxford Shorter Dictionary, the earliest meaning of the adjective 'professed' was this: 'that has taken the vows of a religious order'. By 1675, the word had been secularized thus: 'that professes to be duly qualified; professional', 'profession' originally meant the act or fact of profession. It has come to mean, 'the vocation in which one professes to be skilled in and to follow… . A vocation in which professed knowledge of some branch of learning is used in its application to the affairs of others, or in the practices of an art based upon it. Applied specifically to the three learned professions of divinity, law and medicine, also the military profession' (Hughes, 1963, p. 656).

Those who professed did it because they claimed to know better than the laymen. One proposition underlies the three oldest professions—the clergy, the law and the medicine—that they know better than the laity regarding theology, law and medicine. If professionals claim that they know better, then they should be and they are held responsible for the decisions they make. Thus, a doctor is held responsible for the course of action, which he/she prescribes for a patient.

(c) *A profession has autonomy.*
Since professionals know better than the lay people, the general norms do not apply to them. They have some privileges and responsibilities. A client, a patient and the laity are supposed to make a clean breast before the lawyer, the doctor and the priest. But, on the other hand, the doctor or the priest is not always supposed to tell the truth about their patient or laity. To stretch further about the privileges of professions, it can be said that the doctor can see forbidden parts, the priest can hear forbidden affairs and the lawyer details of the crime. Here, a distinction is made between a customer and a client. One is not a customer to a doctor or a lawyer, but a client. Similarly, a customer is always right, whereas a client is not. That is why, the profession has the privilege of autonomy about its decisions especially with regard to the following matters:
   (i) Control over the admission of new members.
   (ii) Control over the training centres where the members of the profession get their training.
   (iii) Control over licensing for any member to practice that particular profession.
   (iv) Claiming and establishing immunity from outside judgement on technical matters.

This autonomy should be understood as a tacit agreement between the profession, the society and the state. It should be distinguished from some sort of sovereignty. The professions are within society. They must maintain the faith, which the society has on them. Every profession, to be considered as legitimate and to be accepted by the society, has to get recognition by the state. It is the state, which makes the laws, regarding various professions. Doctors and lawyers may contribute in framing these laws. Thus, professionalism is a balance between the need of the autonomy in a profession and the need for public approval. Margaret Lindsay suggests the following framework for teachers as a group to enhance professionalism:

Table 2.1: Teacher autonomy and collaboration with the public to increase professionalism

	The profession's leadership responsibility for the quality of education in schools and colleges	
Joining with the public in	Establishing public policy regarding education. Determining purposes of education. Providing working condition conducive to productivity.	Joining with the profession in
Assuming autonomy for	Determining and utilizing best means for achieving agreed upon purposes. Ensuring competent professional personnel.	Granting the profession the right to make and carry out the decisions in
Joining with the public in	Evaluating achievement of purposes. Apprising public policy regarding education.	Joining with the profession in

Source: Lindsay, 1961, p. 123.

Table 2.1 implies that school teachers have to interact with the public and the state towards the purpose of education and work for better working conditions for them. At the same time, they should also try to maintain more autonomy about how they will carry out education in the classroom. The teacher organizations should appraise the public about the state of education through their research. All these in combination will make teaching more professional.

(d) *A profession has a code of ethics.*
If a profession has got privileges, then how should we ensure that it does not misuse them? Who will judge this? Since the laypersons do not know as much as the professional, how can they judge the professional? How can a layperson say which course of treatment the doctor should have taken? Actually, a profession cannot have it both ways: having privileges and not carrying out its responsibilities. Ultimately, it is the general populace that gives it its privileges. To maintain the faith of populace in it, a profession judges itself. That is why, it has a code of ethics on the basis of which it judges itself and corrects its errant members. A code of ethics serves as

a double-edged weapon. On the one hand, it saves the profession from quacks and charlatans who destroy its *social credit* and on the other hand it saves from inadequately informed prying public. Thus, it is better for a profession to have a code of ethics which defines where their responsibility begins and where it ends. A code of ethics has another advantage. It separates the individual from the act. What should be condemned or eulogized is the act and not the individual. A lawyer should not be blamed personally if he/she loses the case.

A code of ethics may be *partly written* and *partly unwritten*. Though every profession has its own special code of ethics, the following features do apply to most professions:

(i) Emotional neutrality: A professional should not see the particularistic criteria of a client, e.g., doctor should not see the class and caste of a patient before treatment. A patient, whether rich or poor, is a patient.
(ii) Disinterestedness: A professional should do his duty on the basis of the information at hand and not with some ulterior motive. A doctor or a lawyer should not help someone expecting later some quid pro quo.
(iii) No blatant competition: The profession considers itself as a community. All knowledge belongs to the community. Unhealthy competition, to the detriment of other colleagues, is considered as unethical.
(iv) Equal colleague relationship: As the client—whether rich or poor—is a client before the professional, a professional, similarly, is first and foremost a member of the profession, irrespective of his/her caste and class (Larson, 1977).

(e) *A profession has an organization and association.*
Having a code of ethics is one thing and members obeying them another. That is why, a profession needs an organization, which can enforce the code of ethics and keep quacks and charlatans out. It has in its power the 'community sanction'. It can also excommunicate the recalcitrant member.

(f) *A profession has a sense of social service and altruism.*
A professional is not truly a professional if he/she behaves only under the pressure of an organization and a code of ethics. Those are actually meant more for keeping the quacks and charlatans out rather than making the members behave under duress. What

differentiates a professional from a non-professional is some amount of altruism. A doctor will not respond to a call of a patient in the midnight only because there is a code of ethics; the responsibility comes from within. Spontaneous responsibilities like these are inculcated during professional socialization.

> 'Professional behaviour may be defined in terms of four essential attributes: a high degree of generalized and systematic knowledge; primary orientation to the community interest rather than to individual self-interest; a high degree of self-control of behaviour through codes of ethics internalized in the process of work socialization and through voluntary associations organized and operated by the work specialists themselves; and a system of rewards (monetary and honorary) that is primarily a set of symbols of work achievement and thus ends in themselves; not means to some end of individual self-interest' (Barber, 1963, p. 673).

> '(Professionals) may, as in the case of the successful doctor, grow rich; but the *meaning* of their profession, both for themselves and for the public, is not that they make money, but that they make health, or safety, or knowledge, or good government, or good law,....(professions uphold) as the criterion of success the end for which the profession, whatever it may be, is carried on, and (subordinate) the inclination, appetites, and ambitions of individuals to the rules of an organization which has as its object *to promote the performance of function*' (Tawney, as cited in Larson, 1977, p. 58).

Thus, though some kind of pecuniary reward distinguishes a professional from an amateur, it cannot have the ultimate say in what makes a profession. Professionals generally make more than others; but money is not a major distinguishing mark of a profession.

To summarize the above discussion, it can be said that a profession has the following characteristics:

(i) an abstract theoretical knowledge base;
(ii) responsibility for the decision that is made in the name of the profession;
(iii) autonomy;
(iv) a code of ethics;
(v) an organization and association; and
(vi) a sense of social service and altruism.

Carr (2000) also arrives at the same features that characterize a profession. According to Larson (1977), the above features should be added by certain qualifications. First, to have the above features in full degree is an *ideal typical* possibility. Every profession tries to attain, and has attained the above features in degrees and not fully. The important question is not whether a particular occupation is a profession or not, but how much professionalized is a particular occupation. Second, a profession cannot escape the context. The legal profession should be judged keeping in mind the context whether it is India or the United States of America. A lawyer in India is not a lawyer in the United States of America. The contexts are different. Therefore, what is considered as professional will vary from context to context. Rue Bucher and Anselm Strauss consider '...professions as loose amalgamations of segments pursuing different objectives in different manners and more or less delicately held together under a common name at a particular period in history' (Vollmer and Mills, 1966, p. 186).

The Criticism of the Taxonomic Approach

Roth (1974, as cited in Klegon, 1978) notes that the characteristics listed by the same author may vary at different times. Klegon (1978) problematizes one of the most important characteristics of a profession from the taxonomic point of view—possession of a theoretical knowledge base. He contends that it is not the knowledge per se but the social definition that matters. The knowledge of a lawyer is not created by a lawyer or lawyers but by the state and the state can change this knowledge. With regard to the knowledge of priest, Fenn (2003) talks about the processes of 'desacralizing' and 'resacralizing' by which some, were hitherto sacred, are losing their sacredness and some, were hitherto not sacred, are becoming sacred. He also points out that in the present age the people are claiming direct access to god, which is decreasing the importance of the priest. Pfadenhauer (2006) talks about the general loss of the cognitive as well as the moral superiority of the professions. For example, the competition to which orthodox medical practitioners are exposed by providers of natural remedies results from a critique of medicine that is already widespread among the general public. Psychologists and teachers are also increasingly facing similar problems. Gerhards (2001, as cited in Pfadenhauer, 2006) labels this development a 'rebellion of the public'. Launching a broadside on the taxonomic approach, Metzger writes:

> They reasoned that, if *any* occupation could be thus exalted—if there could legitimately be not only a medical profession, a legal profession, and a clerical profession (the 'learned' professions of hoary pedigree) and an engineering profession, an accounting profession, an architecture profession

> (a group of late-comers modelled on the hallowed three), but also a banking profession, an advertising profession, a real estate profession (mere businesses angling for the public's trust), and a cooking profession, a dancing profession, a baseball profession (mere skills looking for a fancy name), not to mention Mrs Warren's profession (that unspeakable skill or business that muddied everything by being called the 'first' profession) – why, then, the term would lose all eulogistic meaning and hardly make any social sense at all. Largely to save an honorific from a usage that was threatening to debase it, *these sociologists took it upon themselves to compose a list of defining attributes that would distinguish the genuine article from the unworthy pretentious rest* (1987, p. 11).

The taxonomic approach is no more considered as the most useful approach. 'The 'trait' approach is now largely assessed as being a time-wasting diversion in that it did nothing to assist our understanding of the power of particular occupations (such as law and medicine, historically) or of the appeal of 'being a professional' in all occupational groups' (Evetts, 2006, p. 519). This does not mean that the taxonomic approach has lost its appeal. There are still people who are convinced with its heuristic value (Sciulli, 2005).

The Power Approach

In contrast to the taxonomic approach, some authors focussed on the power dimension of the professions. The taxonomic approach portrayed the professions in a positive way by focussing exclusively on their contribution to society in contrast to their own status and material gains (for example, Talcott Parsons and Emile Durkheim). They did not focus on the professions' exclusive claim on the knowledge based on market closure for others and the consequent gain of power. David Sciulli summarizes this in the following words:

> During the 1970s, functionalists' manifest failure to support their second proposition in particular set the backdrop for a new stage in the sociology of professions. Anglo-American sociologists critical of functionalism adopted a revisionist posture toward professions that first drew attention to the failure and in time explicitly rejected both parts of the received approach (Johnson, 1972; Larson, 1977; Collins, 1979; Starr, 1982; Freidson, 1989). The revisionists—who call themselves 'power', 'monopoly' and 'neo-Weberian' theorists—soon established, on the basis of a quite different three-part approach, what remains the core of received wisdom in the sociology of professions today (2005, p. 917).

The power approach draws attention towards the self-serving aspects of the profession. The professions derive their power with the aid of the state and, thus, consequently are able to close the market for their services to others. It is not that there is an a priori knowledge base, but the profession defines the knowledge base and protects it from competing knowledge base. To protect itself from others, the profession inflates the credentials required to enter the profession (Collins, 1979).

Professionalism and the Contemporary Society: Lack of Trust and Consequent Hybrid Professionalism

Presently, the professions are no more seen as benign. Volume 54, issue 4 of the *Current Sociology* was devoted to the issue of decline of trust among the public towards the profession. There is now a focus on the changing loss of normative as well as ethical superiority of the professions, including the classic one of the medicine (Pfadenhauer, 2006). Widespread mass media has diminished the aura of the esoteric knowledge of the professions. The rise of alternative paradigms and counter-experts has sapped the public belief in the established professions as the sole possessor of the esoteric solutions for society's problems. Even a classic and established profession like that of a doctors is losing its autonomy regarding the course of treatment and fees to be charged. They are constrained by the critical public as well as the state in this regard (Jenny, Marjoribanks and Pirotta, 2003).

Noordegraaf (2007) identifies the current notion of professionalism as hybrid professionalism which he distinguishes from pure professionalism and situated professionalism. 'Professionalism can no longer be seen as a mere matter of occupational control (pure professionalism) or of organizational control (situated professionalism). It has to be seen as reflexive control—hybrid professionalism does not constitute occupational and organizational control; it is about controlling the meaning of control, organizing and professionalism. Professionalism is used not so much to improve organizational contexts but to improve the idea of professionalism in changing organizational contexts' (Noordegraaf, 2007, p. 775). Tables 2.2 and 2.3 show the differentiation among 'pure', 'situated' and 'hybrid' professionalism.

Professionalism is now increasingly a question of socio-symbolic legitimacy for the occupations, new ways of ordering and controlling collective conduct than the traditional control of protecting a privileged position. However, this does not mean that surrendering professional autonomy is completely good for society. 'Attempts to restore pure professionalism, with

Table 2.2: Different reactions to pressured professionalism

Type of professionalism	Explanation	Illustration
Purified professionalism	The idea of professionalism outside traditional professional domains is rejected; traditional professionalism is defined properly.	Raelin's (1986) clash of cultures; Freidson's (2001) recent emphasis on professional control; Mintzberg's (2004) rejection of professional management.
Situated professionalism	Traditional professionals work in organizational contexts; the idea of professionalism is not restricted to traditional professionals and has to be broadened to include experts.	Wilensky's (1964) recognition of program professionals; Larson's (1977) description of organizational professions; Brint's (1994) emphasis on expert professionalism; Whitley's (1989) occupational professionals.
Hybridized professionalism	Professionals are reflective practitioners; their links with outside worlds are part of professionalism; they form a social category/class.	Schön's (1983) managers as reflective practitioners; Kearny and Sinha's (1988) exploration of professional administration; Grey's (1997) analysis of professional management; Fournier's (1999) managerial professionalism as disciplinary mechanism; Evetts's (2003) emphasis on occupational change.

Source: Noordegraaf, 2007, 771.

Table 2.3: Ingredients of hybridized professionalism in public domains

Three ingredients	Explanation
Linkages between work and organized action	Subtle, soft and selective standards Frameworks for meaning making
Mechanisms for legitimating work	Rhetoric for normative control Symbolic acts
Searches for occupational identities	Work as dealing with trade-offs Communal identity

Source: Noordegraaf, 2007, 779.

strong substantive and institutional control, as well as strict closure, are understandable but nonsensical. Attempts to go beyond professionalism and surrender to businesslike, corporate, and measurement ideals are nonsensical as well' (Noordegraaf, 2007, p. 781). Thus, the notion of professionalism is not useless. 'Hybrid professionalism professionalizes ways of becoming professional without ever really becoming professional' (ibid.).

Teaching as a Profession: The Taxonomic Approach

Both the taxonomic and the market closure/power approach took medicine and law as the archetypal professional groups. Comparing teaching with these groups resulted in teaching being regarded as 'semi-professions' (Etzioni, 1969, as cited in Evetts, 2003). They did not look at the various peculiarities of teaching like its public service character.

Teaching may include from university to school teaching, and liberal education to professional education. It will be ironic if teachers of professional education themselves are not considered members of the profession. Even teachers of liberal education in universities do not have so much of a problem of claim regarding teaching as a profession because historically established professions like medicine have derived their legitimacy from their association with universities and long doses of liberal education (Larsons, 1977). The claim of profession is most acute with regard to school teaching.

There have been many attempts to salvage teaching from this identity problem staying within the so-called taxonomic approach. There are many scholarly works that specifically dealt with this issue (Stinnett, 1968; Spackman, 1991; Carr, 2000; Dhar, 1996). But all of these have dealt with this issue essentially staying within the taxonomic approach. When Rowan (1994) compared teaching with other occupations in American context and found that teaching is only next to the classic professions, it was the triumph of the taxonomic approach rather than the teaching as a profession. This finding may boost the morale of teachers, but may not free teaching from the state of being constantly compared with other professions.

While Behar (1996) in the context of India and Sykes (as cited in Mcclure, 1999) in other contexts are not convinced about teaching as a profession within the taxonomic approach, Carr (2000) equates teaching with medicine and divinity—the two oldest professions. He finds teaching non-problematic as a profession based on its moral purpose. This may be theoretically true as education was initially imparted by the clergy in the West and priest in the East. Thus, there are views, which find the teaching as a profession as non-problematic and there are views which find it contentious. Larson (1977), on the other hand, holds that the important question is not whether something is a profession or not but how far professionalized is a so-called profession. No profession will fully conform to an ideal definition of profession. From this perspective, the question seems to be how far professionalized is teaching. This does not involve a radical break up with the taxonomic approach and the reference to the classic professions because the continuum on which the degree of professionalization is determined is itself bound by taxonomy.

Difference between Teaching and Other Professions: The Debate within the Taxonomic Approach

The comparison of teaching with other classic professions within the taxonomic approach itself is problematic. One reason why the problem for school teaching becomes more acute is that it is contextual like law. A lawyer in one country cannot automatically make a lawyer in another country. Since what is considered as *teaching worthy*, and *the right methods of teaching* are susceptible to the influence of contexts, emergence of a common knowledge base like medicine is a tough problem. Besides, the context influences the minds of pupils. Even with regard to methods, it cannot be said safely, following Piaget, that cognitive stages according to age are same everywhere. Rashmi Sharma (2000) has pointed out this deficiency of contextual studies with regard to India.

The doctors and the lawyers most often deal with single individuals whereas the teacher deals with a whole community. It, therefore, becomes very difficult to judge how much a teacher has contributed to a particular student. It becomes even more difficult due to the fact that students are taught not by one teacher, but by many teachers. But, in spite of all these, primary teachers constantly accept their accountability to everyone (Broadfoot and Osborn, 1993, 1995, as cited in Nias, 1999) and a constant burden of guilt (Hargreaves, 1994, as cited in Nias, 1999). On the other hand, the medical profession is not blamed for the general health of the people. Teacher training is sometimes accused of not imparting the knowledge and skills to the teachers. But, no one thinks that by passing the medical examination one attains the proficiency as a physician (Hoyle, 2001). It takes years to become an expert. In contrast to higher education, pupils are involuntary clients in primary education whose age generally means that they are of a low status than the adults. In contradiction to this, the relationship between the professional and the adult client is voluntary.

The state plays an important role with regard to the professions. The Indian middle class or the professions of doctor, lawyer and teachers were mostly a product of British Raj (Misra, 1961). Siegrist's (2002, as cited in Sciulli, 2005) four-fold classification of four distinct types of 'professionals' during the 19th century shows the important role of the state in creating and sustaining a profession itself. His classification runs as follows:

(i) Those bound to the state directly as civil servants, who are assigned particular tasks.
(ii) Those who are state-appointed and hold public offices but are monitored and not assigned tasks.
(iii) Self-employed practitioners (free professionals) within markets for expert services that are still restricted at least somewhat, whether by the state or associations.
(iv) 'Free trade' practitioners who are left to their own devices to regulate their service markets more informally.

So far, the taxonomic approach and the power/market closure approach have portrayed the self-employed doctor or lawyer as the epitome of profession and autonomy. The focus has been less on the bureaucratization and corporatization of the professions working in large organizations or the biggest of all organizations—the state. Compared to other professions, teachers almost exclusively work as public profession and are most often employed by the state. Their claim for autonomy always necessitates the concurrence of the state (Gleeson and Knights, 2006). Since teaching is a public profession and predominantly employed by the state, it has a consequence with regard to its number too. The number of professionals that primary teaching produces in a year may be produced by other professions like medicine and engineering in ten. This also could be one of the reasons for the perceived low status of primary teachers.

Outright Rejection of the Taxonomy Approach with Regard to Teaching as a Profession

There has been some altogether skeptical as well as rejection of the taxonomic view itself. Klegon (1978) explores the nature of knowledge in each of the trinity and shows the limitations of popular perception about the degree of perfection or the state of knowledge in the trinity of medicine, law and divinity. For example, the state can change the knowledge of the legal profession and it is the court which is the ultimate interpreter of law. Theoretically, the problems related to knowledge ail not just teaching but it is applicable to any profession. There are three kinds of uncertainty, which afflict any profession:

(i) The imperfect mastery of available knowledge.
(ii) The indeterminacy of the professional knowledge itself.
(iii) The inability to distinguish between the imperfect mastery of available knowledge and the indeterminacy of professional knowledge itself (Ben-Peretz, 2001).

Klegon (1978) proposes to increase the indeterminacy or the scope of greater individual judgement rather than a strictly codified technical knowledge. He fears that technical rationality may reduce the autonomy of teachers rather than increase it. He quotes Barbara Melosh who found that nursing lost its autonomy precisely when it became technically proficient. Pratte and Rury suggest, 'The scientific quest for a rational basis for teaching probably has facilitated the deskilling process. But much of teaching is artistic and should be recognized as such…' (1988, p. 85). 'Teachers today are in the somewhat paradoxical position of losing autonomy while they are becoming technically more proficient' (ibid., p. 81).

Burbules and Densmore (1991) criticize the logic by which the taxonomic approach arrived at the characteristics of a profession. The taxonomic approach applied a sort of *post hoc ergo propter hoc* type of logic by a historical analysis of the few classic professions of law, medicine and divinity and then applied it to others without their historical analysis. This is not tenable logically. He also criticizes the professionalization project of teaching as happened in other professions by pointing out the consequent dangers. For example, the professionalism project may segment teachers into elite and the rank and file as happened in other professions. Taking the argument to its logical conclusion, Johnson (1974) found no relationship between the teachers' professional role orientation and their observed behaviour in the classroom in an empirical study. He suggested that it should not be taken for granted that if teachers develop professional characteristics, their teaching in the classroom will be improved. He suggests that the voices about professionalism may have more political value than value for the classroom.

Teacher Professionalism

A profession is a vocation having institutionalized knowledge base, skills, ethics and autonomy. Professionalization is essentially a process by which occupations or vocations institutionalize knowledge, expertise and privilege. The exact content of these knowledge, expertise and privilege will vary from profession to profession. Metzger (1987) calls the exclusive concern with status as 'professionism' rather than professionalism (Metzger, 1987). Thus, professionism and professionalization have somewhat similar connotation of being more concerned with status and privilege.

Professionalism is an ideology, which emphasizes more on knowledge, skills and ethics rather than the material benefits that accrue to a profession. Though a distinction is maintained between profession and professionalism (Evetts, 2003; Vollmer and Mills, 1966), sometimes these two are used almost identically (Carr, 2000; Larsons, 1977). The differences then are not substantial. Knowledge, skills, ethics and autonomy are emphasized as the constituents of both profession and professionalism. Vollmer and Mills say, 'We would prefer to use professionalism to refer to an ideology and associated activities that can be found in many and diverse occupational groups where members aspire to professional status' (1966, p. viii). Professionalism sometimes is a strategy to penetrate the power structure (Hinai and Ahmed, 2007).

While professionalization is concerned with standardization, professionalism is concerned with standards (Goodson, 2000). There can be three aspects of standard—intellectual, practical and ethical. Teacher professionalism should be more concerned with standard than standardization, i.e., institutionalization of status and benefits. Since there are three aspects of professionalism, i.e., intellectual, practical and ethical (ibid.), teacher professionalism should mean enhancing the knowledge base of education (intellectual), finding out more effective paedagogy (practical) and self-responsibility with regard to the total progress of pupils, irrespective of supervision from any external agency (ethical). Goodson (ibid.) distinguishes three phases of teacher professionalism as follows:

(i) Classical: The professionalism of the past emphasizing autonomy and group control of affairs.

(ii) Practical: The professionalism of the present age, which sees the teacher as an educational worker.
(iii) Principled: It is based on morally agreed principles, desire to continuously learn, to positively care and discretionary judgment. This is the professionalism, which we should aim for.

Similarly, Hargreaves (2000) has identified four ages of teacher professionalism—the pre-professional age, the age of the autonomous professional, the age of the collegial professional and the age of post-professional or postmodern. It is not as if the present age has discarded all the vestiges of the previous ages. The present age of post-professional or postmodern also contains the elements of earlier pre-professional age; for example, a naïve conception of teaching which looks at teacher professionalism as depending on enthusiasm and commitment and not on the broader aspects like teacher education and socio-political forces. Hargreaves' analysis focussed centrally on teacher action in the classroom, implying that this is the crucial criterion of teacher professionalism.

At an individual level, professionalism has been associated with the following aspects:

(a) Dedication, commitment and highly skilled practice (Helsby, 1999, as cited in Hinai, 2007).
(b) Expertise, autonomy, commitment and responsibility (Strauss, 1963, pp. 8–9).
(c) Knowledge, autonomy, responsibility (Furlong, 2000, as cited in Bates, 2007).

The issue of professionalism presents itself in many ways at an individual level. Frances Spackman (1991) out of his long teaching experiences suggests the following imperatives for a professional teacher at an individual level:

(a) Teachers should see the health and safety of children, which involves watching the corridor, playground, having primary knowledge about first aids and a list of who to call in what situations.
(b) Staff-room etiquette: Teachers should decide how much time has to be spent in the staff-room. They should maintain a balance between staying aloof and becoming too involved. It is important that they maintain personal privacy as well as pupils' privacy.
(c) Relation with pupils: They should be tough on groups and soft on individuals. The disapproval should be of the deed and not the individual.

(d) Joining the union: This involves a decision on whether they are ready for a strike in case, called for.

All the above imperatives point out that professionalism is most concerned with the quality of service. 'Broadly speaking, *professionalization* is now widely used to describe the pursuit of status and *professionalism* to describe enhancement of the quality of service' (Englund, 1996, as cited in Hoyle, 2001, p. 146). This quality of service can be translated into the following aspects with regard to primary teachers:

(a) Literacy (having an array of diagnostic and assessment instruments).
(b) Mathematics.
(c) Information and communication technologies.
(d) Reflective intelligence (Caldwell, 2000).

The following National Education Association, USA (NEA) checklist of *a good teacher* also indicates the various dimensions of the quality of service:

(a) Does each pupil feel that I am interested in him/her personally?
(b) Do I make a pleasant appearance before my pupils?
(c) Do they like, respect and have faith in my judgment?
(d) Do I have democratic relation with pupils?
(e) Do I value and cultivate relationships with parents?
(f) Am I active in parent–teacher work?
(g) A good teacher in the community
(h) Is my teaching reflected in the lives in the community?
(i) Do I have exemplary conduct?
(j) Am I friendly towards neighbours and at community gatherings?
(k) Am I active in non-teacher group?
(l) Do I participate in community improvement project?
(m) Do I take the advice and ability of laymen?
(n) Do I assist local teachers' group?

(The NEA checklist of *a good teacher in my school and in the community,* as cited in Stinnett, 1968, p. 357)

Teacher Professionalism: Difference Between the Indian and the Western Context

The debate on profession and professionalism has largely drawn upon the Anglo-American and European context (Evetts, 2003; Sciulli, 2005). Similarly, teacher professionalism has often been discussed in an a contextual sense; for example, when teaching is discussed as a profession within a taxonomic approach (Burbules and Densmore, 1991; Carr, 2000; Hoyle, 2001; Pratte and Rury, 1988; Sykes, 1991). Whenever it is contextualized, the literature is dominated by either the context of the United Kingdom (Apple, 2001; Bottery and Wright, 1997; Henson, 1987; Knight, 1984) or the United States of America (Apple, 2001; Burbules and Densmore, 1991; Gideonse, 1993; Hamm-mond and Sykes, 1999; Rowan, 1994; Shanker, 1985; Sockett, 1996; Urbanski, 1998) and to a small extent by the European context (Klette, 2002). The European view is different with regard to the recent spate of reforms with regard to teachers (ibid.). Unlike the major view in the United States of America and the United Kingdom which sees the centralization of standards sapping teacher professionalism, it is contended in the context of Europe that prescriptions can be narrow as well as broad (ibid.).

The Indian context is very different from the Anglo-American and the European contexts. The Anglo-American and the European context is a context where universalization of literacy has happened a long ago, where almost all teachers have either graduate or above as the academic degree and where teacher education is predominantly concurrent. Compared to the West, teaching is not yet considered a feminine profession in India.

Professionalism as a balance between the state, community and market is an issue in the Western context (Day, 2007). In India, it can be the balance between the state measures and one's own conscience rather than the demands of community. The vast majority of parents are illiterate and less demanding. This is probably the reason why private tuition and teacher absenteeism exist in India (Hallack and Poisson, 2007). If the community was demanding enough, then teachers would not have such a scope for being absent.

The classrooms of India are different from the ones in the West. Discipline is a big issue in developed countries (Anderson, 2004; OECD, 2005). However, children in the developing countries are better behaved than their counterparts in the developed countries (Anderson, 2004). In California, half of all the teachers leave the profession within five years mostly due to discipline problems (Marshall, 1998, as cited in Giulio, 2000, p. 5). Teachers of India do not leave the job because of discipline problem. Rather, there is a concern in India to reduce the hierarchical relation between the teacher and the pupil (NCERT, 2005). Achievement standard is perceived to be low in the Western developed countries in comparison to some of the Asian countries like Japan and Korea (Nunes and Bryant, 1996). But in India, the attempt is to attain a benchmark operationalized as 'minimum levels of learning' (MHRD, 1990) rather than comparison with other countries as such.

There are differences with regard to teacher organizations too. While material benefits are universally the concern of teacher organizations including India, teacher organizations elsewhere also do a lot more related to the profession. Teacher unions conduct surveys on teachers, launch campaigns to improve the image of teachers and have been involved actively in teacher professional development (see the country background papers to OECD, 2005; http://www.oecd.org/document/50/0,3343,en_2649_39263231_317 11602_1_1_1_1,00.html, accessed on October 11, 2008). Teacher organizations in India mostly do not have a code of ethics that is helpful to the real-life situations of teachers in a practical way. They are hardly involved in teacher professional development activities (Swami, 1980; Kingdon and Muzzamil, 2003). Teachers in India will rather take recourse to the notion of *guru* than professionalism to improve the salary.

The Indian state wants to bring teachers into the fold of professionalism to improve their performance (MHRD, 2006). Teachers in the West claim professionalism to obviate interference from the state. Most of the scholars in the West are unanimous in their opinion that the state interventions in the form of standards will reduce teacher autonomy and, therefore, may be detrimental to teacher professionalism in the long term (Hinai, 2007). The administration in the United States of America and the United Kingdom moves on a standard-based model of professionalism. The academia disapproves it. Hargreaves and Lo opine that standardization, less support, work overload sap teacher professionalization (1995). Apple (1995) has pointed out this factor of standardization, which he calls managerial techniques. The culture of teaching manuals, ready-made self-instructable materials for pupils, etc. are more concerned with making the teacher an educational worker than a professional. The adoption of these methods by the state would not improve the teacher professionally. There is always the necessity of interpretation of the curriculum in the context of the local variations in its meaning to the pupils. In the new information age with the problem of real virtuality, neither capital nor anything else can compensate for education (Hargreaves and Lo, 2000). Day opines that the state prescriptions usually run contrary to teachers' professional and personal identities that are important for job fulfillment, commitment and self-efficiency (2007).

Though the context is different, the solution to teacher professionalism by the Indian state does not seem different. This is evident by the following actions: The National Council for Teacher Education (NCTE) was made a statutory body in 1993. There has been an increasing focus on teacher curriculum framework. The NCTE brought out in 1998 'Competency-Based and Commitment-Oriented Teacher Education for Quality School Education (Pre-Service Education)'. The National Council for Educational Research and Training (NCERT) too has come out with a 'Curriculum Framework for Quality Teacher Education' in collaboration with the NCTE in 2006. There has been increasing emphasis on in-service training. There has been an effort to catch up with the West by emphasizing the *reflective teacher* in the National Curriculum Framework (NCERT, 2005) without first deciding about the other two models—the charismatic and the competent teacher (Moore, 2004). A teacher should be both competent and reflective and not only one of these two. 'Professional teachers must be capable of profound reflection on practice; competent to enter into a dialogue of the practice they know and the theory or literature they read' (Sockett, 1996, p. 26). The most recent attempt has been the effort to define the grey area of teacher professionalism (MHRD, 2006). All these actions remind one of a standard-based framework that one repeatedly comes across in the literature on teacher professionalism in the West.

3

THE STATE AND TEACHER PROFESSIONALISM

Introduction

As compared to the concept of profession, professionalism has its origin in the 1990s. The concept of profession originated in the nineteenth century in the context of the industrial revolution and the great progress in science and medicine, which gave rise to the modern professions. There is little similarity between the modern professions and their ancient counterparts.

In contrast to 'profession', which is 'standardization of knowledge, status and accountability', professionalism is more concerned with 'standards'. Profession, in addition to standards, is concerned with material and moral benefits. Professionalism is more concerned with the knowledge base from which the profession derives its legitimacy, and the performance of the individual members.

Simply speaking, professionalism in teaching is concerned with the art and the science of teaching. So when we speak of the state and teacher professionalism, we have to take into account the state policies towards teacher education and teaching standards, and towards the material conditions of teachers, like salary. We also have to take into account teachers' responses through teacher unions. Figure 3.1 illustrates this.

In Figure 3.1, the three angled arrows show that teacher education and teacher working conditions are influenced by negotiation and struggle between the state and teachers' union.

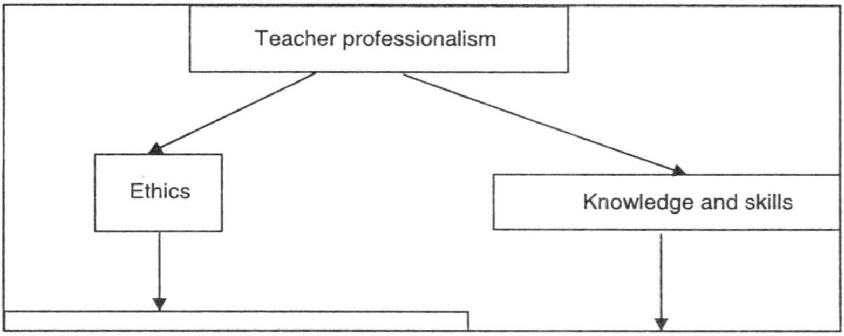

Figure 3.1: Relationship between the state and teacher professionalism

A Brief History of Teacher Education

The school system, as we know, is about two hundred years old. Initially, education was not in the domain of the state. It was imparted by the religious establishments. The content of education was predominantly religious. In England, the earliest forms of present-day schools were entirely connected to religion. They were the 'song scoles' where the poor boys were trained to chant and the 'lecture scoles' where clerks were taught to read in the services of the church (about tenth century). Any kind of systematic state-supported schooling started with the establishment of grammar schools. These were the schools meant for poor pupils. Around 1550, King Edward VI founded 21 grammar schools. In the beginning of the nineteenth century, various societies connected to the church were established in England for the promotion of education. 'They (the various education societies)...created a demand for a system of national education which found its first expression in parliament in 1833 in a grant of 20,000 pounds on motion of lord Althorpe' (Barnard, 1861, p. 332). In 1851, 'the scholars on books' as a proportion to the population were 11.76 per cent. Almost all the schools were established and managed by the religious denominations and were aided by the state—like the present day case of aided institutions. In France, from 1791 to 1794, a system of public schools was projected in which primary education was to be free to all at the expense of the state by various ordinances of the convention (the government during the revolution). In the United States of America, the public school system for the general population was established during the nineteenth century. For example, the school system came into being in Arkansas in 1869, in California in 1800, in Georgia in 1870, in Indiana in

1848 (a system of free schools) and in Kentucky in 1838. There was no systematic state connection with the education before the establishment of the public school system. The first connection came with the appointment of state 'superintendents of education' in various states during the nineteenth century. It was only after this that the focus came to teachers, the quality of teachers and the training of teachers.

History of teacher education follows the general trajectory of education. Teacher education, especially in Europe and England, started first in the religious establishments and was then adopted by the state. In the United States of America, initially, teacher training was first spearheaded by private initiatives and philanthropy and only aided by the state.

> The first school specially destined for educating and training teachers in the principles and practice of their profession was instituted by the Abbe' de la Salle while he was canon of the cathedral at Rheims in 1681 and was perfected into the institute of the *Brothers of the Christian Schools* in 1684. In 1697, Augustus Herman Franke' founded in connection with his orphan school at Halle a teachers' class composed of poor students who assisted him certain hours in the day in his schools in return for their board and instruction. Out of these he selected about the year 1704 twelve who exhibited the right basis of piety, knowledge and the aptness to teach and constituted them his '*seminarium preceptorum*' or teachers seminary. These pupils received separate instruction for two years and acquainted a due degree of practical skill in the classes of the same general establishment. Teachers thus trained, and hundreds of others who resorted to Halle, to profit by the organization and spirit of the schools of Franke', disseminated knowledge of better methods of school organization and instruction throughout Europe in the course of the next half century (Barnard, 1863, p. 753).

The first normal school and the polytechnic school in France was established in 1794 in the context of various ordinances from 1791 to 1794 to establish public schools in which primary education was to be free to all at the expense of the state.

> In England, 'the first step towards the formation of a more efficient body of teachers was taken by Sir J.P.K. Shuttleworth and Mr. E. Carleton Tuffnell, when, in the year 1840, they founded a school at Battersea for training masters for the schools of pauper children, maintaining at their private cost, aided by some of their friends' (ibid., p. 343). 'The state normal school at Framingham, the first normal school under state auspices in America, was opened at Lexington, with a formal address by Governor Everette, on July 3rd, 1839. Three young ladies were all that presented themselves as candidates for examination' (ibid., p. 659). '... these schools (in America) were not at first state schools but

the schools of private munificence aided by the state—the state being responsible neither for success nor failure. Consequently and indeed as a measure of policy also private aid was solicited' (ibid., p. 666).

This is equally applicable in the case of England. Most of the American states had established normal schools for teachers between 1839 and 1867.

In the early period, there was no uniformity about the duration of the teacher training courses. In 1847, the duration of the longer course in Borough Road Normal School (the first teacher training institution in England) was of one year. In 1866, the duration of the teacher training course in Massachusetts State Normal School was two years. The Borough Road Normal School (1847) had two types of courses: one of six months and another of one year duration. Borough Road Normal School was the first normal school in England and Wales. It started as a model school in 1805 conducting the 'training of schoolmasters'. The course content was divided into 12 classes. These 12 classes in ascending order were (pupils would study them as they progressed):

(i) Grammar and English composition
(ii) Elocutions: readings in prose and poetry
(iii) Arithmetic and mathematics
(iv) Model lessons in natural philosophy
(v) Art of teaching (12 weeks)
(vi) Practical simultaneous lessons
(vii) Bible lesson
(viii) Schools of design
(ix) Geography and history
(x) Arithmetic
(xi) Elements of physics
(xii) Vocal music (Barnard, 1861, pp. 435–37).

The total time of the curriculum of the Massachusetts State Normal School (1866) was two years, divided into four terms of 20 weeks each. The course contents included the following in ascending order:

(a) Arithmetic
(b) Geometry
(c) Chemistry
(d) Grammar and analysis of the English language
(e) Physiology and hygiene
(f) Botany and zoology
(g) Algebra

(h) Geography and history
(i) Natural philosophy
(j) *Rhetoric and English literature*
(k) *Mineralogy and geology*
(l) *Astronomy*
(m) Mental and moral science—including the art of reasoning
(n) Theory and art of teaching
(o) The civil polity of Massachusetts and the United States (Barnard, 1868, p. 657)

In the above, the emphasis is mine. I think mental and moral science is necessary in the higher classes of teacher training, but it is difficult to say how far Rhetoric and English literature, Mineralogy and geology, and Astronomy are necessary for teacher training. Probably, these were included to make the course look more wholesome. Another contrast between the English and the American curriculum was the religious education. Bible lesson was in the curriculum of teacher training in England but not in the United States of America. The Americans were influenced a lot by the French revolution. The division between the church and the state was maintained.

Teacher Education in India: A Historical Overview

Teacher education in India has a long past but short history. Gurukul centred tradition of the Vedic period was somewhat modified and enriched under the influence of Buddhist vihara-based system. This continued till the eleventh century AD. The arrival of the Muslims witnessed the rise of a parallel Maktab-based tradition and the two traditions thrived side by side till the coming of the British.

'The first normal school in India was set up at Serampore (Bengal) by Carey, Marshman, and Ward in 1793. This was the result of collaborative effort between the Danish and English missionaries. The Portuguese missionaries also ran a few seminaries to train candidates for the priesthood,' (Devi, 1968, p. 4). Thus, a normal school was established in India much before the United States of America (1839) and England (1840). But some kind of progress was made only in the beginning of the twentieth century. For example, in 1881–82 'the Madras College ...had 8 graduates, 3 first year arts pass students and 18 matriculates on its roll. The Lahore College had 30 students and admitted those who had passed the 1st year arts' (ibid., p. 10). If this was the condition of colleges, then one can imagine the condition of normal schools. The Hartog Committee (1929) was shocked to learn that only 44 per cent of teachers in primary schools were trained and only 28 per cent had completed middle course (ibid., p. 28).

In the initial period, the focus was to study the existing subjects well rather than studying for teaching them well. '...the expression training of teachers had at this time an entirely different connotation from what it is today, and meant general education in Western knowledge, that is to say in subjects as algebra, geometry, astronomy and history of England rather than *instruction in the practical art of teaching*' (Nurullah and Naik, 1943, p. 433). The training given in the year 1826 emphasized on knowledge of content and method of instruction, as theory was unheard of. But they had enough 'supervised practice' under the prevailing system. The new grant-in-aid rules for 1859 required that every teacher for whom grants were made had to have obtained a certificate of training. In 1882, Indian education commission recommended for an examination in the principles and practice of teaching, success in which was to be a condition of permanent employment in any secondary school. In 1919, Sadler Commission recommended a department of education in the universities to promote systematic and practical study of the science and art of education. It also recommended that a postgraduate degree in education be instituted (Devi, 1968).

The government was making gradual efforts to improve the teacher quality. But the task was not easy. The Quinquennial Review of the Progress of Education in India, 1917–22, observed,

> by holding out the bribe of a stipend and perhaps by the use of some thinly veiled compulsion, there are gathered into the guru training schools a number of teachers whose knowledge of the subjects they teach is little above that of the unfortunate taught. Here they attempt in one year or two to go through the whole upper primary or middle vernacular course with a top-dressing of the art and theory of teaching superadded. There are no foundations on which to build, so that it is not surprising to quote the inspector, Dacca division, that 'the actual work done by the training teachers in primary schools is cruelly disappointing. It is in fact a misnomer to class the ordinary product of the guru-training school under the head 'trained'. To undergo training implies the acquisition of professional and technical skill. Training as imparted in Bengal is merely a despairing attempt to supply by special means some point of what is wanting in the teachers' general equipment (Nurullah and Naik, 1943, p. 441).

Teacher education initially arose to strengthen the vernacular education rather than English education. It was only after 1855–60, when the anglicists won the argument over the orientalists, that the education system was geared towards Western education. The *gurus* of Bengal were the teachers of traditional *tols*.

The duration of the training courses varied from six months for *gurus* in Bengal to three years in Bombay and Coorg in 1885. Teacher training curriculum comprised history, geography, mathematics, English, oriental language and grammar in 1828. The curriculum became a little elaborate in 1925. The curriculum in 1925 in the Maharashtra (earlier Bombay) for teacher training included principles of education, mother tongue, arithmetic, history, geography, science—physics, chemistry, physiology, and hygiene and first-aid, drawing, nature study and gardening, physical education, hand work, music (very similar to the early English and American curriculum). As compared to the curriculum in 1910, algebra and second language were removed in 1919 and nature study or geography was added to it.

Teacher Education in Post-Independent India

Teacher education in post-independent India was no one's exclusive responsibility. It was looked after by the Centre, states, the universities and private enterprises. That's why the quality of teacher education varied widely across India. The principal efforts in post-Independent India were to streamline it and make the training quality comparable across India. The principal ways in which this happened were the following:

(a) Some commissions recommended to appoint more women teachers.
(b) There were national seminars and conferences on teacher education.
(c) An exclusive commission for school teachers was appointed.
(d) There were national level efforts to streamline the teacher education curriculum.
(e) National level institutions were established to monitor teacher education (*Policy Perspectives in Teacher Education: Critique & Documentation* by the National Council for Teacher Education, http://www.ncte-india.org/pub/policy/policy_o.htm).

All these recommendations gradually streamlined teacher education and made the teacher education as it is today. There were also direct attempts to streamline the teacher education curriculum. Following is a very brief account of the main recommendations of some of the important committees and commissions with regard to teacher education in India:

a. The University Education Commission (1948–49) headed by Dr Radhakrishnan recommended principles of education, methods of teaching, history of education, school management and hygiene as compulsory papers in teaching (Nurullah and Naik, 1943).

b. The Secondary Education Commission (1953) appointed to examine the conditions of school education made specific suggestions about the preparation of teachers. Among its chief recommendations were:
   (i) Two-year training programme for undergraduates.
   (ii) One-year training programme for graduates.
   (iii) Affiliation of graduate training colleges to universities.
   (iv) Training for organizing curricular activities.
   (v) Organization of refresher courses.
   (vi) Providing residential facilities.
   (vii) Emphasis on research.
   (viii) Exchange of teachers from teacher colleges to schools and vice versa (*Policy Perspectives in Teacher Education: Critique & Documentation* by the NCTE, undated).

c. Indian Education Commission (1964–66) was the first that gave comprehensive suggestions regarding teacher education. Some of the important recommendations were:
   (i) To remove the isolation between teacher training institutions, universities and schools.
   (ii) The duration of the professional courses should be two years for primary teachers who have completed the secondary school course. It should be one year for the graduate students, but the number of working days in a year should be increased to 230.
   (iii) Attempt should be made to recruit first and good second-class students to teacher training institutions and adequate scholarships should be given to them.
   (iv) Every training institution should have an experimental or demonstration school attached to it.
   (v) The duration of the training course for primary teachers should be uniformly two years for those who have completed the secondary school course. Teachers with different educational qualifications should not be put into the same course (ibid.).

d. National Commission on Teachers-I or School Teachers, 1983–85 was appointed to enquire all aspects of school teachers. Some of the important recommendations that it made with regard to teacher education were:
   (i) Considering that the elementary is so crucial a level, we are strongly of the view that the professional training for the elementary

teachers should begin only after the twelfth class and the training should be of at least two years duration.

(ii) Parallel to the four-year-integrated course we have recommended for the secondary teacher, we see the possibility of developing a four-year-training programme for the elementary teacher after class ten.

(iii) Training of teachers should be skill-based.

(iv) The trainees should be provided opportunities to teach for not less than 6–8 weeks in the first year and 12 weeks in the second.

(v) A demonstration school should be attached to every training institute (ibid.).

The next important event was the National Policy on Education (NPE), 1986.

National Policy on Education, 1986

The NPE 1986, called for an *overhaul* of the teacher education system in the country. It emphasized the need for continuing education for teachers to meet the thrust envisaged in the policy. A new centrally sponsored scheme of restructuring and reorganization of teacher education was launched in 1987–88. It had following five components:

(i) setting up of district institutes of education and training (DIETs).

(ii) strengthening of 250 colleges of teacher education (CTEs) and development of 50 of them as institutes of advanced studies (IASEs) in education.

(iii) strengthening of state councils of education and training (SCERTs).

(iv) orientation of schoolteachers.

(v) establishment and strengthening of Department of Education in universities (Working Group Report on Elementary and Adult Education, 2001).

Table 3.1 shows the quantitative progress of the above scheme. The scheme was modified in 1993 and 2000 and the upper limits of central assistance were raised to compensate the escalation in costs of construction, increase in price of equipment, etc. The tenth plan provided additional central assistance for boundary wall and approach road. The Special Orientation Programme of Primary Teachers was also upgraded to include upper primary teachers (Working Group Report on Elementary and Adult Education, 2001). By 2004, 500 DIETs, 87 CTEs, 38 IASEs and 30 SCERTs had been set up for teacher education.

Table 3.1: Progress on teacher education schemes

Item	Target	Achievement (as on March 31, 1998)	IX Plan target	IX Plan sanctioned
Programme for Mass Orientation of School Teachers (1986–90)	2.0 million	1.76 million	—	—
Establishment of DIETs	425 by the end of VII plan	442	100	35
Upgradation of Secondary Teacher Education Institute into CTEs/IASEs	135	110	125 CTEs + 15 IASEs	12 CTEs + 37 IASEs
Special Orientation Programme of Primary Teachers during 1993–97	1.8 million	1.0 million	—	—
Strengthening of SCERTs (29)	All SCERTs	20	—	—

Source: Rajput and Walia, 2002, p. 18; for IX Plan: Working Group Report on Elementary and Adult Education, 2001.

In India, DIETs are now the principal focus with regard to elementary teacher training. The tenth plan-working group (Working Group Report on Elementary and Adult Education, 2001) says that DIETs are not the same in all the states. They are more effective in southern states which have a tradition of education. It emphasized on the linkage of DIETs with schools. Akai (1999) mentions in her study about DIETs of Delhi and Gurgaon that higher secondary teacher trainees of DIETs evaluated theoretical subjects unfavourably. On the other hand, the graduate trainees opined theoretical subjects like 'Education in Emerging India' favourably. Probably, the teacher trainees with higher secondary qualification could not realize the importance of theoretical subjects properly.

DPEP was the major programme from 1996, which stressed on teacher education. The focus was mostly on in-service training, which ranged from three to twenty days. The focuses were joyful learning, child centred instruction, competencies in MLL, multi-grade instruction and gender sensitization. Though most of the trainings had a module on gender sensitization, they did not have one on sensitivity towards SC/ST students. The model, which DPEP adopted, was cascade model. A cascade model has top down approach. Master trainers train block officers and they in turn train the teachers. Most states adapted the existing Special Orientation Programme of Primary Teachers of the NCERT, which was mainly motivational to include activity preparation. Evaluation of DPEP does not convince whether massive short-term training in DPEP (in some cases lasting only three days) will uplift teachers' knowledge and skills (The World Bank, 2003).

National Council for Teacher Education

The NCTE was established in May 1973 by a government resolution to advise central and state governments on all matters pertaining to teacher education, with its secretariat located in the NCERT. The NCTE's status and role till 1993 was purely advisory and it did not have statutory powers to enforce its guidelines. As per the provisions laid down in the NPE 1986 and the Programme of Action for its implementation, the NCTE has been conferred statutory status as per the NCTE Act No. 73 of 1993 passed by the Parliament and assented to by the President. It has come into existence with effect from May 17, 1995. The Act provides for the establishment of the NCTE with a view to achieving planned and coordinated development of teacher education system throughout the country, regulation and proper maintenance of norms and standards in the teacher education system and for matters connected therewith. The NCTE has now prescribed detailed guidelines for teacher education programmes, which cover infrastructure, teaching staff and facility. The guidelines are available on the web. Some of its main features are:

(a) The duration of teacher training will be two years.
(b) There shall be at least 150 teaching days and 30 days of practice teaching in a nearby school.
(c) Both the principals and lecturers should have five years' teaching experience in recognized elementary schools.

In this context, it is relevant to mention the survey of teacher educators carried on by the NCTE in 1999. In India, though there are surveys on teachers by NCERT and others, survey on teacher educators is very rare. Following are some of the characteristics about teacher educators which have a bearing on teacher education:

(a) 79.4 per cent had second class in BA/B.Sc./B.Com.
(b) 59.4 per cent had second class in MA/M.Sc./M.Com.
(c) 94.7 per cent used regional language as the medium of instruction.

At the all India level, out of 150 teacher educators whose age ranged between 41 and 47 years,

(a) 91.3 per cent had no research paper to their credit in the last 5 years.
(b) 80 per cent had no article published in the last 5 years.
(c) 83.3 per cent had never published a book (NCTE, 1999).

The above academic and research credentials of the teacher educators do not inspire confidence. With such credentials, they would not be able to provide leadership to the teacher trainees; for example, very few had worked on any research paper in the last five years. Also, one does not know the quality of the research papers that few of them published.

According to Mehta (2004), 58.55 per cent regular primary teachers had up to higher secondary qualification, which in case of para-teachers was 50 per cent. Graduates and postgraduates constituted 36.69 per cent in case of regular primary teachers while they constituted 42.65 per cent of the para-teachers. Thus, India is yet to attain the position when graduates and postgraduates will constitute the majority in primary school teachers, like the position in the developed countries.

Model Teacher Education Curriculum

The NCTE first brought out a curriculum framework for teacher education in 1978. Another curriculum framework was issued in 1988. But it did not catch national attention because the work for the NPE 1986 had already started. Thereafter, another curriculum framework was issued in 1998 after wide consultation.

In 1972, the theory papers of Principles of Education, Educational Psychology, Teaching of Mathematics, Teaching of Science, Teaching of Social Studies and Teaching of Languages were taught almost everywhere in India. School Organization and Management was compulsory in 12 states. Except five states, other states did not have any optional papers, and these five states had only one optional paper. The procedure for practice teaching varied across different states. Where it was done on a weekly basis it varied between two and three days, and where it was done in a block of time it generally was two–three months (NCERT, 1977). Maximum teacher training courses had the duration of two years and some had one year. Also, those who taught were not much above in qualification than those whom they had to teach. For example in many cases, the qualification required to join the teacher training courses were SSC, high school or VIII pass. After the course, they became eligible to teach classes between V and VIII. They were not in a high pedestal than the subjects whom they taught. This could be due to the shortage of teachers. Almost the same trend prevailed in 1995–96; Table 3.2 shows this.

In 1970s there were some teacher training courses, which accepted VIII pass students. That situation no longer exists. But still, it is very different from developed countries where graduation is the minimum qualification for primary teaching.

The National Council of Education Research and Training (NCERT) also has developed a model curriculum for elementary and secondary teacher education. State governments and universities may adopt/adapt this in their teacher education programmes. The NCERT

Table 3.2: Pre-service training of teachers for different levels of education

Level of education	Type of training institutions	Admission requirements	Duration of the course	Diploma/ degree awarded
Pre-primary Education	Private Unaided	12 years of schooling	One to Two years	Certificate/ Pre-school in Education
Primary Education	Government Private Aided Private Unaided	10/12 years of schooling	One to Two years	Certificate/ Diploma in Elementary Education
Secondary Education	Government Private Aided Private Unaided	Graduation	One year Two years*	Bachelor of Education
Four year integrated course	Government Aided	12 years	Four years	Bachelor of Education

*In 1999, some institutions initiated a two year teacher education programme for secondary teachers based upon the recommendations made by the National Council for Teacher Education

(*Source:* Rajput and Walia, 2002, p. 7)

revises this curriculum from time to time. The curriculum brought out in 1991 for both levels has the following components:

- Foundation Courses
  - Education in Emerging India
  - Educational Psychology
- Stage Relevant Specialization
  - Elementary Education and Teacher Functions
- Language Teaching
  - Teaching of Mother Tongue
  - Teaching of English Language
  - Teaching of Mathematics
  - Teaching of Environmental Studies (Science)
  - Teaching of Environmental Studies (Social Studies)
  - Teaching of Health and Physical Education
  - Teaching of Art
  - Teaching of Work Experience
- Additional Specialization
  - Science Teaching/Social Studies Teaching/Pre-school Education
- Elective—one
  - Adult Education
  - Non-formal Education
  - Social Education
  - Tribal Education
  - Multiple Class Teaching
  - Population Education
  - Special Education
  - Educational Technology
- Practicum
  - Practical Work
  - Internship in Teaching (in Primary and Upper Primary/Pre-school Systems)

The weightage for different components is mentioned below:

• Foundation Course	20%
• Stage Relevant Specialization	30%
• Additional Specialization	10%
• Practicum	40%

The structure discussed above is good. It would have been better if it included a course on philosophy and sociology of education. For example, the kindergarten could simply be reduced to some activities. Alternatively, the teacher trainee can understand Froebel's philosophy behind the kindergarten. Much of the modern psychology of education is based on the ideas of some key philosophers like Comenius, Dewey, Herbart and Montessori. Additionally, a course on sociology of education in India would better enable the teacher trainee to understand the educational scenario in India. Without this kind of course, some of their courses like 'Education in Emerging India' will be reduced to just history, and course of 'Tribal Education' will be reduced to statistics about the progress of education among the tribals.

The NCTE had recently put in its web site a Curriculum Framework for Quality Teacher Education. This latest curriculum framework places teacher education in the current socio-political context. The NCERT too has come out with a Curriculum Framework for Quality Teacher Education in collaboration with the NCTE in 2006. Thus, there seems to be a duplication of work between NCTE and NCERT. There is another instance of duplication of work between NCTE and NCERT. The NCTE brought out in 1998 'Competency Based and Commitment Oriented Teacher Education for Quality School Education (Pre-service Education)'. The NCERT too brought out an edited volume 'Teacher Commitment' in 2003 (Walia K., ed., 2003). Much of the literature of the NCERT and the NCTE with regard to teacher education has of late portrayed a routineness and helplessness about teacher professionalism in India.

In India, all commissions and people concerned with education opine that teacher training should be linked to university. Singh (2003) is probably the only one who voices against this trend. According to Singh, the association of teacher training with universities has made it more academic to the detriment of the skill aspect of training. For him, the role of universities is to strengthen subject-content knowledge while the role of teacher training institutions is to strengthen the skill aspect. One may not agree with his prescription of separation of teacher education from universities. But, it is also true that the present M.Ed. programme for teacher educators is more academic than skill based. Besides, it does not make them specialists in a particular subject area.

The State and Teacher Education

Pre-Service Education

Pre-service teacher education can be of two types—concurrent and consecutive. In concurrent teacher education, the trainee pursues the education course along with other subjects. In consecutive type of teacher education, the trainee pursues exclusively teacher education course after finishing the required amount of general education. While the concurrent model is considered more qualitative, there are advantages of consecutive model too. The consecutive model allows people to enter teaching profession after they finish their education. This gives them adequate time to take a decision to enter the teaching careers, unlike the concurrent model where they have to decide at a young age.

In all Organization for Economic Co-operation and Development (OECD) countries, except France and Germany, primary teacher education is structured along concurrent lines (see Appendix 3.3). On average, the length of primary teacher education programme in OECD countries is 3.9 years. It is five years in Finland and France and between 5.5 and 6.5 years in Germany. In case of India, the duration of integrated courses is like other countries—four years for an integrated B.Ed. course. But, in India, most of the primary teacher training happens outside the university system in exclusive institutions without any link to a university. In China also, primary teacher education is done only in teacher education institutions without being attached to any university. The fallout of this has been the low value, which has been attached to the teacher training programmes (Morris and Williamson, 1998). In most of the European countries, the teacher education institutions are being made university-like so that degrees will be mutually recognizable in the future. This is a result of the Bologna declaration. For example, the teacher training institutes were made university-like in Switzerland recently (OECD, 2005).

Germany, France and Canada seem to give a special emphasis on pedagogy than other countries where pedagogy is at par with other subjects. Pedagogy is given 6–8 semesters in Germany and one year in both France and Canada (Nelson, 1994).

Most of the countries give importance to practice teaching except China (10 days), Japan (24 days) and Taiwan (15–20 days). Practice teaching is not given so much importance in these countries because of the Confucian tradition of giving value to academics rather than the practicality of practice teaching. China, Japan and Taiwan will be on the lower side of the emphasis given to practice teaching. Countries like USA (50–70 days), Canada (8 weeks), Australia (40–100 days), Hong Kong (40 days) will be in the medium range. Countries like UK (32 weeks), Italy (one year) and Germany (18–24 months) almost put a premium on practice teaching (Nelson, 1994; Morris and Williamson, 1998). The NCTE in India has recommended a minimum of 30 days of practice teaching. In the 1970s, it was about two–three months where it was done en bloc and two–three days where it was done on a weekly basis (NCERT, 1977). Recently, practice teaching experience is 'increasingly being incorporated throughout the entire teacher education programme and its scope is being broadened. Teacher trainees are asked to participate in school activities, observe classrooms, tutor young people and serve as teacher aides prior to actual practice teaching' (McIntyre et al., as cited in OECD, 2005, p. 108).

In approximately 50 per cent of the OECD countries, prospective teachers are also required to pass a competitive examination and/or successfully complete a period of mandatory teaching experience before they become eligible for appointment as permanent teachers. Competitive examinations exist in France, Germany, Greece, Italy, Japan, Korea, Spain and Mexico (in some states). This is done either to give a teaching license or to determine the successful candidates for appointment in public schools. Mandatory work experience of between one and three years is also a requirement for permanent positions in Italy, Spain, England, Ireland, New Zealand, Northern Ireland, Scotland, Turkey, Israel (for primary and lower secondary education), and the United States, (OECD, 2005; also see Appendix 3.3). In India, there is no state examination for primary teaching in contrast to lecturership where one has to pass an examination conducted by the state. The examination, which the teacher training institutions hold, is what makes somebody eligible for primary teaching in India.

Teacher Professional Development

'The tendency over the last few years has been to begin to accept teaching as a profession, and consequently the transformation from *teacher training* to *teacher professional development*' (Villegas, 2003, p. 36). Academic programme for teacher professional development manifests itself mainly through pre-service and in-service teacher education. Professional development programmes are meant for updating and broadening the knowledge and skills of teachers. Apart from broadening knowledge and skills, professional development programmes are also conducted to facilitate educational reforms, to make teachers perform new functions and for larger school development (OECD, 2005). Increasingly, teacher professional development is considered as a long-term process, which occurs through both formal and informal channels. There is criticism against the traditional type of teacher professional development through conferences and workshops.

The earliest models of teacher development were the 'trait and factor model' and the 'process-product' model (Sprinthal, Reiman and Theis-Sprinthal, 1994, as cited in Sabharwal, 2002).The earlier models became less relevant when new initiatives happened in teacher education in the 1980s. According to Sparks and Loucks-Horsley, presently five models of staff development exist (1995, as cited in Sabharwal, 2002). Table 3.3 illustrates these five models.

Table 3.4 shows the models of teacher professional development which are practised in the world given by Villegas after reviewing the literature on teacher professional development.

Table 3.3: The five models of staff development: their assumptions

Model	Assumptions
Individually guided model	• The individual teacher can determine his/her learning needs and provide self-direction leading to desired self-learning. • Adults learn efficiently when they initiate and plan their learning activities.
Observation/ assessment model	• Observation of one's practice deepens one's insight into how one can become a better practitioner. • Availability of another person's observation of one's practice furthers the learning of the observed as well as the observer. • Observing positive change in observation-based feedback encourages a person to strive for further improvement.
Involvement in development/ improvement process model	• Persons working closest to the job best understand the inputs needed for improving their performance. • Participation in demanding and challenging programmes brings about improvement in teacher's knowledge base and skills.
Training model	• Certain behaviour and techniques are worthy of replication by teachers in the classroom. • Training, especially when planned well, add to the teacher's repertoire of skills.
Inquiry model	• Teachers are intelligent, inquiring being with legitimate expertise and significant experience repertoire. • They can search for and collect valid data and reflect upon it. • As their new understanding develops, teachers can formulate new questions and strive for their answers.

Source: derived from Sabharwal, 2002, pp. 251–53.

Table 3.4: Teacher professional development model

Organizational partnership model	Small group/individual model
Professional development schools	Supervision: traditional and clinical
Other university–school partnerships	Students' performance assessment
Other inter-institutional collaborations	Workshops, seminars, courses, etc.
Schools' networks	Case-based study
Teachers' networks	Self-directed development
Distance education	Cooperation or collegial development
	Observation of excellent practices
	Teachers participation in new roles
	Skills development
	Reflective model
	Project-based model
	Portfolios
	Action research
	Use of teachers' narratives
	Regeneration or cascade model
	Coaching/mentoring

Source: Villegas, 2003, p. 70

Table 3.4 includes both the formal and informal resources for teacher professional development. For example, the formal resources in Japan include ministry, local boards, universities and the informal resources include teachers' union, voluntary study groups, case study, monthly meeting and journals, schools' in-house study workshops based on classroom observation and self-study (Sato, 1992, as cited in Villegas, 2003). A survey of 3,987 teachers in Japan in 1981 indicated that more than half of them had been active in some kind of voluntary study groups (Shimahara, 1995, as cited in Villegas, 2003, p. 97).

Teacher professional development can happen either in a centralized or decentralized way. In the centralized model, the state plays the main role while in decentralized model other agencies like the universities play an important role.

> Professional development is largely provided by state agencies in France, Germany, Korea and Spain. On the other hand professional development program is decentralized in Flemish community in Belgium, Denmark, Finland, Hungary, Italy, the Netherlands, Norway, Sweden, and Switzerland. These countries are moving from a supply-oriented model of in-service training to one based on demand. Schools are allocated funds to organize in-service training responding to their specific needs and can pay for trainers, researchers or

> advisers. In such countries universities and other teacher education providers sometimes compete with non-government agencies, private consultants and training firms offering professional development activities for teachers. (OECD, 2005, pp. 122–23)

In France, 'missions' have been created in all administrative regions to support the work that pre-existing institutions were already doing. On the other hand, the schools are primarily responsible for the in-service education of their own staff in the Netherlands though they will get the budgetary support from the state (Villegas, 2003). The other countries where in-service programs are being designed and offered by the schools are Germany, Japan, Spain and the UK (Benejam and Espinet, 1992, as cited in Villegas, 2003). In the UK and Spain, in-service teacher preparation focuses on action research, problem-solving, group interaction, etc. (ibid.).

> "In New Zealand, teachers are not fully registered until they have acquired two years of classroom experience, during which they can participate in a programme of 'advice and guidance' which includes mentoring, discussion groups, observation of other more experienced teachers and written record of the induction programme. In addition, schools receive resources from the district in order to support not only the work of the new teachers, but also that of their mentors. In Japan, beginning teachers are given a lighter workload. This allows them to attend in-school training sessions twice a week and out-of-school training once a week and also offers them the guidance and support of the 'guidance teachers" (APEC, 1999; Hawley and Hawley, 1997, as cited in Villegas, 2003, p. 60). In New Zealand, schools which hire newly graduate teachers receive more funding to support a greater number of mentor teachers and provide enough time for the induction activities.

By undergoing professional training, teachers reset the goals, practices, beliefs regarding themselves as well as the students. This in turn influences their actions. Professional development is culture building and not mere skill training (Cochran–Smith and Lyttle, 2001, as cited in Villegas, 2003). 'When looking at professional development, one must examine the content of the experience, the processes by which the professional development will occur, and the contexts in which it will take place' (Ganser, 2000) Fielding and Schalok, 1985, as cited in Villegas, 2003, p. 11). Changing teacher without changing contexts, beliefs, structure, rarely creates a significant change (Darling-Hammond and Mclaughlin, 1995; Fullan et al., 1995, as cited in Villegas, 2003). A teacher professional development model that does not take teachers into account does not succeed. There is a need for professional development of the teacher, by the teacher and for the teacher (Pierce and Hunsaker, 1996, as cited in Villegas, 2003).

Though there are many ways in which teacher professional development is done in different countries, there is a concern about the effectiveness of the models. Hawley and Valli (1999) reviewed the literature for the characteristics of an effective teacher professional development model. According to them, following should be the characteristics of an effective professional development model:

(a) It should be student-centred.
(b) Teachers themselves should be involved in the selection of problems and solutions.
(c) It should be school based.
(d) It should involve collaborative problem solving.
(e) It should be continuous and supported.
(f) It should do an evaluation of multiple sources.
(g) It should involve a theoretical understanding of knowledge and skills.
(h) It should be part of a comprehensive change process which aims for big but starts small (Hawley and Valli, 1999).

Teacher education has drawn considerable attention in the recent past. OECD has prepared a comprehensive report dealing with the teacher situation in OECD countries and also organized an international conference on the theme of 'Teachers Matter' in Amsterdam. The NCTE and UNESCO brought out a report about teacher education in SAARC countries in 1999. The NCTE has also brought out the teacher education situation in the SAARC courtiers in its journal in 2005 (*Anweshika*: Indian Journal of Teacher Education, Volume 2, Number 1, June 2005). All these events point out how much teacher education is in focus internationally.

One reason why teacher education has come into sharp focus is that there is a concern for the quality of school education globally. Achievement tests of students are regular phenomena in the developed countries. These tests put the school education in public focus. Since the teachers are responsible for school education, they come into focus and since teacher education is supposed to be responsible for the quality of teachers, teacher education comes into focus.

In the last decade, teacher education has been restructured. But the issues vary across the world. The issues in the European countries and in the North America are:

(a) Teacher shortage.
(b) Attracting more males to the teaching profession.

(c) Providing channels for those who have higher academic qualification but not the teacher qualification.
(d) Providing some channel for teachers from foreign countries to teach (OECD, 2005; Siniscalco, 2002).

As part of the restructuring teacher education was drawn into the higher education system in Australia, which created its own problem. The department of education could not find an important place amongst other departments in the university system, which reduced its funding and personnel. This is an example of unintended consequences of restructuring. In some of the developed countries like Japan and Taiwan where the status of teachers is high, the problem of teacher shortage does not exist. The issues are different in countries like Korea and the SAARC countries. They do not face the shortage in numbers. They rather face the infrastructure constraint. In many small countries like Maldives and Nepal, the restructuring of teacher education was done with the foreign financial and academic help (see *Anweshika*: Indian Journal of Teacher Education, Volume 2, Number 1, June 2005).

While there seems to be a global consensus of making training a graduate or post-graduate profession, there also seems to be a global concern about university education not equipping teacher trainee for real-life classroom situations. There is a consensus to increase the involvement of schools in teacher education. In England, there is a school-based postgraduate programme in education. Schools are also actively involved in teacher training in England more than other countries. Globally, there is a concern to increase the classroom and school exposure of the teacher trainee.

States intervened more directly in teacher education in the 1990s. There were two dominant trends in the 1990s—centralization of standards and decentralization of finance. States assumed the role of arbiters of standards which so far they were not doing directly. On the other hand, they were partially withdrawing the financial support, which so far they were doing rather unconditionally.

In England, the Teacher Training Agency (TTA) was created in September 1994 under the Education Act of 1994 to oversee the training programmes imparted by the institutions through Office for Standard in Education (OFSTED) (Bate, Gough and Stammers, 1999). The OFSTED inspects English and one of the core curricula. In Taiwan, after the new Teacher Education Act, 1994, students in teacher training institutions are no more given free meals and boarding and not guaranteed by the government a job. They have to compete in the open market (Fwu and

Wang, 2002). In China, institutions of teacher education, like all the other higher education institutions, have been given more freedom in curriculum decision making. The 'price' of this freedom is that institutions have to raise a certain percentage of their budget, which had always been provided in full by the state (Shen, 1994). In America, since 1998, the secretary of education is required to issue annual reports to the congress on the state of teacher quality nationwide. In return, the secretary receives reports from every state on teacher quality (US Department of Education, 2002). All these point towards a movement towards the centralization of standards.

Teaching Standards: What to Teach

Professionalism is more concerned with standards than anything else. State policies towards standards in teaching could take any or all of these issues: who to teach, what to teach, how to teach and how much to teach. When translated into academic jargon, these mean the prescription of the standards of teacher education, the prescription of the standards of curriculum which the teachers are supposed to teach and the prescription of standards and amount of work that teachers are supposed to do.

In the USA, schools have to perform in a particular way to attract federal grant under different programmes. In the UK, the school results and OFSTED inspection reports are public and these put tremendous pressure on teachers. Many countries in the world have a state-specified curriculum for almost all subjects. Except Canada and the USA where these standards about curriculum are decided provincially, in most of the countries standards are set at the national level (Nelson, 1994). In England, there are detailed national curricula for core subjects like English, Mathematics and Science at the primary level and it is on the web. Recently the USA has also introduced national standards, which the teachers are supposed to pass, which most of the states have adopted and will be forced to adopt in future to receive funds. So, in the near future the standards will be decided centrally in the USA (US Department of Education, 2002). Broadly, we can say that there is a move towards centralization. Alexander (2000) has dealt at length on the centralization of primary education in the UK after 1985. This is the case in India also, in the 1990s.

Choosing a textbook is decentralized in the USA, the UK, Italy and Canada while it is centralized in Japan and India (Nelson, 1994). In decentralization, teachers can choose a textbook from different publishers keeping in mind the state-specified curriculum. In India, the primary teacher, specially in the first three grades, is expected to teach mainly literacy, numeracy and life skills. Besides these, the teacher is required to have knowledge of the process of a child's growth, development and learning. At the secondary stage, a teacher is expected to be familiar with adolescent psychology and social processes, in addition to the knowledge of the school subjects. The curriculum for primary teacher education is developed by state governments/state boards of teacher education and is reviewed from time to time. The curriculum for secondary teacher education developed by universities is also reviewed and updated periodically in the light of changes in the school curriculum, advances in pedagogical science, societal demands, technological advancements and changes in the socio-economic structures in the country. The National Curriculum Framework of 2000 by NCERT can be considered as the Indian equivalent of the centralization of curriculum in the USA, England and in many other countries. It was available on the web. It contained the detailed guidelines on primary curriculum. The content guidelines in the UK (available on the web) were similar to this.

There was a lot of reaction to the National Curriculum Framework of 2000. The NCERT came out with another National Curriculum Framework in 2005. The predominant feature of this framework is that it endorses the social constructivist approach towards learning. This curriculum framework was ostensibly made to make up the shortcomings of the Curriculum Framework of 2000. But, this too drew criticism. Batra (2005) points out that though the Curriculum Framework 2005 restored the voice and agency of children, it was silent and ambivalent about the voice and agency of teachers. It did not underscore the importance of the teacher as the vital mediating agency who translates the curriculum in the classroom.

Workload of Teachers

A teacher's work includes both teaching and non-teaching activities. There are four countries that prescribe more than 1,000 hours of teaching time for teachers—India, Indonesia, the Philippines and the United States. The hours of teaching for other countries are:

- 900–1,000 hours of work – 7 countries
- 800–900 hours of work – 15 countries
- 700–800 hours of work – 11 countries
- 600–700 hours of work – 8 countries.

Among the 17 World Education Indicator (WEI) countries which are economically developing or underdeveloped except Russian Federation, the mean is 872 hours of work per year. Among the OECD countries, which are mostly economically developed countries, the mean is 805 hours of work per year (see Appendix 3.7; UNESCO, 2006, Table 5.f).

If the total number of hours of work is divided by the total number of weeks, we get the weekly teaching load. The highest teaching hours per week prescribed is in the United States (30 hours). The WEI mean is 22.36 hours of teaching time per week and the OECD mean is 21.18 hours.

A teacher's work includes non-teaching duties too. While the teaching time is relatively uniform in the European Union countries, lot of variations exist in the statutory non-teaching time. While the allocation of time between teaching and non-teaching activities is decided by the head teacher in England and Ireland (at the primary level), it is statutorily prescribed in other countries. In 55 countries out of 70, the total working time of teachers was between 20 and 40 hours per week. In the OECD countries, it was between 30 and 40 hours per week. Amount of working time did not change in most of the countries during the 1990s (Siniscalco, 2002).

There are only two countries which have more than 30 as the pupil–teacher ratio: India and the Philippines. While the WEI mean is 24.3, the OECD mean is 16.9. Among the OECD countries, only three have pupil–teacher ratio more than 20: Mexico (28.5), Republic of Korea (29.1) and Turkey (26.5).

In India, education codes in different states specify the number of class or periods teachers at different levels have to teach. A sample study undertaken by Goyal and Chopra (1990) reveals that about one-fourth primary school teachers teach 31–35 class periods and a similar number teach more than 36 class periods a week. In middle schools, nearly half of the teachers teach 31–40 class periods a week whereas 12 per cent teach more than 40 class periods. The workload of teachers is often judged in terms of amount and type of work done by them. The study by Goyal and Chopra (1990) indicates that 42 per cent primary school teachers teach two classes or more at a time. About 50 per cent upper primary/middle school teachers report that they teach four or more subjects. More than 60 per cent of teachers teach about 50 students on an average, 34 per cent teach between 51 and 100, and about five per cent more than 100 students. This means that on average, about 39 per cent teachers teach more than 50 students in the primary school. At high/higher secondary levels, however, the teacher–pupil ratio was 1:16 in 1994–95. It is evident that there is too much stress on primary school teachers, especially those handling multi-grades. Besides teaching, elementary and secondary school teachers have to spend a fair amount of time on co-curricular activities, especially in private schools. In addition, teachers have to do clerical work and other miscellaneous works like organizing relief work, collecting census data, participating in family planning campaigns and population control drive and helping in the smooth conduct of elections.

One can say that in terms of sheer time, Indian teachers work more than their counterparts internationally, taking into account the class size and multiple class teaching.

Salary

A professional gets paid for the professional work rendered. In the US, the highest paid profession is that of a physician (Seshadri, 2000). 'In most OECD countries teachers' salaries are lower than those of equally qualified workers...The unfavourable position of teachers in relation to other qualified professionals in both OECD and non-OECD countries has also been noted by the ILO' (Siniscalco, 2002, p. 40). State policies towards teacher professionalism have to take into account teacher salary if it wants to attract and retain talent in the teaching profession. In countries like Japan and Taiwan where teachers get very good salary and compensation, teaching draws the best talent (Morris and Williamson, 1998). In contrast, there is always a concern about attracting people to teaching in countries like the USA, the UK and India. In terms of salary, teachers are better off than other equivalent public servants in Australia, Japan and Taiwan; more or less equal in China and Singapore and lower in Hong Kong and the USA (see Appendix 3.2; UNESCO, 2006, Table 5.h.i).

Teachers in the OECD countries may be better paid in absolute terms but when teachers' salaries relative to per capita GDP are compared, many low and middle income countries pay more than the OECD countries (UNESCO, 2006; Siniscalco, 2002). When teacher salaries relative to GDP are compared, then Indian teachers are the highest paid in the world (more than four times of per capita GDP; see ibid.). The UNESCO (2006) data reveals the following facts about teacher salaries:

(a) There are five countries where teachers get the salary that is more than two times of the GDP per capita of their respective countries–India, Philippines, Jamaica, Jordan and Turkey. None of these is a developed country.
(b) The countries where the salary rises steeply in the first fifteen years but remains the same afterwards are—India, Jamaica, Australia, New Zealand and Scotland.

(c) The countries where the salary rises steeply between the fifteenth year till the end of their career are—Malaysia, Austria, France, Mexico and Luxembourg.
(d) The countries where the salary rises steeply throughout the career are—Jordan, Japan, Republic of Korea and Portugal.

In the 1990s, teachers' salaries increased or remained stable in OECD, high-income and many middle-income countries. But it deteriorated in the low-income countries (Siniscalco, 2002).

In India, the pay for a teacher was INR 15 per month in 1826. The Sargent Report, 1944 recommended that no teacher should receive less than 20 per mensem. In 1972, the basic salary ranged between INR 75 and INR 136 (Andhra Pradesh) to INR 165 and INR 320 (Delhi). In 1977, there were two scales INR 285–550 and INR 235–345 (NCERT, 1977). Over the years, various commissions and committees have recommended salary scales for teachers. Notable among such commissions was the National Commission for Teachers I, 1983. At present, in India, teacher salary compares very favourably with other government employees with similar level of qualification (World Bank, 1997).

Status

The National Commission on Teachers I (1983–85) agreed that status is a complex sociological concept. It quoted the 1966 Inter-governmental Conference of UNESCO for the definition of status as 'both the standing and regard the society accorded them as evidenced by the level of appreciation of the importance of their function and competence in performing it, as well as working conditions, remuneration and other material benefits accorded to them relative to other professional groups' (NCT, 1986, p. 24). This definition emphasizes not only the purely social aspect of status but also the economic aspect. The pioneer sociologist Max Weber in his essay 'Class, Status and Party' located status not only in social and economic context but also in a context of power. 'Now "classes", "status groups" and "parties" are phenomena of the distribution of power within a community' (Weber, 1994, p. 113). This power aspect did not escape the notice of the National Commission on Teachers I (1983–85). 'The school teachers' desire for a higher status is simply a desire for a salary and working conditions that can save her/him from humiliation and indignities suffered so often' (NCT, p. 24). The power aspect is also reflected in the fact that professions demand 'respectable remuneration' rather than 'remuneration for work done' (Weber, 1994).

Eric Hoyle (2001) differentiates between prestige, status and esteem. '*Occupational prestige* is ... the public perception of the relative position of an occupation in a hierarchy of occupations (139)... *Occupational status* is ...which knowledgeable groups allocate a particular occupation (144)... *Occupational esteem* is the regard in which an occupation is held by the general public by virtue of the personal qualities which members are perceived as bringing to their core task' (147). Hoyle's concept of occupational prestige is more close to the NCT's employment of the term status. Figure 3.2 shows how prestige is influenced in a complex way by a host of factors.

Figure 3.2 shows that prestige or the social standing of teaching is determined in a complex way by the following determinants:

(a) Children as the principal clientele of teachers living in a world where the status of adults are high as compared to children.
(b) The nature of knowledge in teaching.
(c) Teaching as a public profession having its implications on its number and salary.

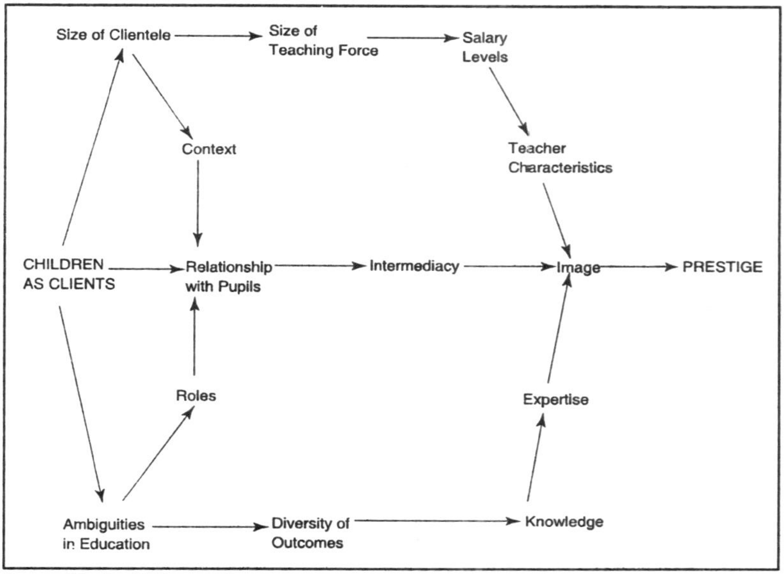

Source: Hoyle, 2001, p. 142.

Figure 3.2: Hypothetical determinants of the occupational prestige of teaching

The National Commission on Teachers-I quoted 'the five determinants of teacher status as identified by the WCOTP[1] study' on the status of teachers in India; these are:

(i) The academic and professional requirements for entry into the profession.
(ii) The financial and other economic benefits.
(iii) The professional responsibilities assumed.
(iv) The freedom of teachers to take part in public affairs.
(v) The degree of public recognition.

The National Commission on Teachers-I mentioned the other factors that will influence the status of an individual teacher—'the sex of the teacher, the social class of the pupils, the social origin of the teacher, the age of the pupils, the subjects taught and the qualifications of the teachers' (1986, p. 25).

Hoyle differentiates between 'the *formal status* of teaching which is authoritatively determined and the *semantic status* of teaching which is determined by the way in which groups refer to teaching as a *profession*—or seek to withhold this status—in which contexts and with what intent' (2001, p. 144). Thus, formally, primary teachers may be placed in a high pedestal but they themselves may not feel that.

Apparently, the status of teaching is high in most countries of the world. 'The scattered findings do not provide a solid basis for generalizations, and can be taken as indicative only. Based on the material included in the country background reports, however, the social standing of teachers seems quite high, and seems to have changed little over the years' (OECD, 2005, p. 81). However even where it is high, there seem to be contradictory views. Usually, Japan is considered as a country in which the status of teachers seems to be high. An official document of the Government of Japan has the following words:

> The relatively high public appraisal of teachers' social status seems to be due to the following factors: First of all, in Japan, a country with few natural resources, a certain level of importance and significance is recognized for the teaching profession that cultivate the human resources who will shoulder the next generation. Secondly, teachers' job consists of teaching knowledge and skills necessary for every citizen to live as a member of society. Moreover, the following factors can be given in view of the system. Teachers in public schools have the status guaranteed as education officials. From the perspective of securing human resources, teachers are paid good salaries compared to ordinary public officials (Japan Country Background Report to OECD, 2005, pp. 19–20 http://www.oecd.org/dataoecd/58/20/29163349.pdf).

However, an in-depth investigation by a researcher reveals a different picture. 'Teachers in Japan are no longer held in high esteem simply because of their position in the Confucian hierarchy of status and authority. Gone is the time when the word of the Sensei would bring silence and order to a classroom. Ironically, the fruits of a postwar first-world nation—increased parental education, material affluence and a liberalization of educational practices—have placed teachers in a precarious position' (Gordon, 2005, p. 459). Everett Hughes points out that as non-industrial societies have moved to becoming industrial societies, they have been influenced by Euro-American views about the prestige of occupations. Thus, 'the physician appears to be the world champion of this popularity contest' (1959, p. 46). All these point out the difficulty of arriving at a consensus on status. There seems to be multiple stakeholders projecting different status images of an occupation because of various reasons. They could be the following:

The government: It may project a high image of teachers to boost their morale.

The population: It may project an image based on inadequate information and it may be susceptible to propaganda; Everett Hughes points out the fragility of public perception of a profession based on 'name' only.

> As a matter of fact, many of our leading named occupations are inwardly so varied that to call them by one name is close to misleading. Ratings based on the name alone tell us little or nothing about the actual images, which people have, of the occupation. They also tell us nothing of how the images held by people of one kind (class, age, ethnic group, religion and region) varies from those held by some other kind. For the kinds of doctor, teacher, businessman, lawyer, or soldier visible to one kind of people may be quite different from those visible to others (1959, p. 47).

The media: It might have its own bias. An OECD document mentions, 'as most Country Background Reports note, media coverage of schools often focuses on the negatives such as student violence and misbehaviour and this undoubtedly makes teaching seem a less attractive career' (OECD, 2005, p 81). Unlike the West, in India, the media in its day-to-day report does not report the student violence, but mostly the commissions and omissions of teachers, rather than their positive contributions. The positive contributions are mentioned in a perfunctory and ceremonial manner on 'Teachers' Day'.

The members themselves: The members of the teaching profession themselves may not feel what others assign to them.

It well could be that whatever high status the public accord to teaching may be because of the public disdain for manual labour rather than the love of knowledge. Max Weber (1994) writes that it seems that the public accords higher status to a style of life removed from manual labour or labour for livelihood than that which is connected with it; for example, 'the sculptor working like a mason in his dusty smock as over against the painter in his salon like "studio" (p. 120)... 'Honour peculiar to status absolutely abhors that which is essential to the market: higgling' (p. 120). He points out that it is not the parvenu but his descendants, who have never engaged in the struggle for economic survival, are accepted. Thus, the popular accordance of high status is not based on only knowledge base of a profession or ethics.

The State and Teachers' Organizations

An account of the state and teacher professionalism remains incomplete without an account of the state and teacher organizations. Teachers' organizations, whether called unions or associations, negotiate or fight with the state over the issues of salary, working conditions or professional development of teachers. But the relative emphasis on particular issues varies across countries. The strength of teacher unions vis-à-vis the state also varies across countries.

In the United States of America, the first national teachers' organization (National Education Association [NEA]) started in 1857. In England, the first teachers' organization (National Union of Teachers [NUT]) started in 1870. Before these, there were regional organizations in both the countries. Gradually, they felt that there should be a national organization. Thus, regional organizations were the precursors of national organizations. This is true in case of India too.

In England, before the National Union of Teachers came into being, teachers' organizations were based more on religion because education itself was linked to the church (Manzer, 1970). When national level organizations came into being, eventually one organization became preponderant in both the USA and England. For example in 1960, 68 per cent of the teaching profession belonged to NUT in England (Manzer, 1970), and in 1967, 52 per cent of classroom teachers belonged to NEA in the USA (Stinnett, 1968). We will see subsequently that this is not the situation in India. Generally, the services of teacher organizations in the USA and England are the following:

(a) Publication.
(b) Lobbying for the right kind of legislation.
(c) Research and fact-finding.
(d) Field services and public relation.

(e) Other services—legal counselling, insurance, educational films, radio programs, recreation and housing (Spackman, 1991; Stinnett, 1968).

What is the power by which teacher organizations can protect teachers' interest? The NEA has a permanent Defense Commission within it with the responsibility of overseeing teachers' interest. Its chief weapons are:

(a) To arouse public opinion.
(b) To mobilize members not to take employment in the school considered unjust.
(c) Also, it can provide legal services and financial assistance to the suspended teachers when they are off the job (Stinnett, 1968).

The NEA is a federation of state organizations. The aggrieved teacher or teachers first have to route their grievance/s through the state organization. Then, the Defense Commission visits the area and investigates the case. The report is widely publicized. It is the public pressure, which mainly works because few authorities would want to see themselves in poor light. For Ronald Manzer (1970), in the context of England, teachers' organizations have following two powers:

(i) To affect the electoral fortunes of politicians.
(ii) To affect the policies being carried out.

According to him, a teacher organization can succeed if its claims are moderate and it is supported by technical evidence.

After considering the history of teachers' organizations in England and the USA, the following issues generally emerge before a teacher organization (Spackman, 1991; Stinnett, 1968):

(a) Member, dismember, fee.
(b) Strike and other tools of sanction.
(c) Tools of controlling members.
(d) Relation with rival organizations.
(e) Who dominates in the organization?
(f) What services they provide?

All of the above issues are relevant in India too.

Teachers' Organizations in India

Evolution

The initiative came from women rather than men for forming a teachers' organization in India. The first teachers' organization in India was

Women Teachers' Association, Madras (1890). Miss Keely, principal of The Doveton Girls' School, Miss Arnold, superintendent of The Presidency Training School for Mistresses and Miss Ive, headmistress of Bishop Gorries Girls' High School were associated with its activities. In contrast, initially, the oldest teacher organization in the USA, NEA, was not open to women. The NUT of the UK had to wage a struggle for parity between male and female teachers. Now little is known about the Women Teachers' Association, Madras (1890) as it has ceased to exist. The real foundation for teacher organization was laid in India by Madras Teacher's Guild (1895). Its later transformation, The South India Teacher's Union (SITU) (1908), played a pioneering role in teacher organization formation in India. Initially, SITU was mainly concerned with the academic issues, which were discussed in its educational conferences organized every year. SITU started bringing out its official monthly journal *The South Indian Teacher* from 1928 that went on uninterrupted till 1966 (Swami, 1980). Thus, 'the emergence of teacher organizations in India was in the initial stages motivated primarily by academic considerations and they started gradually drifting towards trade unionism during the post-world war period' (ibid., pp. 221–22). This is true in case of the USA and the UK also.

The growth of teacher organizations was slow till 1920. Teacher organizations came up in almost all the states and provinces between 1920 and 1930. But, the real spurt came only after 1940. Out of the 100 organizations that Swami (1980) studied, 78 came into existence after 1940. Table 3.5 shows the chronology of some of the oldest teacher organizations in India.

The first national level organization was All India Federation of Teachers' Associations formed in 1925. Its name was changed to All India Federation of Educational Associations in 1933, as it was felt that teachers' associations smacked of trade unionism. The new name would also allow purely academic associations to get affiliated. Along with the growth in numbers, teachers' organizations also got differentiated over the years in India. Following are the reasons why there is a multiplicity of teacher organizations in India at present time:

(a) **Variety of categories of teachers:** Gradually, primary teachers, secondary teachers and university teachers formed their own exclusive organizations. For example, following organizations were formed for particular categories of teachers at the all India level:

(i) All India Primary Teachers' Federation (1954).
(ii) All India Secondary Teachers' Federation (1961).
(iii) All India Federation of University and College Teachers' Organization (1962).

Table 3.5: Chronology of the oldest teachers' organizations in India

State	Name of the organization	Year of founding
Tamil Nadu	Women Teachers' Association	1890
Maharashtra	Maharashtra State Primary Teachers' Association	1914
West Bengal	All Bengal Government School Teachers' Association	1920
Uttar Pradesh	U.P. Non-Gazetted Educational Officers' Association	1920
Madhya Pradesh	Madhya Pradesh Pradhamic Siksak Sangha	1922
Gujarat	Baroda Secondary Teachers' Association	1924
Bihar	Bihar and Orissa Subordinate Educational Service Association	1924
Orissa	Bihar and Orissa Subordinate Educational Service Association	1924
Andhra Pradesh	Hyderabad Teachers' Association	1925
Rajasthan	Marwar Teachers' Association	1925
Punjab	Non-Government School Teachers' and Managers' Association	1926
Haryana	Non-Government School Teachers' and Managers' Association	1926
Kerala	Travancor Teachers' Association	1927
Karnataka	Mysore State Education Federation	1927
Delhi	Delhi School Teachers' Association	1942

Source: Swami, 1980, p. 47.

(b) **Diverse management:** Government and private school teachers formed their own organizations.
(c) **Administrative divisions in the states:** During the process of states' reorganization, the original organization was split into the respective state organizations into which the original state was reorganized.

(d) **Regional heterogeneities:** There are historic-geographical regions like those of Marathawada and Vidarbha in Maharashtra, Telengana in Andhra Pradesh. Since the loyalty towards the region is strong, some teacher organizations operate exclusively within the region.

The National Commission on Teachers (1983) mentioned ten all-India teachers' organizations. Ravi Kanta Chopra's study (1993) mentions 102 teachers' organizations at state level of which 41 are for secondary and higher secondary teachers, 31 for primary teachers, 15 for primary and secondary both, seven for headmasters and eight for language, science, physical education and craft teachers. In the study, the number of members ranged from 200 to 2,00,000 and membership fee ranged from INR 1 to INR 25. Multiplicity of teacher organizations is prevalent in the USA and the UK also. Sex is also a criterion there for multiplicity. But the extent of multiplicity of teacher organizations is far greater in India as compared to the USA and the UK. Because of such bewildering multiplicity, teachers are not able to achieve professional unity (Swami, 1980).

Finance

Teacher organizations in India are far from being financially well off. Often, members evade subscriptions when there is no agitation going on. Besides, group rivalries and questions on the integrity of the functionaries affect collection. The financial handicap prevents them from acquiring assets. Out of 100 organizations that Swami (1980) studied, only 11 had permanent buildings, 22 were situated in rented buildings and 67 operated from the residences of the functionaries or the educational institutions they serve. Of the 33 organizations having offices in permanent or rented buildings, only 21 could acquire minimum institutional assets like furniture, typewriters and duplicating machines.

In contrast to the USA and the UK, majority of teacher organizations in India do not have full time office bearers aided by secretarial staff. Often, the head office moves from place to place along with the office bearers after every election. Thus, many teacher organizations have mobile head quarters in India. The office bearers do it voluntarily and are not paid for it.

Politics, faction fights and group rivalries: One of the main factors which generated factionalism was the creation of teacher constituency in the legislative assembly of some states. Rival groups either broke away or formed new organizations. For example, Telangana Teachers' Union was formed as rival to Andhra Pradesh Primary Teachers' Association in 1972. But later, the leadership of both the associations decided to merge in 1974 and work under the banner of the original association—State Teachers' Union. A recent study (Kingdon and Muzzamil, 2003) has documented the group divisions of Madhyamika Siksak Sangha of Uttar Pradesh.

Politicization of teachers has certainly benefitted teachers but has affected education adversely. The above study says:

> Teachers' participation in politics also has a direct effect on the functioning of schools; it keeps them away from schools because they are engaged in union/political activities... showed a high degree of participation by teachers in protest action suggests that a substantial number of hours of teaching time must be lost for a large number of teachers in most years in union related activities, such as pen down strikes, mass casual leave, pickets and sit ins, demonstrations and jail terms, etc. Moreover the few MLAs and MLCs who are teachers, continue in their teaching posts that are often not filled by replacement teachers, thus leading to a loss of teaching activity. Teacher union leaders and teacher MLAs and MLCs continue to draw their teacher salaries (plus their MLA and MLC salary) for the full term of political office, though they do not teach during this period. These financial resources could arguably be better spent in other ways (Kingdon and Muzzamil, 2003, pp. 262–63).

Teacher Organizations and Strikes in India

There is no institutional mechanism for consultation between administration and teacher organizations regarding academic and salary matters in India. What happens in India is that teacher organizations give suggestions unilaterally and the state accepts or rejects them unilaterally. For example, while the Government of India categorically committed itself to the implementation of the UGC scales of pay in 1966, it gave no commitment with regard to Education Commission's (1966) recommendation regarding teacher's pay. In fact, much of the strike and agitation by teachers in India is for implementation of such recommendations or improvement of salary or dearness allowance (Swami, 1980; Kingdon and Muzzamil, 2003).

The absence of institutional consultation mechanism in India is probably one of the main reasons for frequent strikes in India. But the presence of such mechanism abroad has not entirely precluded strikes. Swami (1980) in his study points out that most of the agitations launched by teacher organizations in India are for increasing pay, dearness allowance, private teachers' security of service and parity with government teachers. The few cases where teacher organizations did agitation for purely professional purposes are:

(a) A day's mass casual leave by the teachers of Osmania University in 1967 for the preservation of university autonomy.
(b) A demonstration in 1971 and a weeklong strike in 1972 by the teachers of University of Delhi demanding participatory right in the internal administration.

There are also instances where teacher organizations joined agitations for purposes that are not of direct concern to their profession. Some such instances are:

(a) Teachers' strike in Andhra Pradesh in 1973 demanding bifurcation of the state.
(b) Teachers' struggle in Gujarat in 1974 pressing for the dismissal of the ministry and dissolution of the assembly.
(c) Teachers' demonstration in West Bengal registering their protest against the USA in Vietnam War.

Some of the protracted long strikes between 1966 and 1974 are:

(a) Private college teachers in Kerala for sixty three days (1971).
(b) The private college and school teachers in Orissa for sixty days (1969).
(c) The teachers and other employees in Andhra Pradesh for fifty six days (1971).
(d) Secondary teachers in Bihar for fifty two days (1972).
(e) Teachers and other employees in Kerala for forty six days (1973).
(f) Private college teachers in Andhra region in Andhra Pradesh for thirty eight days (1973) (Swami, 1980).

The strikes and other agitations by the teachers in India in different states over the years have achieved higher pay package for teachers. Swami's study (1980) says that teachers could not get exactly what the Kothari Commission recommended in many states. But, in a few states, teachers were able to achieve scales higher than what the Kothari Commission recommended. Regarding security of service, following are the achievements of teachers' struggles over the years:

(a) Orissa Education Act, 1969.
(b) Punjab Aided Schools (Security of Service) Act, 1969.
(c) Kerala Universities Bill, 1972.

(d) Delhi Schools Education Act, 1973.
(e) Gujarat Secondary Education Bill, 1973.
(f) Tamil Nadu Recognized Private Schools (Regulation) Bill, 1973.
(g) Mysore Private Educational Institutions (Discipline and Control) Act, 1973.
(h) Uttar Pradesh Salary Disbursement Act, 1971.
(i) Uttar Pradesh Basic Education Act, 1972 (Swami, 1980; Kingdon and Muzzamil, 2003).

The National Commission on Teachers-I said:

> the main preoccupation of teachers' organizations particularly since independence has been with the improvement of salary and service conditions of teachers. And in this they have, without question, achieved considerable success. The principle of parity of scale, status and service conditions between teachers of government schools and those of aided institutions for instance, is now fully recognized and implemented in most parts of the country. The organizations have also been effective to some extent in drawing attention to the unsatisfactory service conditions in some of the privately managed schools (NCT, 1986, p. 73).

Academic Programme

Teacher organizations in India have been more successful in improving socio-economic status and less in improving professional competence of the teachers. Seventy three out of hundred organizations that Swami (1980) studied had no publication to their credit. They were not even bringing out their organizational journal. Only 33 per cent out of 750 teachers who responded to the questionnaire in the above study were active participants in the academic programmes of the organization. Forty one per cent were non-participants and 26 per cent were passive observers. The reasons for their lack of academic activities were preoccupation with emolument and service conditions, lack of adequate finance and lack of interest from teachers themselves. The leadership of these organizations is voluntary and their little time is preoccupied with material problems. Besides, they can do little with inadequate finance.

The State and Teacher Unions in Other Countries of the World

The position of teacher union vis-à-vis the state varies across the world. The country background reports for OECD (2005) not only includes

European countries but includes countries like Mexico, Israel, Chile and the Republic of Korea also. According to it, there are broadly two kinds of environment that prevails in the states—centralized and decentralized. Teacher unions are dominant, and have equal or less than equal footing vis-à-vis the states. Similarly, their behaviour can be restricted to either material benefits, professional activities or both. So, there can be any kind of combinations between the environment of the states, the strength of the teacher unions and the behaviour of the teacher unions.

In Chile, Sweden and Finland, where local authorities are the employers of teachers, associations of local authorities have been formed. Teacher unions have to negotiate with these associations of local authorities in these countries. These central agreements influence the relation between teacher unions and the local authorities.

Teacher unions are dominant in Italy, Mexico and France. Teacher unions are placed relatively on an equal footing in Sweden, Austria, Belgium, Denmark, Finland and Germany. On the other hand, there does not seem to be a smooth relation between teacher unions and the state in Greece, Israel, Chile and the Republic of Korea.

The scope of teacher unions' activities varies across countries. While in some countries teacher unions may be content with safeguarding the material benefits of teacher, in some countries teacher unions try to even better the image of teaching profession itself. Teacher unions agreed for individual performance-related pay in Sweden. The Danish Union of Teachers set up an internal working group to examine the contents and organization of teachers' training with the purpose of suggesting possible changes of the training. In late 2002, the Trade Union of Education, the dominant teacher union of Finland, launched the 'Finland Needs Teachers' project to increase awareness of teaching work and of the profession's effectiveness in society. In Australia, subject associations have come out with documents like *Standards for Excellence in Teaching Mathematics in Australian Schools* in 2002 by the Australian Association of Mathematics Teachers, *Professional Development for English Teachers* in 2001 by the Australian Association for the Teaching of English. In Greece, teacher unions were influential in the transformations of the two-year (non-university level) initial training of primary teachers (pedagogic academies) to four-year (university-level) training during 1984. In Israel, teacher unions have supported the government attempt to make the teacher education more academic. Teacher educators were sent to universities to earn higher academic degrees as part of the academicization process (country background reports for OECD, 2005).

Conclusion

Teacher professionalism now is truly at crossroads. Recently, countries across the world have taken definitive steps to regulate teacher professionalism. The word 'professionalism' is now explicitly mentioned as a qualification to be attained by teachers. In countries like the UK, it has also been translated into particular activities and sentences. In the USA, teacher standard now broadly refers to subject content knowledge and verbal ability for which there are national standards, which the states are to follow within a definite time period. In India, the government is soon going to have more control over teacher education through the NCTE.

Along with this, countries are also defining what to teach. For years, teachers have been exercising some autonomy regarding what to teach. In India, Taiwan and the UK, it has taken the shape of national curriculums for core subjects. It has made a definitive framework for teachers with regard to what to teach.

While the standards have been defined, increasingly, the state is withdrawing financially or linking finance to reform. In England, the candidates in teacher training have to pass the test by OFSTED on the basis of which the institute's credibility to get money for teacher-training programme from Teacher Training Agency depends. In China also, teacher-training institutes have to raise some part of their finance. In Taiwan the teacher training institutions, which so far were state managed, have been deregulated.

The teachers' responses through teacher unions have been to oppose any kind of deterioration in their material conditions in which they have succeeded. They also have opposed reforms that aim at linking salary to performance and objectifying teacher certification.

Note

1. 'Franklin E.W., 1967, Status of Teachers in India'-prepared by WCOTP, 16A/10 Western Extension Area, New Delhi; WCOTP – World Confederation of Organizations of the Teaching Profession; merged with IFFTU in 1993 to form Education International, the largest federation of teacher unions.

4

DEVELOPMENT OF EDUCATION IN ORISSA

The Historical Legacy

A lot of the energy of the Oriya people was spent in creating a province of Oriya-speaking people and protecting Oriya language. Until 1936, Oriya people had to grapple with the task of creating a province of Oriya-speaking people on the face of the opposition of the people of Bengal. The interest of the Bengalis in opposing a separate Oriya province was that they could garner most of the lucrative government jobs in Orissa because of their educational advancement so long as Orissa remained a part of Bengal-Bihar-Orissa Province. Today, somebody could hardly imagine that Medinipur and Bankuda were ever in Orissa. Oriya language was wiped out from Medinipur and Bankuda between 1850 and 1870. The next targets of Bengalis were Cuttack, Puri and Balasore. But fortunately, they could not succeed. Initially, there was a lot of support from the British to the Oriya people in this matter.

All these also happened because of the collective effort of the people of Orissa. The collective effort materialized itself into the establishment of Utkal Sammilan in 1903 with the aim of a separate Orissa province. Their principal task was to influence the British government, promoting and propagating Oriya language through writing books, starting newspapers, writing Oriya primers, etc. Utkal Sammilan held its various meetings in the coastal areas and later in the feudal states of western Orissa. The movement to promote Oriya language resulted in a general emphasis on education. Utkal Sammilan started in Cuttack and the hubs of the Oriya language movement were the districts of Cuttack, Puri and Balasore. Radhanath Roy and Fakirmohan Senapati wrote extensively in Oriya. They also became high officials (inspectors) in the education department. Thus, one of the reasons why coastal districts like Cuttack, Puri and Balasore are educationally more advanced today is because they started early on the path of education. Koraput and Ganjam, which are educationally backward, joined Orissa as late as 1935. The princely states (in western Orissa which are the educationally underdeveloped region) joined Orissa only after independence (1948–49). There was no pressure on the feudal lords to improve education in their areas. They were not like the Raja of Travancore or the Sahu Maharaj of Kolhapur. Thus, the educational underdevelopment of some of the districts of Orissa (Koraput, Kalahandi, etc.) is historical.

Growth of Schooling

The Pre-independence Period

Hunter wrote in 1870 that Orissa was full of ignorance. Illiteracy was 97 per cent in Orissa in 1905. From this, one can guess the situation of Orissa regarding education before the starting of the twentieth century. Here education means education in its contemporary sense, which was introduced by the British. Orissa's neighbour Bengal was an early beginner in this sort of education. But, education in a traditional sense existed in Orissa before the arrival of British system of education. Fakirmohan (1843–1918) has written in his autobiography that there were *chatsalis* in a big village or one for two-three small villages. Pupils were taught reading, writing, mathematics, and letter-writing and multiplication chart. The teachers were mostly from *karan*, *astrologer and ojha* caste. They used to get 1–4 *annas* as monthly fees from every child they taught. Higher education was in Sanskrit, where *brahmins* were predominant (Mahapatra, 1977).

The early education efforts were concentrated in the coastal districts of Orissa and became widespread much later than Bengal. This will be evident from the following important dates in the origin of modern education in Orissa:

- 1804: First Oriya letters were made up of wood.
- 1809: First Oriya printed text *The New Testament of the Bible* came out.
- 1823: Missionaries established schools in Puri and Cuttack. Puri Zilla School was established by the East India Company.
- 1841: A higher English school was established in Cuttack.

- 1845–1848: Two vernacular schools were established in Orissa.
- 1853: A higher English school was established in Balasore.
- 1855: A higher English school was established in Berhampur (Senapati, 1996).

Missionaries came to Serampore of Bengal in around 1770s. But they came to Orissa at the beginning of the nineteenth century. Like in the rest of India, the missionaries were the pioneers of education in its modern form. They brought out the first printed book in Oriya *The New Testament of the Bible*. They established the first schools. The East India Company came about fifteen years later.

Orissa was adjoined with the Bengal presidency. From 1813 to 1834, though Bengal presidency was getting more money for education than the other two presidencies, nothing reached to Orissa ever. The government adopted the policy of grants-in-aid after the Wood's Despatch in 1855, which broadly recommended the policy to mix public and private effort towards education. As a result of this policy, those traditional schools which were outside the ambit of the government were tried to be brought within the ambit through the grants in aid. For this purpose, Cuttack, Puri and Balasore got 12,000, 6,000 and 6,000 rupees, respectively. The conditions for the grants-in-aid were that the local population will provide the house for the school, would not stop their traditional support to the teacher and the teachers will attend the *guru* training school if required. These traditional schools were called *chatsali, tol* or *maqtab.* These institutions were imparting a narrow type of traditional education to a narrow clientele (Samal, 1984; Dwibedi, 1968).

The grants-in-aid policy was not giving any good result. As soon as government started giving some money to the school or to the teacher (*avadhan*), people tend to withdraw their traditional support to the teacher and the school. Because of this, the teachers themselves did not like to be aided. The matter went so far that teachers started propagating against the government schools in *brahmin* strongholds in Puri district. The traditional *avadhans* were either *brahmins* or *kayasthas*. For them, the sacred palm-leave texts were worth studying and not the printed texts. For a long time, they hated to touch the printed texts. Also, education open to all including the *shudras* must have been very revolting for them (Mahapatra, 1977).

Payment by results instead of grants-in-aid was introduced after some time. In this system the teacher of any child, who qualified for the scholarship, got five rupees per month. The teachers of the first six students of a circle who passed got two rupees. The students themselves got two rupees. The least amount that the teacher got per student was eight annas. But even this did not work. When local self-government was introduced under Lord Ripon after 1885, the schools were placed under municipalities and district boards. From 1885, local district boards started managing education. They were getting some money earmarked for education from the government. The DPI was the CEO of the district board as far as primary education was concerned. The district board had one education committee to make suggestions with regard to education. It was decided in 1902 to introduce the *quarterly subsistence allowance* instead of payment by results. By this, schools got between one rupee and half rupee per student. This was considered better than payment by results. This allowance could shift from the school where there was no student to those where there were students.

The government had declared in 1857 that from thenceforth, those who are educated in vernacular will be preferred in government jobs. Model schools were established and free printed books and slates were distributed among the children. Provisions for scholarship were made. Another policy change in 1872 was a milestone in the history of education in Orissa. That year, Bengali was removed from Orissa as the mother tongue and Oriya became the mother tongue of Orissa. Till then, Oriya did not have the recognition from the government as a separate language. Thus, only by 1873 did Oriya gain recognition from British government as a separate language and till then instruction was carried out in Bengali in Orissa. Also, the name of the province changed from '*Udisya*' to '*Orissa*'. Due to the effort of Ravenshaw, Orissa was separated from the Vardhaman education division in 1875 (see Appendices 4.1 and 4.2).

In about 1925, compulsory education was introduced in Banki and Parlakhemudi. In 1927, 36 cases were referred to court against guardians who did not send their children to school in Banki Union, which had adopted the Bihar and Orissa Primary Education Act of 1919 involving compulsion.

The ill-effects of privatization were manifest as early in as 1935. By 1935, government was concerned about the mushrooming growth of private primary schools started by half educated gurus in unsuitable houses and surroundings which was considered detrimental to the cause of children's education. A system of recognition of three classes of schools (A, B, C) was introduced in 1936. These A, B, C were different grades of schools according to their quality. So, the disease of privatization is not as recent as we may think (Samal, 1984). The next important event was in 1942 when a committee was formed to bring the parity between the primary education of the northern Orissa (six years) and southern Orissa (five years). Co-education was introduced in primary education in 1943 (ibid.).

Development of girl's education: In as early as 1850, government had given instruction to the commissioner to encourage the people to send their girl children to school. Before this, all the money was being spent on boy scholars only. From 1854, it became a part of the government policy. Missionaries like Reverend Philips and Mrs Buckley helped the efforts of the government through orphanages and *zenana* associations. In 1865–66, priests started girl's education in orphanages. But, the government noticed that the girls were not going to the government schools in spite of the government effort including the establishment of a model school because the people trusted the *avadhanas* (the traditional teachers) more than the government-appointed teachers. Therefore, the government made special provisions for those *avadhanas* with whom there were large number of girl pupils. Slowly, girls and women showed interest in education in Orissa. The missionaries started training schools for women teachers in Cuttack, Balasore and Berhampur. By 1872, the girl students were allowed freeships. There were nine girls' schools by 1875.

Table 4.1 shows the growth of schools in Orissa in the pre-independence period (collated from Samal, 1984).

Table 4.1: Growth of schools in Orissa in pre-independence period

1858	3 Zilla schools 18 Vernacular schools 7 Aided vernacular schools 786 Students
1872	3 Higher English schools 11 Aided middle English schools 21 Middle vernacular schools 18 Aided middle vernacular schools 2527 Students
1937	1988 Primary schools 193 Minor schools 36 High schools 5 Colleges

The Post-independence Period: Till 1960

The literacy of Orissa was 15.80 per cent in 1951. The literacy among SC and ST was 3.3 per cent and 1.5 per cent, respectively before independence (Das, 1970). With such less literacy, one can very well imagine the struggle which was waiting ahead to fight illiteracy. After independence, the government initially got bogged down with the issue of basic education versus the non-vocational primary schools having English as their only attraction. The concept of basic education, which emphasized vocational education, had started since Wardha Congress, 1937. Honestly enough, the government pushed through the programme of basic education from 1951, especially when it had the power to shape the state of education. In the budget of 1949–50, the state made provisions for raising the pay scale for primary school teachers and establishing 60 new basic schools. But slowly, resistance to basic education built up because it was not teaching English, which the middle class found necessary for jobs. The colonial hangover had not got over. The aim of education was to become a clerk in the secretariat. Some of the legislators brought out the queer logic that the government is discriminating against the students who are taking to basic education, thereby excluding from the pie of government jobs. Running a basic school was much more expensive than running an ordinary primary school from the financial point of view. In 1955, while the annual expenditure incurred by the government on a primary school on an average was 551 rupees, that of a basic school was 3,355 rupees (Rath, 1977).

There were steps towards the unification of control over basic and primary education. A deputy director of public instruction was appointed in 1957–58. In December 1958, inspector of basic schools was transferred from the Organizer, Basic Education to the inspecting officers of the education department. The syllabi for basic and primary schools were made the same in 1959. Gradually, basic education lost ground. We do not find reference to basic schools in the statistics of later period.

There were 48,000 villages in Orissa in 1953–54 and three-fourth of these did not have any primary school (Rath, 1977). The government prepared a plan of education in 1954. The education plan of 1954 prepared by a special officer established a scheme of universal, free and compulsory primary (or junior basic) education for all children between six and eleven years of age. The plan estimated that about 26,000 teachers would be needed to serve the estimated number of 18 lakh children in the age group of six to eleven years. But, in 1953–54, Orissa had about 11,225 primary schools (9,614 lower-primary, 1,056 upper-primary and 555 *sevashrams*) served by 18,917 teachers of whom 8,312 were trained.

In 1954–55, Orissa started implementing a novel scheme *Relief of Educated Unemployment and Expansion of Primary Education* sponsored by the Government of India. Orissa was aided in opening a large number of new primary schools under this scheme—1,200 in 1953–54, 1,350 in 1954–55, and 100 in 1955–56. There was also a weeklong drive for enrollment in May 1960. After discounting dropouts, the net increase was considered to be 1.6 lakh (Rath, 1977).

Education between 1960 and 1980

In 1968, Directorate of Public Instruction (DPI) was divided into Directorate of Higher Education and Directorate of School Education. Later, in 1983, Directorate of Primary Education was separated from Directorate of School Education. Directorate of Adult Education was created in 1988 (Senapati, 1996). These were the administrative changes to cope with the new programmes and to focus more on particular sectors of education. Besides this, the government also took the following administrative measures to improve elementary education in 1974:

(a) 16 new class II posts were created.
(b) 3 new class I posts were created.
(c) Education area were made at par with revenue area.
(d) Examination in classes I and II was abandoned.
(e) From August 1976, new time tables for primary schools were introduced; 7–11 AM for all children and 11–12 AM for weak children (Finance Minister Binayak Acharya's Speech, *Utkal Prasanga*, June 3, 1974).

At the start of the eighties, the government targeted to give all 6–11 year olds primary education and 50 per cent of all 11–14 years old upper primary education by March 1990 (Dr Sitakanta Mahapatra, Education Secretary as cited in *Utkal Prasanga*, Nov/Dec 1983, p. 25). The major planks of government actions were intended to be enrollment drive, bringing back dropout children by persuading their parents, enrolling girls and popularizing primary education. The decade started with a primary education campaign from September 5 to 14, 1981. It officially fulfilled the target in Orissa about enrollment of 6–11 and 11–14 year olds (Gangadhar Mahapatra, Education Minister as cited in *Utkal Prasanga*, October, 1983, p. 11). Only 40 per cent were reaching class V at that time and primary education was taking half of the budget. The administrative structure included 56 education districts and 21 tribal sub-plan areas where there was additional fund and education programmes from the Harijan and Tribal Welfare Department.

Operation Black Board

The National Policy on Education (NPE), 1986 had recommended Operation Black Board to improve the infrastructure of the primary schools of the country. Its main aim was to have two all weather rooms in a primary school and provision of teaching learning material (TLM). Accordingly, Government of India started Operation Black Board in 1987–88. In Orissa, under this scheme, 3,272 teacher posts were sanctioned initially and 2,242 school buildings were made at a cost of INR 15.91 lakh. In 1993, Operation Black Board was operative in 30,940 primary schools out of a total of 55,052 primary schools. Nearly 13,190 teacher posts had been sanctioned under Operation Black Board by December 1995 (Government of Orissa, 1996).

Apart from this, the Government of Orissa took the following steps towards education between 1989 and 1993:

(a) In 1989–90, 500 new schools were established, 400 teacher posts filled up and 1,000 new teachers appointed.
(b) In 1990–91, again, 500 new schools were established, 400 teacher posts filled up and 1,000 new teachers appointed. Also, 377 new deputy inspector posts were created.
(c) Between 1990–91 and 1991–92, 3,292 teachers were appointed.
(d) From April 1, 1991, 3,802 aided middle schools were taken over by the government and the rest 1,294 were planned to be gradually taken over.
(e) In March 1993, government decided that those working as temporary teachers in government high schools up to December 31, 1984 were to be made permanent (Ghadei, 1993).
(f) Between 1989 and 1992, six aided teacher training colleges were brought under direct government charge.

School Education in the 1990s

The nineties are marked by two big programmes: the Total Literacy Campaign (TLC) and the District Primary Education Programme (DPEP). Total Literacy Campaign was meant to improve adult literacy and the DPEP was meant to improve school education.

District Primary Education Programme (DPEP)

The DPEP was a centrally sponsored programme of Government of India (with funds from the World Bank) and Government of Orissa in 85:15 proportion. The main objectives of the programme were:

(a) To reduce the differences in enrolment, dropout and learning achievement among gender (boys and girls) and social groups (SC, ST, and general category) to less than five per cent.
(b) To reduce overall primary dropout rates for all students to less than 10 per cent.
(c) To raise the average achievement levels by at least 25 per cent over the measured business level (i.e., at the beginning of the project).
(d) To provide according to national norms access to all children to primary education classes (class I to V), i.e., primary schooling wherever possible or its equivalent alternative education (alternative schooling or employment guarantee scheme).

The DPEP was launched in Orissa in 1996–97, initially in five districts. It was extended to three more districts in 1997–98 and to eight more in 2001–02. The initial eight districts of the first phase (with World Bank' money) of five years duration were Balangir, Baragarh, Dhenkanal, Gajapati, Keonjhar, Kalahandi, Rayagada and Sambalpur. The eight districts of the second phase of seven years duration (with DFID money) were Boudh, Kandhamal, Koraput, Malakangiri, Majurbhanj, Nawarangapur, Nuapada and Sonepur. The maximum limit for each district was INR 40 crore. The Orissa Primary Education Program Authority (OPEPA) was the implementing agency. Till 2002, Government of India had released INR 148.37 crore for the scheme and the contribution of Orissa government was INR 20.55 crore. The total amount of expenditure in phase I covering eight districts was INR 168.93 crore as on October, 2002 (OPEPA, 2001, as cited in CYSD, 2003). Appendix 4.3 gives the details of new primary schools, education guarantee scheme centre and alternative and innovative education centres opened districtwise in DPEP phase I and II.

The Sixth All India Educational Survey (NCERT, 1998) provides us with an insight into the situation with regard to elementary education around this time. According to it, the educational situation was the following (NCERT, 1998):

(a) A total of 96.3 per cent of population in Orissa had access to a primary school within a distance of 1 kilometre against the all India percentage of 93.03. 91.73 per cent of population in Orissa had access to an upper primary school compared to 87.91 per cent of the population at the all India level.

(b) About 11,655 habitations did not have primary schools within a distance of 1 kilometre, which requires provision of schooling facility.
(c) Around 16,317 habitations did not have upper primary schools within a distance of 3 kilometres.
(d) Without exception, these schoolless habitations were in the tribal and remote rural areas.
(e) Dropout rates at the primary and upper primary stage were 43.5 and 57 per cent, respectively.
(f) Levels of learner achievement measured in terms of the quantum and quality of learning acquisitions were abysmally low. Wide variations in levels of learner achievement among boys and girls, urban and rural children, children from SC/ST and non-SC/ST communities shows poor functioning of schools and inadequate teaching inputs especially in rural schools (Baseline Assessment Studies, DPEP, 2001 as cited in Government of Orissa, 2003).
(g) There was no reliable or quantitative assessment of minimum levels of learning, which was partly due to the no-detention policy.

Education after 2000

There were two programmes which started after 2000. They were the Sarva Shiksa Abhiyan (SSA) and Employment Guarantee Scheme/Alternative and Innovative Education Programme (EGS/AIE). The aims of SSA are as follows:

(a) All children in school, EGS centres or alternative schools by 2003.
(b) All children complete five years of primary schooling by 2007.
(c) All children complete eight years of elementary schooling by 2010.
(d) Focus on elementary education of satisfactory quality with emphasis on education for life.
(e) Bridge all gender and social category gaps at primary stage by 2007 and at elementary education level by 2010.
(f) Universal retention by 2010.

The scheme started with the approval of annual work plan and budget for two months, i.e., for February and March 2002 for 14 non-DPEP districts (OPEPA, 2001, as cited in CYSD, 2003).

Employment Guarantee Scheme, a centrally sponsored scheme with 75:25 sharing between the Centre and the state, was introduced in

2001–02 in place of the earlier non-formal education. Efforts were to be made through this programme to ensure primary school facility to the children in a habitation where there is no such facility within 1 kilometre (where formal school is not possible due to lack of sufficient population) in a period of 100 days on receiving the demand of such facility by the local community. In Madhya Pradesh, the place of origin of EGS, it was 90 days. By the end of December 2001, a total number of 1,631 EGS centres had been opened in eight DPEP districts in the state and a sum of INR 12.30 crore had been released by Government of India under the scheme (OPEPA, 2001, as cited in CYSD, 2003; see also Appendix 4.3).

Elementary Education in Contemporary Orissa

Figure 4.1 shows the administrative set-up of school education in Orissa at present.

Presently, more than one department is responsible for school education. They are:

(a) Department of School and Mass Education, which is responsible for the majority of the schools.
(b) Harijan and Tribal Welfare Department which maintains residential schools for tribal children.
(c) Orissa Primary Education Programme Authority, which was in exclusive charge of DPEP and now SSA.

Department of School and Mass Education

↓

3 Regional Joint Directors

↓

19 CI + 4 CI (Harijan & Tribal Welfare Department)

↓

75 DI + 8 DI (Harijan & Tribal Welfare Department)

↓

SI at Block Level

(Note: DI—District Inspector of Schools, CI—Circle Inspector of Schools, SI—Sub-inspector of Schools)

Figure 4.1: Administrative set-up of school education in Orissa

(d) Directorate of TE and SCERT (Teacher Education and State Council of Education, Research and Training), which looks after teacher training.

Co-ordination among various departments remains an issue. Besides, there are issues at every level. At the level of SI, there is the issue of their training. They have to learn effective school supervision. For this, there is a need for them to know education management and administration. Recently, the BRC and CRC teachers have been aiding them in their supervision. At the level of DI, the large number of schools per DI is a concern. Appendix 4.4 shows that the minimum number of schools that a DI is to supervise is 384 in Rayagada. It is difficult for a DI to supervise qualitatively such a large number of schools. There is a need for some administrative innovation with regard to this.

There are many agencies, which are responsible for the early childhood care and education (ECCE) as shown in Table 4.2. In 2001, the population of children of 0–6 years age group in Orissa was 52 lakh which

Table 4.2: Access to pre-primary education in Orissa

Coordinating agencies	Types of programmes	Coverage
ICDS, Government of Orissa through Panchayati Raj Department	Anganwadi centres for children of 2–6 years age group and advisory role to pregnant women	176 projects in 176 blocks with 17,190 centres
Government Recommended (Education and Panchayati Raj Department)	ECE centres (independent) for 3–6 years age group	85 non-government organizations covering about 2,000 centres
Government of Orissa Education Department	Children independent centres	76 centres on experimental basis
State Council for Child Welfare, Bhubaneswar	Crèches and balwadis for children of 0–6 years age group	42 crèche units by non-government organizations
State Social Welfare Advisory Board, Bhubaneswar	Crèches and balwadis for children of 0–6 years age group	About 400 units by non-government organizations
Director of Elementary Education (Recognition Authority)	Pre-school education sections attached to schools	104 private registered bodies

Source: Panda K.C., EFA in Orissa, 1992, as cited in Government of Orissa, 2003a, p. 68

was 14.1 per cent of population. Various government and non-government ECCE schemes covered only 19.6 per cent children of 3–6 years age group in 1997. There are 18 blocks which were not covered by ICDS in 2002–03.

Education of Scheduled Castes (SCs) and Scheduled Tribes (STs)

There are 62 tribes having 25 dialects in Orissa. In 1981, SC population was 16.66 per cent and ST population was 22.43 per cent of the total population. One-third area of Orissa is declared as scheduled area where 56.85 per cent STs live. These are mostly the western districts. 52 per cent of the SC population lives in Puri, Ganjam, Cuttack and Balasore (Das, 1970). The literacy of SC and ST before independence was 3.3 per cent and 1.5 per cent, respectively. It was 11.6 and 7.4 per cent, respectively in 1961 (ibid.). About 86 per cent of tribals were illiterate in Orissa in 1980s.

The special effort for education for the SCs/STs has been the opening of residential schools and hostels for them under the Tribal Sub-Plan (TSP) in the name of Integrated Tribal Development Agency (ITDA) projects which started from Fifth Five-Year Plan (1974–78) onwards. Tribal sub-plan strategy ensured quantification of funds, identification of tribal concentrated areas, and multisectoral approach for tribal development. The TSP area or scheduled area consists of 118 blocks out of 314 blocks of Orissa. Currently, 21 ITDAs, 46 modified area development approach (MADA) pockets in 47 blocks, 14 cluster area approach pockets, 17 microprojects for 13 identified primitive tribal groups in the state are functioning for exclusive development of tribals (Mahapatra, 2003). The 13 primitive tribal groups of Orissa for whom there are microprojects are Bonda, Didayi, Dongria Kondh, Kutia Kondh, Chuktia Bhunjia, Lanjia Saora, Juang, Lodha, Hill Kharia, Mankirdia, Paudi Bhuyan and Saora. Table 4.3 shows the literacy rates of some of the primitive tribes, which show the extremely low level of literacy among them.

Besides these, there were microprojects for SCs in Jajpur and Bhadrak subdivisions of the erstwhile Cuttack and Balasore district (*Utkal Prasanga*, August, 1978). These districts have large SC population. Majority of the SCs live in Puri, Ganjam, Cuttack and Balasore districts and these districts are educationally better off. The chief obstacle in the progress of education in Orissa is the large-scale illiteracy among the tribals and not even the SCs.

Table 4.3: Literacy rates of some of the primitive tribes of Orissa

Tribe	Literacy (in per cent)
Khond	7.9
Gond	13.5
Santal	9.1
Kolha	5.8
Bondo	5.66 males (1990 survey)
	0.69 females (1990 survey)
Didayi	7.89 (2001–02 survey)
Kutia kanda	12.60 (1991 survey)

Source: For Bondo, Didayi, Kutia Kanda – Mahapatra, 2003; for the rest – *Utkal Prasanga*, September, 1978.

The government-run schools and hostels exclusively meant for tribals in ascending order are sevashrams, avasika sevashram, ashram and high schools, respectively. All these are residential schools where the pupils are given food and basic clothing. Besides these, there are exclusive hostels attached to the primary schools of the education department. All these residential schools and hostels come under the department of Harijan and Tribal Welfare and not under the education department. Table 4.4 shows the progress of the number of these hostels and residential schools.

Table 4.4: Progress of hostel facilities for tribal children in Orissa

	1969–70	1973	1975	1978	1979	1989	1992	1993–94
Boys High School	—	47	51	—	—	117	—	138
Girl High School	—	7	8	—	—	33	—	42
Total	—	54	59	64	—	150	167	180
Ashram & Kanyashram	94 (22)	55 (18)	57 (19)	60 (20)	—	85	100	104 (31)
Avasika Sevashram	13	25	28	36	36	50	94	103
Sevashram	1,185	—	1,185	1,185	1,185	1,091	1,032	1,014
Chatsali	135	—	105	84	—	—	—	—
Primary School Hostel	773	819 (68)	932	982	1003	—	1200	1,411

Note: Figures in brackets are for hostels exclusively for girls.
Source: Collated from various issues of *Utkal Prasanga*.

Table 4.5: Districtwise distribution of schools for tribal children

District	Ashram	Kanyashram	Sevashram	Avasika sevashram
Balasore	1	—	7	—
Mayurbhanj	2	4	93	7
Sundergarh	5	4	86	6
Samabalpur	—	—	8	1
Keonjhar	8	2	28	10
Ganjam	1	2	47	3
Koraput	26	7	223	31
Kalahandi	—	1	3	2
Phulbani	4	1	93	8

Source: Government of Orissa, 1996.

Table 4.5 shows the districtwise distribution of these schools (only in scheduled areas) in 1993–94.

From Table 4.5, we can see that the erstwhile Koraput district (whose present break-up new districts are Rayagada, Malkangiri, Nawrangapur, Koraput), which has the lowest literacy rate, has no dearth of exclusive schools for the SC/STs.

Literacy Programmes

Orissa had adult education programmes since 1949. The three programmes for adult education are:

(i) General Adult Education Programme.
(ii) Vocational Adult Education Programme.
(iii) Non-formal Adult Education Programme.

From 1977, the state started emphasizing on adult education because the Central Government itself had started the Adult Education Programme. The state made the following provisions after 1978:

(a) A separate cell for adult education in the secretariat.
(b) A separate department in the education directorate.
(c) A planning officer at each district level.

In Orissa, every Adult Education officer in a district had to open 50 centres under this programme, preference being given to backward areas. It was to run for six months and each one was to cater to about 20 pupils.

Slate, pencil, books, cloth, blackboards, etc. were to be given. INR 75 was for kerosene and supplementary expenses. The teacher was to get INR 50. There was a total of INR 300 for six months.

Adult literacy in the 1970s was dismal. On September 23, 1976 in a meeting of the education minister, it came out that 39,000 (40 per cent) out of 1,06,000 people in Bhubaneswar (the state capital) were illiterate. It was disquieting. A plan was made whereby there would be display boards in key visible public places declaring 'illiteracy is a scourge, to remove it is the duty of every educated person'. There was a Mutual Education Scheme conceived by the vice chancellor of Utkal University in the same year whereby students will go up to 8 km from Bhubaneswar and spread literacy. From the same year, ME (middle English) school students were asked to chip in the adult education programmes. The Upper Primary Teacher Association agreed to help the Adult Education Programme. They opened 162 centres. NGOs opened about 600 adult education centres. A publication division was established to provide primers for literacy centres. By February 1977, there were 70 primers including a *kui* (a tribal dialect) primer for tribal areas (Tripathi, 1977). In 1977, the deputy DPI commented that the state is making 28,000 people literate by spending INR 10 lakh. By October 1978, there were an estimated 55 lakh adult illiterates in the state (ibid.).

There were special centres for disadvantaged groups too. In 1977, there were 25 adult education centres (1,000 students) in tribal areas and four teacher-training centres. There were 21 village-based adult education projects in 1983–84. There were 3,868 centres for males having 1,21,735 students, 2,832 centres for females having 84,778 students. There were 25,104 SC students and 46,182 ST students in these centres. Between 1980 and 1983, 50 per cent of all adult education centres were reserved for women to increase women education. There were 560 adult education centres exclusively for women.

While adult education/non-formal centres were meant for adult illiterates who were outside the formal system, the *chatsalis* were meant for drop-out children to bring them into the fold of education (Kabi, 1985). The number of *chatsalis* was increased after 1980. A *chatsali* was supposed to be established wherever 25 or more out-of-school children were found. The school building and supervision of the teacher was to be the responsibility of the villagers. The teacher was paid INR 105. There were 4,000 *chatsalis* before 1983–84 (2,979 primary + 1,021 middle). 3,000 co-educational and 560 *chatsalis* exclusively for girls (non-formal) were opened in 1983–84. Co-*chatsali* was financed 50:50 by the Centre and the state and the Centre gave 90 per cent for exclusive girl *chatsalis*. No new *chatsali* was opened due to finance crunch in 1984–85. There were 1,59,000 pupils in primary *chatasalis* and 9,000 in middle *chatsalis* in 1984–85. The seventh plan target was to open 2,000 new *chatsalis* and enroll 50,000 students.

The nineties saw the deficiencies of earlier adult education programme. Primary and Adult Education Department became Department of Mass Education from 1989. A separate Directorate of Adult Education came into existence on September 21, 1988. So far, there was only a separate cell since 1977. After 1989, the State Resource Centre was reconstituted. There were 13 posts of District Adult Education Officer. In 1989, there were 51.8 lakh adult illiterates. We have seen earlier that there were an estimated 55 lakh adult illiterates in 1978. Why was the progress on adult literacy so slow? One main reason was that the neo-literates were relapsing. Around 1990, 14 per cent of the currently enrolled and half of ex-enrolled were on the verge of lapsing into illiteracy (CYSD, 1990). The principal huddles according to the study were:

(a) Women did not feel comfortable sitting with others in open space.
(b) Caste (sitting of lower and upper caste together).
(c) Sheer lack of space.

Though the programmes had made people literate temporarily, people had relapsed. Besides, there was the population increase. Around 1990, the enrolment of women was 51.9 per cent and that of SC/ST was 35.1 per cent in the adult education programme.

Janasiksa Nilayam Project, another programme meant for adult education, started from 1989–90. One Janasiksa Nilayam was meant for a population of 5,000 people. There were a total of 604 Janasiksa Nilayams in 1991. The Janasiksa Nilayam Preraks received their first 10 days in-service training in 1990. A study commented that there was loss in transmission in the process of training master trainers who in turn trained the Preraks (ibid.).

The nineties were marked by the Total Literacy Campaign (TLC). The State Literacy Mission Authority was formed in 1989 for the TLC. The erstwhile Adult Education Programme got merged with the National Literacy Mission. 72 blocks were chosen for TLC. TLC was a new addition. So far, there were *chatsalis*, adult education centres and non-formal centres; all meant to cater to different segments of the population who are out of the formal system of schooling. Table 4.6 shows the target and achievement of TLC in the initial period.

Table 4.6: Progress of total literacy campaign till October 1992

District	(1) Target	(2) Success	Literacy rate in 1991	Literacy rate in 2001	Change
Sundergarh	3.50	3.26	52.97	65.22	12.25
Rourkela	1.00	7.10	—	—	—
Ganjam	8.06	7.10	46.72	62.94	16.22
Keonjahr	4.70	2.57	44.73	59.75	15.02
Dhenkanal	4.90	—	54.91	70.11	15.2
Kalahandi	3.50	3.00	31.08	46.2	15.12

Source: Col. 1, 2 – Majhi, 1991.

These are the official figures. If we see the figures, then the programme is successful. Most probably, it was. I have added the literacy figures to show whether the 2001 census reflect all this effort. The census reflects to some extent, especially when the change in case of an educationally advanced district like Cuttack is no more than 10 per cent over that of literacy in 1991 census. Following was the position of TLC in 2002:

(a) The TLC was in operation in 11 districts (Cuttack, Kendrapada, Jagatsinghpur, Jajpur, Boudh, Deogarh, Koraput, Nawarangpur and Rayagada).
(b) Six districts were proposed for post-literacy programmes (Sonepur, Baragarh, Kandhamal, Bhadrak, Khurda and Nayagarh).
(c) Post-literacy programme was continuing in two districts (Puri and Balasore).
(d) Proposals for continuing education had been submitted to the Government of India for 11 districts (Bolangir, Ganjam, Kalahandi, Keonjhar, Malkangiri, Sundergarh, Angul, Dhenkanall, Jharsuguda, Nuapada and Sambalpur) and one special project (Rourkela).
(e) Out of 11 districts and one special project ready for continuing education (Rourkela), three districts and one special project had received sanction for continuing education programme (Government of Orissa, 2003).

Teacher Education

Pre-independence Period

In 1849, there were three normal schools in Calcutta, Dacca and Gowhati in the Bengal presidency. There were two scholarships for Oriya students to go to Calcutta, but nobody went. It is easily understandable that it was because of the lack of communication and the cost involved. When Radhanath Roy was the DPI, he used to set out and travel by bullock carts, elephants and foot to see the schools and used to come back after 2–3 months. If that was the state of communication, then it is understandable how people could go to Calcutta to take teacher training. After more than a decade, the first training class for primary teachers started in Cuttack in 1863 due to the effort of the education director Atkinson. It reminds the situation when teacher training started in the USA first as a class rather than as a school or college. The training class in Cuttack became the first normal school for primary teachers in 1869. It may be mentioned that teacher training schools were called normal schools in their beginning world over. Its (training class in Cuttack) later incarnation was Radhanath Training College, which was the centre of the movement for promotion of Oriya language. Its first principal was a Bengali, Dwarakanath Chakraborty. Even though he was a Bengali, he did his best to promote Oriya education. That time, *guru* training was of one year and *pundit* training was of three years. The second teacher training school opened in Anugul in 1883. Ten guru training schools were opened in Orissa by 1902. The number of gurus who received training in each school was limited to 10. The students spent their time partly in acquiring some knowledge of drawing, school gardening and other subjects and partly in learning a manual on the art of teaching. They also spent time in teaching the children in the nearby school during a course of two years. It was too common for a *guru* who received seven rupees while under training to return to his school and draw there a stipend of one rupee or two. Therefore, there was discouragement for the trained *gurus* to stay in education. In 1923, Cuttack Training School became Cuttack Training College. During the five years ending 1921–22, 1,500 teachers were trained for various primary schools of Orissa. But by 1936, only 900 more were added. There is be no doubt that a large part of this wastage was due to the fact that trained teachers found other walks of life more attractive (Samal, 1984).

Post-independence Period

In 1950, about 50 per cent of the 16,000 male teachers in primary schools had no formal training. In the 1949–50 budget, the state made provisions for raising the pay scale for primary school teachers and establishing 60 new basic schools. The government prepared a plan of education in 1954. The education plan of 1954 prepared by a special officer established a scheme of universal, free and compulsory primary (or junior basic) education for all children between six and eleven years of age. The plan estimated that about 26,000 teachers would be needed to serve the estimated number of 18 lakh children in the 6–11 years age group. But in 1953–54, Orissa had about 11,225 primary schools (9,614 lower primary, 1,056 upper primary and 555 *Sevashrams*) served by 18,917 teachers of whom 8,312 were trained. In 1954–55, Orissa started implementing a scheme 'Relief of Educated Unemployment and Expansion of Primary Education' sponsored by the Government of India.

The government tried to increase the quality of teacher education. Guru Talim, which existed in the British period, was slowly changed into certified teacher (CT). ET schools for teacher education were gradually withdrawn because of low quality. ET schools for teacher education accepted candidates whose qualification was below matriculation. As a result of government policy, the number of ET schools decreased from 83 in 1965–66 to 6 in 1977. Instead, the number of primary and elementary teacher training schools increased from 18 in 1965–66 to 100 in 1975–76.

The government tried to appoint more number of teachers to cater to the growing demand for schooling. Between 1969–70 and 1970–71, 3,500 teachers were appointed. The Governor's speech to the assembly on March 22, 1974 stated that 2,000 teachers were to be appointed and 750 new upper primary schools to be opened in 1974–75. Besides, the government adopted a host of policy measures to better the condition and performance of teachers which are as follows:

(a) Private school teachers' salary was to be at par with the government teachers.
(b) Teachers would get salary directly from the government rather than through the governing body of aided schools (except local-self government and minority institutions). Earlier, the governing bodies used to dilly-dally with regard to salary and exploit the teachers.
(c) The Orissa (Aided Teachers Condition of Appointment) Act was passed to strengthen their (teachers in aided schools) position. They could now go to the tribunal for their grievances.
(d) Teachers who qualify a certain examination for education in tribal areas would get extra pay.
(e) 8,000 primary teachers got training from 850 monitors.
(f) A *siksa udyoga kendra*, fully-funded by the central government, was opened in the education directorate on February 28, 1974 to improve the quality of education (Mahanty, 1977).

(g) 50 per cent of B.Ed. students would get 80 rupees stipend each.
(h) 50 per cent of M.Ed. students will get 100 rupees stipend each.
(i) There were 63,000 scholarships for students in 1972–73.
(j) Women were given preference for teachers from 1983. Between 1980 and 1983, almost all the teachers appointed in the coastal and developed areas were women (Jadunath Dash Mahapatra, Education Minister as cited in *Utkal Prasanga*, June, 1988, p. 8).

A national policy on education (NPE) came out in 1986 as adopted by the Government of India. Orissa took the following steps after the NPE 1986:

(a) All elementary and secondary teachers underwent a centrally sponsored project titled 'Mass Orientation of School Teachers'.
(b) Radhanath Training College, Cuttack, Government Training College Sambalpur and Berhampur were upgraded.
(c) Three teacher training colleges of Orissa were upgraded to the status of 'Colleges of Teacher Education'.
(d) 13 DIETs were created.
(e) District resources units were established.
(f) Substandard teacher training institutes were decided to be phased out.
(g) SCERT was strengthened. Elementary and secondary training institutes merged under a single Directorate of Teacher Education (TE) and SCERT (Government of Orissa, 1993).

The above programmes had their focus on teacher training. Earlier, the government had tried to phase out *guru talim* (in the 1970s) and ET because of their low quality. The efforts after 1986 were to strengthen teacher education further. Apart from this, the late eighties saw the starting of two important programmes: Operation Black Board and Siksa Karmi. Operation Black Board started in 1987–88. Under this scheme, initially 3,272 teacher posts were sanctioned and 13,190 teacher posts had been sanctioned by December 1995 (Government of Orissa, 1996). The Siksa Karmi project started in 1989–90. The number of teachers appointed under this project was 1,441 in 1989–90, 9,309 in 1990–91 and 3,225 in 1991–92.

The new incarnation of the Siksa Karmi project was the Swechchasevi Siksa Sahayaka (SSS) scheme. They are the temporary teachers. Compared to the Siksa Karmi, who used to get INR 400, SSS started with INR 1,500, which has now increased to INR 3,000 rupees for those who have spent five years on the job. But one deficiency marred the whole scheme: the salary was never given regularly. Therefore, the SSSs got a valid excuse for absenteeism. Appendix 4.5 shows the latest numbers of SSS.

There was another scheme which continued in this tradition of appointing temporary teachers. This was the Employment Guarantee Scheme/Alternative and Innovative Education Programme (EGS/AIEP). Employment Guarantee Scheme, a centrally sponsored scheme with 75:25 sharing between the Centre and the state, was introduced in 2001–02 in place of the earlier non-formal education. The EGS teacher was appointed on the basis of recommendation of the VEC. They used INR 1,000 per month. Salary was issued by the block resource centre (BRC) and jointly in the name of VEC president. But one deficiency marred the whole purpose: the salary was never given regularly. Therefore, the EGS to get a valid excuse for absenteeism.

Besides the above, the government took the following measures in the 1990s with regard to teachers:

(a) 1989–90: 500 new schools, 1,000 new teachers, 400 posts filled up.
(b) 1990–91: 500 new schools, 500 new teachers, 400 posts filled up and 377 new deputy inspector posts were created.
(c) Between 1990–91 and 1991–92, 3,292 teachers were appointed.
(d) From April 1, 1991, 3,802 aided middle schools were taken over by the government. Rest 1,294 were planned to be gradually taken over.
(e) In March 1993, government decided that those teachers working temporary in government high schools up to December 31, 1984, were to be made permanent (Ghadei, 1993).
(f) Between 1989 and 1992, six aided teacher training colleges were brought under direct government charge.

Teacher Education in Contemporary Orissa

Most of the teachers are now nominally trained. But the minimum qualification for teacher training in Orissa is low compared to other states. While in many other states, the minimum qualification is twelve years of education for primary teacher, it is 10 years of education in Orissa. Besides, there are two qualities of teacher training institutions in the state for teachers. While the DIETs accept 12 years of schooling as minimum qualification, other teacher training institutions in the state accept ten years as the minimum qualification. The DIETs are well endowed as compared to others. Because of this, there are two grades of primary teachers in the state; though nominally, their qualifications are the same.

Besides training, the quality of teachers remains an issue. Presently, most of the teachers have either ten or twelve years of schooling (Appendix 4.6). The low level of qualification probably shows up in the teachers' subject knowledge. What to speak about minimum levels of learning for children, the performance of teachers themselves is a concern. Appendices 4.7 and 4.8 show the performance of teachers in two vital subjects—English and Mathematics. These show that majority of teachers perform below 50 per cent level. This is a test of their subject knowledge and not 'teaching of the subject knowledge'. It seems that neither higher entry qualification nor training is enough. It seems there is an urgent need to look at the whole issue of teacher recruitment and selection. No amount of training can compensate for teacher dedication and professionalism. The teachers should have the willingness to constantly improve themselves and the state can only aid in this process. The teachers also have to take the initiative themselves.

Presently, the selection of candidates to the pre-service teacher education courses (CT and B.Ed.) is done exclusively on the basis of career assessment. This has inevitably led to the selection of candidates who do not have the right kind of attitude, aptitude and interest that are required for an effective teacher. Selection of candidates solely on career assessment has been obsolete. What is required, therefore, is a selection based on performance in an entrance examination of tough order and followed by a rigorous mechanism for personality appraisal.

The Financial Support to Primary Education: Walking the Tightrope

Unfortunately if one looks into the post-independence Orissa, illiteracy was not the only big problem, there was the basic problem of livelihood also. Orissa is known for the poverty and the natural calamities like flood, drought and cyclones (see Appendix 4.15). 64 per cent people were below poverty line in 1960–61, when the poverty line was 15 rupees in rural areas and 22.5 rupees in urban areas. With such high level of poverty, one does not know whether the government should spend more on irrigation or education.

The link between education and development has dominated the thinking of policy makers only in the present time. The various budget speeches of finance ministers of Orissa show this kind of transition in emphasis. So, as I will show later in the financial statistics, it is only after 1974–75 that one sees any significant increase in the money spent for education. The state has relied a lot on centrally sponsored schemes like the

Adult Education Programme (1977), Operation Black Board (1988), Total Literacy Programme (1990), DPEP (1996) and now SSA (2000). But even if we assume that the financial condition today is worse than the earlier years, the state's commitment to education is more as compared to the earlier times. Revenue expenditure on education as a percentage of total revenue expenditure is more now as compared to the earlier period. The predicament of capital expenditure is that there is not much left after debt servicing. In this context, the 2003–04 budget estimate earmarking 1.03 per cent of the total capital expenditure for education is more as compared to earlier period (see Appendices 4.21–4.23). Levels in spending for education compared to previous years have increased significantly in 1974–75, 1984–85 and 1989–90. In these years, total spending on education attained higher levels and stayed at that level in the following years.

It can be seen from the Appendix 4.21 that 1974–75 is the year when the financial support to education did a quantum jump. How could the state afford it? There was first a cyclone in 1970, then a flood and then a drought. Again, there was a tornado and a cyclone in 1971. Natural calamities are almost recurrent in Orissa (see Appendix 4.15). But because of the loan relief scheme of Finance Commission, the state had to pay Rs. 52.99 crore instead of Rs. 287.37 crore to the central government by March 31, 1974. The plan support had also increased from the Centre. The Fifth Finance Commission recommended Rs. 287.33 crore as plan support as compared to the total fourth plan of Rs. 252 crore (for Orissa) which included both the state and central outlay. In contrast, the total outlay in fifth plan was Rs. 567 crore. The Sixth Finance Commission recommended Rs. 577.32 crore for the state (Finance Minister Binayak Acharya's speech, *Utkal Prasanga*, June 3, 1974). Besides this higher plan allocation from the Centre, the state had surplus in the previous two years—Rs. 0.36 crore in 1972–73 and Rs. 0.59 crore in 1973–74. That's how the state could afford a significant increase in the financial support to education. This support was reflected in the next year.

The state gradually introduced more and more schemes in education after 1975—the Adult Education Programme in 1977, Operation Black Board and Siksa Karmi projects in 1988, Total Literacy Mission in 1991, DPEP in 1996 and EGS in 2001. These were possibly the reasons why the spending in education has gone up and up since 1984–85.

The data on the budgets for 2000–01 to 2003–04 show the following:

(a) The state depends on central loan in terms of grants-in-aid to the tune of 25 per cent of its total revenue receipt.

(b) Between 47 and 50 per cent of the total revenue expenditure is spent on general services, which is basically administration.
(c) Between 32 and 35 per cent of the total revenue expenditure is spent on social services.
(d) In the social services sector, expenditure on education, youth, art and culture constitutes between 48 and 51 per cent of the total expenditure.
(e) From amongst the total revenue expenditure on general education, sports, art and culture, expenditure on general education averages a little more than 97 per cent of the total expenditure.
(f) The state is dependent on Government of India loans and advances from the Reserve Bank of India for its capital receipt to the extent of two-thirds of the total capital receipt.
(g) Around 80 per cent of the money received in capital account goes in public debt repayment telling about a debt-trap.
(h) Capital expenditure on economic services is about 9 per cent, less than 2 per cent on social services (where education belong) and less than 1 per cent on general services.

Most probably, the state support to education does not depend on just the financial health of the state but also the prevailing ideology. Natural calamity, poverty, etc. are prevalent even today (see Appendix 4.15). The finance may be even worse because of debt servicing. But, the overall spending on education has increased. May be, initially, the state was bogged down with the task of building some basic infrastructure and industry and was relaxed enough to devote more resources to education after the mid-seventies. Once the expenditure is increased, then it is probably very difficult to cut it down. For example, in the years 1985–86 and 1986–87, the expenditure went up. The state established DIETs, teacher training institutes, etc. to revamp the education. Once it was done, the expenditure (revenue) went up and did not come down from the next year onwards because once something is established, it cannot be abolished easily. In this case, the push was from outside the state—the NPE, 1986.

The Educational Backwardness of the Koraput and Western Districts: The Issue of Poverty

Orissa is the poorest state in India, now replacing Bihar. This speaks about the extreme administrative inefficiency. Southern region of Orissa is the poorest region in India exceeded by only the hills of Assam (54 per cent). Northern Orissa too falls among the five poorest regions of the country (Haan and Dubey, 2003. as cited in Panda, 2004, pp. 167–182). What is of concern is that the poverty ratio of the southern districts has increased while that of the coastal districts has declined over the years. The poorest districts of Koraput, Bolangir and Kalahandi (KBK) are in the southern region. The 4 per cent increase of poverty ratio of northern districts may be more due to change in the methodology to count the poverty ratio between 1993–94 and 1999–2000. But among the districts, poverty of Koraput, Kandhamal and Kalahandi has consistently increased rather than decreasing. Between 1993–94 and 1999–2000, poverty ratio of many districts increased. This is partly because of change of methodology to count the poverty ratio. But, Koraput, Kalahandi and Kandhamal districts stand out. Poverty in these three districts has consistently increased rather than decreasing. Between 1983 and 1987–88, poverty ratio decreased very marginally in these districts—between one and three per cent. Between 1993–94 and 1999–2000, poverty ratio increased substantially in these districts. Even if we discount the factor of methodology change to count the poverty ratio between 1993–94 and 2000, these were substantial increases. In case of Kandhamal, the poverty ratio has remained same since 1983. If we compare 1983 data with the data of 1999–2000, poverty ratios of all other districts has declined (see Appendices 4.9–4.11). Besides poverty, these three districts are in the bottom with regard to important indicators of development (Appendix 4.12). The erstwhile Phulbani district now includes the Kandhamal district after the districts reorganization. Appendix 4.12 shows that the three districts constitute the three bottommost districts in the overall ranking of development. The table is arrived at after taking into account seven indicators for agricultural development, four indicators for industrial development and 15 indicators for basic infrastructure and services that includes primary and middle schools also per 10,000 people. Thus, it gives a fair idea about the overall position of districts.

Amongst the social categories, the tribals constitute the bottommost rung with regard to poverty. While about one-third people among the non-SC and ST population are below the poverty line, they are little above half among the SCs and about three-fourth among the ST (see Appendix 4.13). While the SC and ST constitute about 40 per cent of the population, they contribute about 64 per cent to the number of poor. The southern districts have the highest concentration of tribals. Thus, what comes out of the above discussion is that the tribals and the SCs now remain the social categories constituting the major chunk of poor in Orissa. A special, vigorous and honest effort is required to lift this social segment out of poverty. Often, poverty is a main reason for non-enrollment and dropouts. Southern districts have very low literacy rates. Therefore, removal of poverty is almost non-negotiable in the effort towards universal enrollment and retention.

Conclusion: The Continuing Concern

Removal of poverty, adequate financial support to education and people's awareness are probably the three main pillars on which will rest 'education for all'. It is going to be an uphill task for Orissa. Poverty is often considered as the culprit behind non-enrollment and dropout's. Lack of financial support to primary education has been traditionally considered as a factor for the low quality of education. Though we have not yet won the war on quantity, the issue of quality has been slowly acquiring centre stage. This is certainly a good sign. The DPEP and now SSA are slowly improving the quality of infrastructure. Hopefully, they will improve the human factors—the teachers, school inspectors, etc.

What is the contribution of the programmes? Most of the early beginners in DPEP programme (Bolangir, Baragarh, Dhenkanal, Gajapati, Keonjhar, Kalahandi, Rayagada and Sambalpur) were low literacy districts and are still so, except Baragarh, Dhenkanal and Sambalpur. The districts proposed for post-literacy programme or where post-literacy programme is going on (Sonepur, Baragarh, Bhadrak, Khurda, Nayagarh, Puri and Balasore) were high literacy districts and are still so, except Kandhamal. But the early beginners (except Rayagada) in DPEP have improved between 15 and 16 percentage points over that of 1991 literacy rate, which is at par with the all Orissa situation of 14.7 per cent. But, according to this rate, the gap between advanced districts and backward districts in terms of literacy will always remain so because it is not significantly above the state average of about 15 percentage points. So, a new thinking in policy is required. Recent programmes like DPEP and SSA take into account the differential enrollment of SC/ST and general category. The sooner they take into account the same factor with regard to the teachers, the better it will be.

At 63.61 per cent, Orissa is not more than three percentage points lower than the all India figure. There were 11 districts (total 30 districts) having 70 per cent or more literacy rate in Orissa in 2001. On the other hand, there were 10 districts having literacy rates lower than 55 per cent. The erstwhile Koraput district was having literacy rate of less than 40 per cent. So, the literacy rate of 63.61 per cent for the state hides more than it shows. The state has not consciously adopted a strategy to correct the historical wrong of the western tribal-dominated districts. As discussed earlier, these districts have started late in education since pre-Independence period as compared to the coastal districts. Besides, they are in the bottom in other development indicators like agriculture, industry and basic infrastructure (see Appendix 4.12). Probably Orissa, just after Independence, thought it more important to build up irrigation and industry rather than education. When it finally turned the attention towards education, it did so taking the cue from the Centre, especially after the eighties. When it focussed the attention, it did not have a region- or district-specific strategy. Therefore, the early beginners in education (the coastal districts) stayed ahead of others in education. Khora (2005) has argued earlier that the right amount of representation of females and SC/ST among teachers would have corrected the situation much earlier. Initially, it might have been difficult to get SC/ST teachers. But if it is not done after even 30–40 years, it signals a policy anomaly. This is of course apart from the generic factors like corruption, teacher absenteeism, etc., which require more political and administrative will and the minimum necessity like the availability of teachers and schools.

5

TEACHER PROFESSIONALISM IN RURAL AREAS: A CASE OF LAXMIPUR IN ORISSA

The Problem: Teacher Professionalism—Much Needed But Unexplored Area

While surveys on teachers exist in India, qualitative studies on teacher professionalism are probably non-existent. Survey literatures on teachers focus more on their numerical adequacy, training and their material conditions (see Goyal and Chopra, 1990; Chopra, 1993). There are a few ethnographic studies on education (Thapan 1991, about one school in all aspects; Alexander 2000, about classroom and teaching; Prema Clarke 2001, about teaching styles; Sarangapani 2003, about classroom). So far, probably, there does not exist any qualitative study that has teacher professionalism as its focus by studying 'teachers-in-action'.

The cognitive dimension of professionalism is generally stated as 'highly skilled practice'. It is also conceptualized in the specific context of primary teaching. There are four areas that can be considered as constituting teaching expertise—subject matter knowledge, knowledge of classroom management, instructional techniques and diagnostic knowledge (Weinert, Schrader and Helmke, 1990). Shulman (2004, p. 227) provides seven categories of knowledge-bases of teaching—content knowledge, general pedagogical knowledge, curriculum knowledge, pedagogical content knowledge, knowledge of learners and their characteristics, knowledge of educational context and knowledge of educational ends, purposes and values. Caldwell (2000) envisages four types of knowledge and skills as essential aspects of teacher professionalism in the classroom in the present age—literacy (having an array of diagnostic and assessment instruments), mathematics, information and communication technologies, and reflective intelligence. These various conceptualizations suggest that the cognitive dimension of teacher professionalism is manifest in teacher actions in the classroom. The notion of professionalism shifts our attention from the macro aspects of the teaching profession—its status, the politics around it and the issue of a code of ethics—to the teacher action in the classroom. The macro issues are important but rest on the bottom line, if one may say so, of the teacher action in the classroom. Without the right teacher actions in the classroom, the superstructure of status, code of ethics and the politics of professionalization may look vacuous. Though teacher professionalism can be construed after taking into account the teacher in relation to the pupils, parents, the local community and the society at large, teacher actions, in the classroom is the most important manifestation of teacher professionalism.

It can be a naive assumption that the classroom can be either entirely child centred or teacher centred. Literature on education may project that the classroom has moved from a teacher-centred to a child-centred education after years of espousal by the government and the academia. However, it will be naïve to assume that the classroom indeed has become child centred without seeing the classroom itself.

The classroom will look different from the sociology of knowledge perspective, symbolic interactionist perspective and from the point of view of professionalism. The sociology of knowledge will try to see how knowledge is constructed in the classroom, the symbolic interactionist perspective will unravel the social dimension, but the point of view of professionalism will try to see whether such construction and such dimension conform to spatio-temporal judgements about teacher professionalism or not. For example, from the point of view of professionalism, the construction of knowledge should conform to 'scientific temper' and the social dimension should conform to 'democratic' values.

Concern with the primary teacher and the primary classroom without using the recently popular term of professionalism has been there in the studies of sociology of education in India. 'The meek dictator' (Kumar, 2005) captures the sociohistorical position of Indian primary teacher well. Kumar has convincingly shown the historical roots of some aspects of classroom and teachers that are presently criticized—the hierarchical relation between the teacher and the child and the transmission mode of teaching. Thapan's (1991) ethnographic study brings out the uncomfortable co-existence of ideological and professional commitments amongst teachers in a private school that can be considered unique in the sense that its founder does not propound a schooling based on an ideology of competition and meritocracy.

One of the important findings of this study was to bring out the complexities of a school that may look to an outsider quite orderly, based on an ideological consensus. Clarke (2001) has more explicitly tried to bring out teaching styles of teachers in an urban context. It shows how the textbook is still considered the only authoritative source of knowledge.

There is a transition of emphasis from teacher education and training to teacher professional development and teacher professionalism on part of the government. The National Commission on Teachers I (NCT, 1986) focussed more on teaching as a profession and not professionalism. Its central concern was the status and performance of teachers, which were considered to be interrelated. It gave recommendations on teacher training, working conditions and hoped, somewhat unreasonably, in a code of ethics. However, one does not get a picture of a teacher-in-action, even of a low performing one, from this document. There are mentions about the low performing teacher (NCT, 1986) or making the classroom more democratic (NCERT, 2005), but one becomes curious as to how good or bad Indian primary classrooms are. The National Curriculum Framework 2005 talks about the reflective teacher. But, is it achievable in the near future? Do teachers in the classroom believe in something called reflexivity? An example of the increasing focus on classroom in the notion of professionalism is the Advancement of Educational Performance through Teacher Support (ADEPTS) document by the Government of India (MHRD, 2006). This document suggests ways of transacting in the classroom and deal with both the social and cognitive dimensions.

It is a question of both academic and practical interest as to what is the reality of teacher professionalism in India after a decade that witnessed District Primary Education Program (DPEP; started in 1993–94), Sarva Shiksa Abhiyan (SSA; started in 2000) and the National Curriculum Framework 2005? Whether teachers are regular? Whether they make an effort to teach? What is the teaching style in the context of nearly one decade of emphasis on 'play-way'? What is the discipline style in the context of the emphasis on democratic relationship and prohibition of physical punishment? What is the reality of classrooms in the tribal areas in the light of the growing realization that the tribal pockets are where illiteracy is concentrated? How far have we to go in the context of the effort to transition to quality?

The Methodology of the Study

The broad objective of the study was an exploration into teacher professionalism and classroom processes in a rural area. One of the main reasons for which a qualitative approach was chosen was that there is hardly any qualitative study of teachers or classroom processes in India. There are surveys on teachers. But, there is a lack of any qualitative study on teachers and classroom processes.

In a qualitative study, whatever the respondents say cannot be accepted at face value. One source of data has to be validated by another source of data. What the subjects say has to be verified against one's own observation. Some non-local teachers in my interviews said that local teachers do not have dedication. However, I found in my observation that both local and non-local teachers have dedication and shirking of duty can be found among both local and non-local teachers. Many teachers in their interviews projected the image of a professional teacher. Over the years, primary teachers have inherited some stock phrases about primary teaching like 'primary teachers are all-rounders' meaning that they have knowledge and skill in all the subjects. But they are circumstantial all-rounders and not real all-rounders. Observation of classroom processes revealed, sometimes, a totally different picture. Merely using the interview method can be quite deceiving.

I stayed approximately eight months in the block (November 2005–April 2006; January–February 2007). Eight schools were visited during this period. Live classrooms of 19 teachers were observed. The maximum length of distraction to children because of my entrance to the class was 15 minutes. Distraction means the deviation of children from the task or behaviour they were at when I entered. Twenty teachers were interviewed. Formal interviews lasted between one and two and a half hours, which mostly took place in their homes. However, there was a lot of discussion in the schools.

I took a few teachers and few classrooms out of more than lakh primary teachers of Orissa and millions of classroom teachings for my qualitative study. How far are these representative of teachers and classroom processes of Orissa, if not India? Alexander (2000) grappled with this question in his multi-country study, which included India also. He was satisfied after the study that even few classrooms represent a country to some extent. This can happen because quality compensates to some extent the absence of quantity (large sample size) in a qualitative study. For example, while a quantitative study will merely bring out whether teachers are regular or not, this study shows that there are kinds of regularity—spontaneously regular and regular because of community pressure. While spontaneous regularity will gradually improve education of children, regularity out of compulsion is not useful. I believe that this study represents Orissa to a great extent, if not India. This is also because DPEP and SSA have been influencing every school. They are meant to do so.

Limitations

A qualitative study is a series of subjective judgements. The data is subjective, the interpretation is subjective and the conclusions can also be subjective. Objectivity—both interpersonal and intrapersonal—is ensured by triangulation of the data and other material evidences like cassettes and photos. But, the reader still has to rely on the account of the ethnographer.

Tools of Data Collection

The primary data was collected through two tools of data collection—interview and observation. In-depth interviews were conducted with teachers. Classroom teaching of the teachers interviewed were observed. But classroom teaching could not be observed in some cases and in some other cases interviews could not be done. Those reasons have been accounted for.

The Selection Procedure of Teachers

- **State: Orissa**
  Knowledge of language and context helps greatly in a qualitative study. Since I know the language and hail from Orissa, it was very helpful. It is not a highly literate state and, moreover, is the poorest state in India. Thus, a study of teachers and classroom processes may help in understanding teacher professionalism in a condition of poverty and backwardness.
- **District: Koraput**
  It is the poorest, educationally backward, tribal dominated district in Orissa.
- **Block: Laxmipur**
  One rural block was chosen randomly because poverty and illiteracy are concentrated in rural blocks.
- **Primary Schools**
  Five schools of education department, one school each maintained by Department of Tribal Welfare, one Employment Guarantee Scheme (EGS) centre and one private school were chosen for a fair representation of schools in this area.

- **Teachers**
  All the teachers of any school so chosen were the subjects of the study.
- **Classrooms**
  Classroom teaching of the above teachers were chosen for the study.

The Field Site: Introduction to Laxmipur

Laxmipur is situated in Koraput district, Orissa, India (see the maps below; Laxmipur). Laxmipur is a predominantly tribal population inhabited block with most of the population below poverty line. The tribe which inhabits this area is Khond. Their language is called Kuvi. It does not have a script. There is Kuvi bible in Oriya script. I also found 'A Grammar of Kuvi Language' (Israel M. 1979, Dravidian Linguistics Association, Trivandrum), but very few people know about it. Table 5.1 presents its socio-education indicators.

Laxmipur has close to half the teachers belonging to Scheduled Caste (SC) and Scheduled Tribe (ST) communities. Thus, they are not under-represented. Almost a fifth of the teachers are temporary teachers known as Swechchasevi Siksa Sahayaka (SSS). Also, one fifth of the teachers are female teachers. Female teachers dominate the two schools located in the

Map showing Koraput district in Orissa state

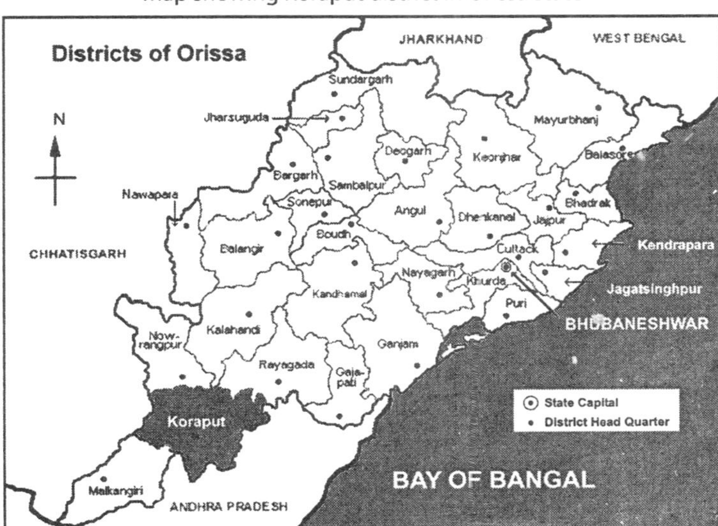

Map showing Laxmipur block in Koraput district

only two towns in the block—Laxmipur and Kakiriguma. While there are six female and two male teachers in Laxmipur primary school, there are four female teachers and three male teachers in Kakiriguma. This shows their preference for urban area. The details of the teachers studied are presented in Table 5.2.

Interviews of teachers and observation of classroom teaching of all the above teachers were to be done. But, interview and observation of a few teachers and classrooms could not be done for various reasons.

Reasons for which classroom observations could not be done are as follows:

Manty (SSS): Manty could not be observed because he travels from Koraput (60 km distance) and whatever little he does is considered sufficient. He is employed for non-academic purposes rather than for teaching.

Kasinath (head teacher): There is some sort of convention in this school and many other schools whereby the head master manages the school instead of teaching. This school has a hostel. The head teacher mainly looks after the hostel. He probably believes that this is reasonable work for him.

Table 5.1: Indicators related to population, education and teachers in Laxmipur

Population indicators	Education indicators	Teacher indicators
Date of starting of the block: 1.1.1960 Area: 45,323 sq km Population: 48,240 (1991) 54,154 (2001) SC: 7,109 (15%) ST: 32,973 (68%) Total households: 14,419 (1997) 15,177 (2002) BPL: 12,663 (87.82% in 1997) APL: 1,756 Total number of gram panchayats: 13 Total revenue villages: 100 Hamlets: 75 Wards: 150 SC: 24 ST: 100 Others: 26	Colleges: 1 High schools: 2 Private high schools: 2 Department of Tribal Welfare high schools: 3 Total primary and upper primary schools: 75 Upper primary schools: 14 Upper primary schools DPEP: 14 New primary schools by DPEP: 4 Department of Tribal Welfare Sevashrams: 5 JELC (Christian Mission)Primary: 1 NCLP Primary: 1 Saraswati Sisu Mandir: 1 Public School: 1 EGS centres: 45 S.I. Circles: 2 (Laxmipur, Kakiriguma) BRCC: 3 CRC: 7 MCS: 14 ECCE: 28	Total primary teachers: 189 Total SSS: 35 (18.51%) Female teachers: 41(21.69%) SC teachers: 54(28.57%) ST teachers: 39(20.63%) Teachers with qualification above HSC: 40(21.16%) Teachers with qualification below HSC: 15(7.93%)

Source: Information was collected from the block office

Mahesh: For reasons not known, only Mahesh from Bakar School is always employed by the Block District Officer for administrative works like survey, voter list, etc. Though he sounds professional and others say so, he could have escaped these non-academic duties at least some times. Probably, he himself does not mind this. During my long stay, I tried several times but I could never attend his class.

Munuaka: Education Guarantee Scheme people hardly go to the school. EGS now has only some meaning because of Mid Day Meal. I told him many times that I could take him by motor cycle if he informs me which day he goes. During my long stay, he never informed me.

Table 5.2: Profile of teachers in the study

Schools	Teachers	Sex	Age	Education	Community	Experience (in Years)	Distance from block headquarter	Mode of transport used by the teacher
Raigad	Magan	Male	36	B.Com, B.Ed.	General	10	3 km, Metal + 5 km, Mud	Scooter
Baisakh	Kasla[£]	Female	50	HSC, CT	ST	31	4.5 km, Metal	Bus + 2 km Walking
	Pajhi	Male	53	BA, CT	General	33	-do-	Bus + 2 km Walking
	Manty (SSS)[¥]	Male	33	B.Ed.	General	5	64.5 km, Metal	Bus + 2 km Cycle (stays in Koraput)
	Jyoshi (SSS)[£]	Female	34	BA, B.Ed.	General	4	4.5 km, Metal	Bus + 2 km Walking
Cisakh	Kasinath[¥]	Male	53	HSC, CT	SC	26	3 km, Metal + 2 km, Mud	Cycle
	Kota	Male	43	BA, B.Ed.	General	25	-do-	Cycle
	Shakir	Male	34	HSC, CT	ST	11	-do-	Cycle
Bakar	Kosa	Male	49	10th, CT	ST	32	5 km, Metal	Cycle
	Mahesh[¥]	Male	33	BA, CT	ST	11	5 km, Metal	Motor cycle
	Virendra	Male	47	9th, ET	ST	26	35 km, Metal	Bus (stays in Kakiriguma)
	Pranati[£]	Female	37	HSC, CT	SC	8	5 km, Metal	Bus
	Alpana (SSS)	Female	33	+2, CT	General	5	35 km, Metal	Bus (stays in Kakiriguma)

(*Continued*)

Kesli	Aminash	Male	51	HSC, CT	General	30	8 km, Metal + 3 km, Mud	Colleague's motor cycle
	Noyak	Male	46	HSC, CT	General	30	-do-	Motor cycle
Tikung	Tima	Male	52	HSC, ET	SC	34	12 km, Metal	Stays in the school
	Meeta[£]	Female	50	HSC, CT	ST	30	-do-	Bus
	Gajendra	Male	52	BA, CT	General	23	-do-	Stays in the school
Upai Public School	Junoka	Male	18	+2	ST	1	0	Stays near the school
	Kabir	Male	32	PG, CT	General	10	0	Stays near the school
Rup-guda	Prabin	Male	55	Matric, CT	ST	35	1 km, Mud	Motor cycle
	Tupur (SSS)	Female	40	+2, CT	General	2	-do-	Walking
	Tejmayi (SSS)	Female	36	+2, CT	General	4	62 km	Bus + 2 km Walking
Daliamb	Munuaka[¥]	Male	24	+2	ST	4	8 km, Metal	Rarely goes

Notes: ¥ - Classroom observations not done; £ - Interviews not done; Names are pseudonyms; wherever residence is not specifically mentioned, residence is block headquarter.

Some of the reasons for which classrooms could not be observed on particular days are doing paintings on the walls, fixing up the swing given by DPEP, BRC meeting, cold cyclonic rain, local haat (weekly market) and so on.

Reasons for which interviews could not be done are as follows:

Kasla: Though being the head mistress and a little professional, she was shy in giving interview. I construe that it was her lack of confidence in herself. Interview is considered something serious here. People fear that they may face problem later because of what they say in the interview. This problem generally is about their superiors like School Inspector (SI). She also could see that she is not going to face any problem for not giving the interview unlike many official works.

Jyoshi and Kosla are close friends. Taking the cue from Kosla, Jyoshi also was unwilling to give interview.

Pranati: In her case, it was extreme lack of confidence almost to the point of hesitation to give the interview to me.

Meeta: Hers was extreme lack of confidence, extreme lackadaisical attitude to the point of laziness towards interview. She is so lazy that she tells another boy to beat the boy nearby for discipline reason instead of herself getting up and beating the boy if that was necessary at all!

In all the cases, the refusal was not direct and confrontational. It was tactful and in a round about way like, 'If two others are giving interview then what's more if I give?' It is also striking that all of the teachers who were unwilling to give interview were women.

Some of the teachers gave a very short interview because they thought that was enough. Since they themselves are not much professional, they can't think of an interview as an elaborate affair. Some interviews were long and satisfactory. But some were short because some were not articulate enough, some were shy and some were taciturn. In one case, the interview could not be tape-recorded because I got the opportunity after much effort and I wanted to take the interview without waiting for the tape-recorder. I had to reconstruct the interview out of memory. In another case I was having fever, but could not let go the appointment for interview. In most cases, I could not look at the schedule because that would have stopped the flow of the interview. But I had memorized the interview guide and I could take more than one interview.

The Categorization of Teachers

Ideally, a professional teacher should have subject knowledge, teaching skills and ethics related to teaching. Such ethics could be his/her concern for children, good relation with children, etc. This can be presented as shown in Figure 5.1.

The present study follows the conceptual framework discussed above. These can be known only through in-depth interviews and observations. It is not easy to classify teachers into professional and non-professional. Larson (1977) opined that the useful question is not whether a vocation is a profession or not, but how much professionalized a vocation is. The useful question seems not to be whether a teacher is professional or not, but how far professionalized is a teacher. No teacher was found to be fully professional from an ideal yardstick—knowledge, skills and ethics. A teacher may have one of these and missing another. Having the three attributes in sufficient degree is, I think, generally a rarity.

Often, teaching in a rural area does not require so much subject knowledge as skills. For example, knowledge of the tribal language (Kuvi) is probably one of the biggest assets that a teacher can have in this area. But this is not imparted by training. On the other hand, lack of knowledge of the tribal language (Kuvi) does not become a big barrier for a teacher who has the willingness to teach. Since the teachers may not have got enough skills during training, often what matters is the willingness to teach. 'Doing whatever is necessary in order to achieve these goals (*learning goals*) rather than doing certain things in certain ways or using certain methods or techniques is a hallmark of an effective teacher' (Anderson, 2004, pp. 24–25; italics mine). Willingness to teach will result in at least two actions—going regularly to the school and attempt to impart some

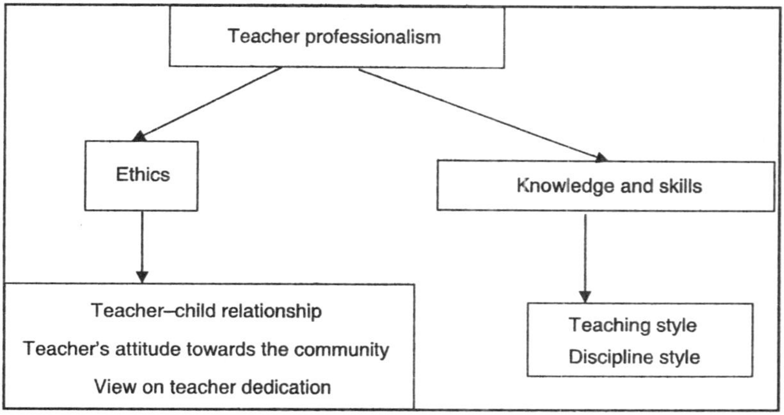

Figure 5.1 Teacher professionalism

training to the children. A teacher must go regularly before he/she can teach and attempt to teach before he/she teaches well. But there are variants of attempt to teach. There is a difference between *attempt to teach* and *attempt to teach to succeed*. In other words, there can be teaching that has an objective and teaching that has none. This is one aspect, which marks out the professional teachers from the non-professional.

Table 5.3 shows that there are many kinds of regularity and many kinds of teaching. There can be various combinations of teaching and regularity. Mere regularity does not improve education. In spite of all the hue and cry about the play-way method, it is not practiced above class I or II. Most of the teachers with little bit of professionalism teach through the direct method rather than play way. A teacher may not be regular but might have the skill to teach. On the other hand, a teacher may be regular because of circumstantial reason. However, that regularity does not improve education in the village. On the top of this, if a teacher is irregular because he/she is always deputed for administrative duties, as happened with one teacher in this study, then it is the government that is to be blamed and not the teacher.

Regularity out of compulsion and mechanical teaching cannot be considered as signs of professionalism. Strictly speaking, mechanical teaching is not teaching as such. It is either reciting or talking. Spontaneous regularity and attempt to teach can be the signs of professionalism. Often, teachers achieve learning goals to some extent through the direct method. They have been teaching through the direct method for decades. Now, play-way method is practiced in a very limited scale for class I or II. Thus, initially, regularity and attempt to teach to succeed can be considered as signs of professionalism.

In India, teacher absenteeism is an important ethical issue. It has recently been construed by the government and academia as violating the ethics of teaching. Teacher absence rate was 25 per cent for 19 states in 2002. The absence rate varied from 15 per cent in Gujarat to 38 per cent in Bihar (Chaudhury et al., 2003 as cited in Hallack and Poisson, 2007). Anand (1996) points out that at any given time, 50 per cent of the sections in primary schools were unattended to by a teacher which is disguised absenteeism. One has to take into account regularity and making an effort to teach as the important ethical dimensions of dedication and commitment amongst Indian primary teachers. These two aspects reflect open and disguised teacher absenteeism. Anitha (2005) took into account *active instructional time* in her conceptualization of quality of schooling in a rural area. Regularity and making an effort to teach can be considered as part of practical and ethical standard mentioned by Goodson (2000). It also reflects dedication and commitment, which are emphasized by official bodies like NCTE (1998) and NCERT (Walia, 2003).

A teacher's primary duty is teaching and not administration. Many head teachers in the study were regular but busied themselves primarily in administration. This administration is necessary, but they can't be characterized as professional as they are unable to do the primary job of a teacher, i.e., teaching.

Finding a teacher who is professional in all subjects and all levels is a rarity (Anderson, 2004). I could not find any teacher as fully professional with all its dimensions—having adequate subject knowledge, teaching skills and ethics. But, scientific endeavour remains incomplete without classification. Classifying in a qualitative study is difficult because each subject is unique and much of the data is subjective.

The teachers of the study can be placed along a continuum of regularity of going to the school and making an effort to teach, though the notion of making an effort to teach is dependent on a subjective judgement. While eight teachers were regular all the time and made maximum effort to teach, three teachers were neither regular nor made any effort to teach. Other teachers' regularity and effort to teach were to a greater and lesser extent as compared to these two categories. They can be placed in between these two categories on the two extreme ends of the continuum. Teachers along this continuum can be considered, though in a simplistic manner, to have various degrees of dedication and commitment. For the purpose of analysis, one can consider calling the first group of teachers as professional, the intermediary group as less professional and the last group as least professional (Figure 5.2 and Table 5.3).

Though this gives an indication of the degrees of commitment among teachers in a simplistic manner, it does not give an idea of the full gamut of professionalism. Professionalism is not only about the commitment and dedication but also about the quality of practice—how teachers teach in the classroom. The following sections deal with these aspects.

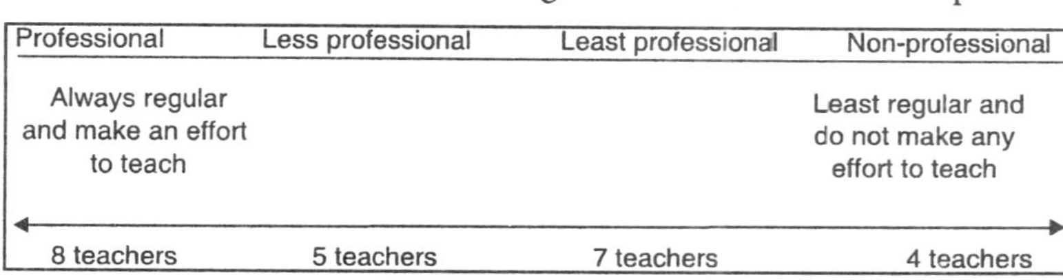

Figure 5.2: Teachers along a continuum of regularity and making an effort to teach

Table 5.3: Categorization of teachers in this study

Teachers	Whether they are regular	Whether they try to teach	Categorization
Gajendra	Stays in the school premise alone. His family stays elsewhere.	Tries very hard to teach; mostly through direct method.	Visibly, *professional* as they have regularity and their class has a learning objective as part of their sincere attempt to teach.
Kosa	Spontaneously regular.*	Tries to teach innovatively.	
Pajhi	Spontaneously regular.	Tries hard to teach mostly by direct method but also gets irritated and frustrated.	
Kota	Spontaneously regular.	Tries hard to teach through direct method.	
Virendra	Regular in his own way; comes around 11.30 am and goes at 4 pm.	Tries to teach hard but mostly through direct method.	
Tima	Stays in the school premises.	Tries to teach skillfully rather than in a mechanical way.	-do-
Noyak	Regular.	Tries hard to teach.	-do-
Manty (SSS)	Regular by SSS standard, that is, 2–3 times a week. Also leaves by 1 pm.	No teaching; but other works like fixing up a swing during my observation period.	
Prabin	Regular and has to be regular as he is the head master, there is a hostel and other two lady teachers are SSS.	Does not teach not very frequently; but whenever teaches, tries hard.	Categorized here as *less profession-al*as they mostly busy themselves in administrative, non-teaching tasks except Junoka. However, since they do their administrative duties well they can be categorized as *less professional.*
Junoka	Has to be regular as it is a private school.	Has to try hard; but mostly rough and ready method like using a little bit of physical punishment.	
Kasinath	Regular.	Does not teach; according to the prevailing culture, teaching is generally not considered as the foremost duty by a head master.	
Mahesh	Irregular because of assignment of administrative duties; but others say that he makes it up even on a Sunday by taking special classes.	Teaching could not be observed. But as others say that he teaches even on a Sunday, it can be construed that he has a willingness to teach.	
Kabir	Principal of the private school; stays very close to the school.	Does not try skillfully; rather applies the method of physical punishment. Minds administration rather than teaching.	-do-

(*Continued*)

Table 5.3: *(Continued)*

Shakir	Regular.	Teaches mechanically through play-way method and direct method.	Mostly carry out teaching like some chore or routine though they do not have any administrative burden; no serious attempt to deliver something. They are categorized here as *least professional.*
Tupur (SSS)	Regular but reluctantly.	Teaches mechanically.	
Tejmayi (SSS)	Irregular or goes by 1 pm.	Teaches skillfully rather than trying hard.	
Jyoshi (SSS)	Regular but leaves by 1 pm.	Teaches mechanically through rote method.	
Kasla	Regular because there is pressure from the village.	Teaches mechanically through TLM.	
Alpana (SSS)	Irregular; or if she comes, then goes by 1 pm.	Teaches mechanically through direct method, also uses TLM sparingly.	
Magan	Does not go once in a while. Once I had gone and he had not come to the school. But he can't entirely avoid because of MDM and he is the single teacher. But he may not be going on Saturdays.	Does not attempt much.	
Aminash	May be regular.	Does not try to teach.	Clearly *Non-professional* as they do not even try to teach mechanically. Munuaka hardly goes to the school.
Meeta	May be regular but leaves by 1 pm.	Does not try to teach at all.	
Pranati	Irregular.	Does not try to teach.	
Munuaka (EGS)	Irregular.	Rarely goes to the school.	

*Spontaneously regular means when somebody is regular not because of the fear of administrative supervision, not just to be *present* in the school but goes to the school to teach.

Strictly speaking, only the teachers who are categorized as *professional* in the Table 5.3 can be considered as professional. This does not mean they have attained the ultimate standard. But, they have a commitment towards the profession. That is why, they go regularly and attempt to teach. Teachers who are less professional and least professional are professional/non-professional to various degrees. This is how the categories are employed in the discussion that follows.

6

FACETS OF TEACHER PROFESSIONALISM: SUBJECT KNOWLEDGE, TEACHING SKILLS AND DISCIPLINE STYLE

Subject Knowledge

Singh (2003) points out that primary teaching is more skill intensive as compared to knowledge. Often, teaching in a rural area in India does not require so much subject knowledge as skills because the students may not progress very fast. Nevertheless, it is also contended that a minimum subject knowledge base is required for primary teaching. Shulman (2004, p. 227) emphasizes content knowledge as a requirement for the teaching profession.

Most primary teachers studied said that they are *all-rounders*, meaning that they can teach all subjects well. A professional teacher said, 'I can tell all subjects but I like science, MIL (first language (Oriya), Art. I have some idea; I can do.' (Pajhi). But, in reality, the teachers are *all-rounders* by compulsion and not real *all-rounders*. They have to teach all subjects because of lack of enough teachers. Observation pointed out that most teachers in this study are good in social studies and first language (Oriya) rather than in mathematics and science. Following observation excerpts of the teaching of two subjects by the same teacher will show this:

> Observation about a lesson on multiplication (1089 × 3) to class VI—'The teacher arrived at the solution through multiplication but did not elaborate that multiplication is continuous addition. He got embroiled in explaining

place values to children. Children have not understood the relation between digits and tens, hundreds, thousands, etc. The method—trial and error (Pajhi).

Observation about a lesson on history—'Teacher: 'Non-independence—depending on others. Your pen I take. This is losing independence. You all cultivate. Tomorrow 100 people come and tell you to go; Leave the field. You go. That's losing your independence. They (British) did not take away the fields. They stayed and took away the wealth' (Pajhi).

In this history lesson, the teacher was clear about how the British exploited the country economically. His subject knowledge of history is better than mathematics. The teacher's knowledge of Subhas Chandra Bose (violent path), Indira Gandhi (*Vanarsena*—monkey brigade meaning children participating in freedom movement) is quite good. I found it was tough to explain non-independence to children. Another difficult concept was constitution. The teacher tried to explain it in the following way:

Constitution—Dr. Ambedkar wrote the constitution in 1950. (January) 26 is called the republic day; means we choose our rulers. But there are rules for whimsical acts. If one of you get drunk and beat another three slaps, police will take him'. A child said that there would be hang order. Teacher—'how can be hang order for three slaps. (There is always the effort to explain to the degree of precision). 'There will be jail. There are high walls in jail. There are jails in Koraput (correct), Rayagada (not correct). Such rules are in the constitution. Ambedkar wrote that. That's why we remember him (Pajhi; author's comments are in the bracket).

I found his understanding of the constitution satisfactory. But, he does not remain focused while describing and deviates a bit from the topic. During another observation, the teacher frequently gave the examples of the village Laxmipur, etc. He is rather good in first language (Oriya) than mathematics.

Some teachers' proficiency in first language is derived from the context. The textbooks are all in the language of coastal Oriya (Oriya spoken in seacoast areas of Orissa). In case the teacher is from coastal Orissa, he does not find any difficulty with regard to the first language (Oriya). This is also applicable to social studies. Though they may be good in first language in the eyes of the researcher or some external authority, their teaching would not be so effective among children because tribal children here are not comfortable with coastal Oriya. Thus, their subject knowledge in first language may be good but teaching may not be equally effective. This is exemplified by a professional teacher, Kota. Though he is good in first language, it was found during observation that his usage of literary words like *garistha* (majority) and *sankhya garistha* (numerical majority) obstructed children's understanding. His using of literary and difficult words is probably the only lacuna. Otherwise, he is good in social studies and first language. He has good story-telling skills. Another professional teacher Gajendra has good story-telling skills. But, he uses coastal Oriya, which reduces his effectiveness. During observation while explaining a lot, he used the literary Oriya word *prachura*. Had he known the local word *gada*, children would have understood easily.

Though language is certainly a hurdle, it does not act as a hurdle for a committed teacher. For example, Gajendra is using the coastal Oriya since the beginning. Still he is able to contribute. Many students have passed. This is because language becomes a barrier at lower classes, i.e., classes I, II or III. It does not become a big barrier beyond that because children would have acquired some amount of Oriya by that time. Therefore, the teachers are able to teach if they are teaching the higher classes.

Language is not the only barrier. The content of the textbook itself may be difficult to understand for the children. I found two such topics during observation—Evening in *Kalijai*' (*kalijai*—an island in the Chilika lake) and about *bauala kumbhira* (a particular type of crocodile) of *Bhitarkanika* (the area of Orissa where these crocodiles are found). Children from this hilly area may not be able to visualize sea, lake, wave, boat and crocodile, etc. that are found in the textbooks. In one case, the children replied that they have never seen a green frog which was mentioned in one English textbook.

Observation pointed out that teachers need more skill than subject knowledge at the primary level, especially at classes I, II and III. For example, teachers have no problem about the place values. However, how to impart the notion to children becomes very difficult. Tenacity and patience is required in teaching. These are the implications of commitment. This is exemplified by Virendra, a professional teacher. His approach is basically task giving. First, he shouts to make the class silent. Then he takes the questions from the textbook and solves them on the blackboard while teaching mathematics. He uses the lecture method. He tries also to impart conceptual understanding. But, since the students would not be clear about the place values, a three digit multiplication becomes difficult for them. Also, he thinks a little of every child rather than the mass teaching. He speaks *Desia* (the variant of Oriya spoken in this area). He employs neither much praise nor rebuke. During my observation, one pupil did the sum wrong. He did not rebuke. The following excerpt from the observation of a lesson on multiplication (class IV) will illustrate his patience while teaching:

Teacher- '5 pencils 25. Like wise radio; you have seen; in your village; what do you do with radio? Dance! (mix a little bit of humour to make the lesson pleasant). Now see, I am doing it. How much one radio?' Children could not say four hundred seventy five.

Teacher- '8 radios? We have to bring 8 × 5 = 40. Keep 0, take 4'. Teacher went step by step.

Teacher- '3800'. (The children are not at home about the place values).

Teacher- 'understood?'

Children- 'yes'.

Teacher- 'I will erase'. Teacher did the second sum. Children said yes, yes all the while. (Children are comfortable about single digit multiplication).

Teacher- 'Now whoever would not do will get beating'. Children came running.

Teacher to the child- 'you have not done this. Where you had stopped? Write that' (Virendra; author's comments are in the bracket).

Lack of progress amongst children creates a sort of diffidence in him. The above excerpt shows that he moves on without children fully understanding the sum. This is probably because it is very difficult to go back and teach place value at class IV.

Teaching Skills

There is no one right way of teaching (Joyce and Weil, 1972, as cited in Hansen, 1979). Style is like a glove; it must fit the hand that wears it. Good teaching style is honed through continuous experimentation (Rubin, 1985, as cited in Ivie et al., 2001). Some teachers may look like authoritarian and some may look like giving too much authority to children. There is no fixed successful model to follow for being a successful teacher. The child does not look to a young teacher the same way as to an old teacher. A young teacher behaving like a senior to children may be acceptable to children, but an old teacher may not.

Observation of the classrooms found the following methods, which are prevalent in the schools of study:

(a) Direct.
(b) Play-way.
(c) Mechanical.

In direct teaching, the teacher mostly 'lectures', 'gives directions' and 'criticizes' in an authoritative way (Flanders, 1970, as cited in Ziv, 1979). This is in contrast to the play-way which was characterized as 'indirect' by Flanders. The teachers' using of the terms 'direct' and 'indirect' in their interviews probably is the result of the influence of Flanders in their teacher education programme. Probably, most of the teacher education programmes in India are yet to take a cognitive turn.

Most of the teachers, including the teachers who are categorized as professional, still believe in the direct method. This is exemplified by Virendra. He does not like the play-way and activity method.

> DPEP teaching, I do not like. No doubt we teach through play-way, song; but no discipline. The matter is the same but now the only difference is that children will be writing in the textbook. Children do not know the concept of separate writing books because of this. They can write in the textbook itself—science notebook, MIL notebook. We have still kept it; we see it how we were writing. Teacher has signed it.

The difference between his opinion and the opinion of a non-professional teacher is that he does not like district primary education programme (DPEP) for some academic reason.

The play-way is propagated so much by DPEP that it is called the DPEP method. Both professional and non-professional teachers disapprove the play-way method for different reasons. I guess that one reason why many non-professional teachers do not support the play-way method is that it involves more hard work and preparation on the part of the teacher. All professional teachers approve play-way and activity method in principle. They do not approve it in practice on the ground that the progress is slow and discipline becomes difficult to maintain. Most teachers do not use it because of circumstantial reasons like the lack of adequate teachers, multigrade classroom and lack of progress among children.

Play/games are occasions for laughter, lightening the mood and remove boredom. But in some cases, play-way becomes only play. The means become an end in itself. Teaching learning material (TLM) is simply distributed among children. Left to themselves, children are likely to focus just on the play aspect and would not mentally bridge the learning aspect.

Why is this so? Teachers cannot teach play-way, activity method or self-learning habit among children because they themselves were probably not taught like that. The direct method was most probably prevalent in the earlier days. Virendra still remembers how one of his teachers taught about the Apollo Mission of America. Huibregtse et al. (1994) showed that even with experienced teachers, there is a strong relationship between their preferred way of teaching and the way they themselves are used to learning (as cited in Korthagen and Kessels, 1999). I guess that the direct method is prevalent among teacher training institutions even now. One cannot imbibe the spirit of play-way or activity method through the direct method.

Method is a means and not an end. If the end is lost sight of, then the method can backfire. There can be the reification of both the direct and the activity methods. Children memorize the multiplication chart through rote. But, they are not able to say when asked randomly because they can say it only sequentially. To say 2 × 7, they have to rote all the way from 2 × 1, 2 × 2... and then 2 × 7. This is a reification of the direct method. There can be reification of play-way method too. It was seen during observation that one teacher personified children into planets and sun. The children could not mentally bridge their game and the solar system. They focused on which child was moving around whom rather than the planets moving around the sun. In another instance, the children were distributed stones and asked to divide them in pairs. The objective was to make them understand the concept of even numbers. They simply distributed the stones among themselves and kept quiet. The teacher did not do appropriate bridging. Play-way and activity method do not become successful unless appropriate games and activities are chosen and directed towards learning objectives in a reflective manner.

Competence and reflectivity should go together. Professional teachers' classes have an objective. However, they themselves are not aware about the factors that reduce their teaching effectiveness because of their lack of reflectivity. Observation found that the teaching effectiveness of the following professional teachers was reduced by the individual specific reasons:

(a) Pajhi: verbal assault.
(b) Kota: use of highly literary words and the response trap (looking at only the side of the class from where response comes).
(c) Gajendra: no response from students and using of coastal Oriya both of which may be mutually influencing each other.

These give some examples of the various subterranean factors that reduce teaching effectiveness. Teachers can be aware of these subterranean factors if they practice reflectivity.

Observations found that a method does not differentiate a professional teacher from a non-professional teacher significantly. Both the professional and non-professional teachers use direct method. Some teachers said that they believe in play way. But, in reality they were not employing the play-way method. What differentiated a professional from a non-professional teacher was the *goal orientation* in classroom processes. In other words, the professional teachers' session or lesson had a goal or objective while the non-professional teachers' had none. The word which the children in a non-professional teachers' class say most often is 'yes', which sounds like 'yes boss' of a popular Hindi film. The predominant occupation of the children in a non-professional teachers' class is copying mechanically from the textbooks to their notebooks, which probably gives them nothing. Though all teachers might have been taught about the objective of a lesson in their training days, remembering objective in a multigrade classroom is not easy. Professional teachers have achieved this over the years because of their willingness to impart some knowledge to the children.

Teachers and children enter the classroom to carry on teaching-learning. Whatever is the outer veneer of the relationship, task orientation is necessary if they are to progress in teaching-learning. This is marked in the relationship between professional teachers and the children. The non-professional teachers just manage the class. The classroom processes under them do not have a learning objective. Children will carry on their own like mechanically copying from the textbook, filling up the drawings in the textbook with colour pencils or playing with each other. Occasionally, the teacher may take some discipline measures or show the child some alphabets. But, learning may or may not progress. The relationship is not characterized by task orientation. Professional teachers' relationship with children is marked by either affection or authoritarianism. Non-professional teachers' relationship with children is marked by either friendliness or distance. But, the distinguishing aspect is task orientation in the relationship between professional teachers and children.

It is not easy to maintain time-on-task in schools consistently every day even in purely quantitative terms. Observation pointed out that the teachers who are characterized as professional teach two–three hours in a day. A professional teacher teaches for about one to one and a half hours in the morning and a similar amount of time in the afternoon. Rest of the time goes in managing the children as well as the school. The school really starts at 11 am in the morning; breaks at 1 pm in the afternoon for mid-day meal (MDM); really restarts at 2 pm in the afternoon and closes at 3.30 pm in the afternoon or thereabout. So, a theoretical notion of at least four–five hours of time-on-task for children is quite far fetched. Expectation from non-professional teachers would be even more far fetched. Unlike in towns, classes in rural schools do not have a sharp beginning and end. It crawls into beginning and peters into end. Children may enter the class jumping. The fortune of class changes in minutes by a small external event. If there is any non-academic activity in a school on a particular day, then it affects teaching. Saturday, which is the day of local *hat* (weekly market), may be unproductive from teaching point of view.

Multigrade does not seem to be successful here. Observation pointed out that higher classes may be engaged with enough textbooks, pen, writing pads, etc., but, class I, II and III may not do anything without the association with the teacher. Lack of sufficient teachers prevents teachers from paying individual attention. Most teachers in the interview said that they pay extra attention to the students who do not progress. This is easy to say. But, I did not see it among many. Prabin and Pajhi do this a little in government schools. This type of culture (individual attention) is prevalent only in the Upai School, which is a private school. But, the number is small there and children are well endowed materially and cognitively because of parental support. Even if a teacher has such skill and orientation, it is not easy to maintain over a long period.

Teaching in the Classroom: Voice and Language

Talking is the medium through which teachers deliver lesson. Observation pointed out that a primary teacher should not be hesitant about even singing and dancing. A talkative, dramatis persona with loud voice seems to be suitable for primary teaching. Voice and the language used are important in teaching. Two aspects of voice were discovered from the observation of the classrooms of the teachers. The professional teachers have two characteristics about their voice—they have a loud voice and their voice portrays affection. It is difficult to say whether a loud voice is an essential requirement for a good teacher. But, a reasonable loud voice is necessary to drown the noise of the children and establish an order. It acts as a tool of discipline also. This is exemplified by Virendra, a professional teacher. His approach is basically task giving. First, he shouts to make the class silent. Then he takes the questions from the textbook and solves them on the blackboard. He uses the lecture method principally.

The tone of the voice is more important than the volume of the voice. Emotion is important in teaching in many ways (Emmer, 1994). The tone of the professional teachers always portrays affection. In some cases, it looks authoritarian from outside but affection exists. Following excerpt of classroom observation of Virendra shows this:

> '12.20 pm—He is inquiring from a boy about Maguni who has not come today. He saw that the same boy is without a pen. Teacher—'you fool, where have you come without pen. Take my pen, give me back after writing'.

Affectionate relation can also be known by the children's interaction with the teacher. During the observation of the class of Noyak, I saw one scheduled caste boy telling the teacher very comfortably in *Desia* how to write *o, a.* (the first two letters of Oriya alphabet). This shows that children do not have the feeling of fear and distance towards the teacher. On the other hand, the tone of the non-professional teachers project distance and indifference. Following observation excerpts about two teachers categorized as least professional and non-professional will show this:

> ...She uses pure coastal Oriya in her teaching. Children have total lack of fear or punishment. Teacher gives little verbal punishment. Children probably think that if they do not know they just have to stand up, face down; but nothing more. During observation three boys at the end were playing a little. Her teaching style is like a question answer session. She asks questions from textbooks, children stand up, teacher corrects if they are wrong (Tejmayi).

> ...Her method is characterized by chanting and meandering (Jyoshi).

Voice may be a subtle factor. But, language is clearly a manifest factor which can aid or hinder the learning of children. Yet, it hardly gets the requisite attention at the school level or among the administration. There are three languages prevalent in this area—coastal Oriya (spoken in the seacoast area of Orissa), *Desia* (variant of Oriya spoken in this district) and *Kuvi* (the language of the tribe that inhabits this block). All the teachers, including the professional teachers, do not use the local variant of Oriya. Some of the professional teachers use coastal Oriya, which is not comfortable to the children. They would have been more effective if they used Desia (the local variant of Oriya) and even more if they knew Kuvi (the local tribal dialect).

The influence of the Oriya is so much that even the teachers whose mother tongue is Kuvi use it sparingly. Kosa is a professional teacher whose mother tongue is Kuvi. He employs TLM skillfully. Since the three classes are seated in one room, he makes them sit in three clusters, walks around and manages each class. He says himself that he employs Kuvi and others confirm it. But, I did not see him using Kuvi during observation of the class. This implies that he uses Kuvi sparingly only when students do not understand Oriya.

Learning Oriya by the tribal children is considered a great feat. Language seems to be a principal barrier. Unless this barrier is overcome, children would remain handicapped. Not employing tribal language makes teaching difficult in this area. The teacher should explain the meaning of an English word in English-Oriya-Kuvi. But if the teacher does not know Kuvi, a break happens in the understanding of the child, as she/he does not know the bridge language Oriya. All the books are in pure Oriya; for example, *eka* (one), *dasa* (ten), *hazara* (thousand), *misana* (addition), etc in mathematics. Tribal children have to master all the Oriya words related to mathematics before they can engage with mathematics successfully.

All teachers say that making children understand Oriya takes time. There seems to be widespread awareness about this. But, there seems to be no motivation either amongst teachers or higher administration. The educational administration could have organized training programs for teachers to learn Kuvi language. If the teachers know Kuvi, then they can establish more clearly the link between Kuvi and Oriya words. Kuvi–Oriya bilingual textbooks in formal schools are absent. There is no teacher manual for Kuvi language. A mini Oriya–Kuvi primer for teachers is absolutely essential in this area, which can be taken up even by the District Institute of Education and Training (DIET). This can be done by translating the class I books into Kuvi by tribal teacher/s and then printed en masse.

Discipline Style

Like there is no one good teaching style, there is no one good discipline style also. Hansen mentions as many as ten various discipline styles (1979, p. 42). However, Stefanich and Bell (1985, p. 21) point out that discipline measures can be 'preventive', 'supportive', 'corrective' and 'adaptive' along a continuum from 'most desirable' to 'least desirable' measures. Teachers in this study seemed to follow a corrective model of discipline rather than a preventive model. They deal with discipline after the issue arises. They do not have an overall plan for discipline. However, there was variation in discipline problems amongst professional and other teachers.

Discipline problem here is defined as deviation from learning. Time-on-task and discipline problems seem to be inversely proportional. While discipline problems do not happen during the teaching of professional teachers, they happen during the teaching of non-professional teachers. Since the professional teachers' class has an objective, the need for discipline measures does not arise always. But, the teachers who are *less* professional and *least* professional use discipline measures rather regularly because their class does not have much goal orientation. Small discipline problems keep happening.The teachers who are non-professional do not use any discipline measure at all. Therefore, their class is marked by laissez-faire. It seems that they do not have the moral courage to enforce discipline probably because they do not try to teach.

Discipline can be maintained through physical or verbal punishment/reward. While professional teachers are likely to use physical punishment for academic reasons, non-professionals use it for non-academic reasons. Interviews pointed out that even professional teachers still believe in physical punishment. I think this is the remnant of the era when they became teachers and took training. This is illustrated by Virendra. Interview with him pointed out that he believes strongly in physical punishment. 'Our time my father himself will tell, 'beat my child' to the teacher... Earlier we used to say in fearful tone, 'hey, the teacher is coming'! Now children say, 'here comes the teacher, the rascal'. Though he sounded the most authoritarian in the interview, physical punishment was not found in his class during observation. He maintained discipline simply by shouting. Another professional teacher Pajhi seemed to believe in physical punishment which came out during the course of interview. However, observation showed that he did not use physical punishment while teaching. Rather, a rough calculation indicated that the teacher's verbal rebuke is about twice that of verbal praise. But, the influence of DPEP on him about joyful learning is also visible. Following observation excerpt illustrates this:

> Teacher— 'Next how much'?
> Child— '*saula, sohola*' (sixteen). Child to child—'do not say laughing'.
> Teacher— 'teacher has to teach smilingly and student has to learn smilingly'.

DPEP has brought some change in the attitude amongst teachers. Though many teachers believe in physical punishment, they hardly use it. Most teachers use verbal discipline, usually just shouting. Rather it was surprising to see the systematic use of physical punishment in the private school. The maximum regular use of physical punishment for academic reason was observed in Upai School, which is a private school. Very little physical punishment was observed in government schools for academic reason.

Table 6.1: Subject knowledge, Teaching style, Discipline Style and Teacher-child relationship

Categorization	Teachers	Subject/s-knowledge S/he is good at	Method believed	Method employed	Discipline mode/style believed	Discipline mode/style employed	Teacher-child relationship characterized by
	Pajhi	History, Oriya	Both direct and play-way	Predominantly direct; employs little bit dramatics and drawing	Physical punishment and a little freedom	Strong verbal discipline; regular	Authoritarianism
	Kota	Oriya	Both direct and play-way	direct method, story-telling Multi-grade teaching,	Physical punishment	Mild verbal discipline; rarely Physical punishment	Friend
	Kosa	More skill-based as he teaches lower classes	Play-way	Activity method with TLM	Verbal discipline	Verbal discipline but not regular	Affection, Grand-Fatherly
	Virendra	Not good but comfortable about mathematics	Strongly believes in Direct method	Direct method	Strongly believes in physical punishment	Regular verbal discipline;	Authoritarian paternalism
	Noyak	Oriya	Play-way	Not much could be observed as the school is at an earlier stage of evolution (see Page-147)	Verbal discipline	Occasional mild physical punishment	Affection
	Tima	Not good but comfortable about Mathematics	Direct as well as play-way	Direct	Verbal discipline	Verbal discipline occasionally	Affection
professional	Gajendra	Oriya	Play-way	Direct, a little play-way	Verbal discipline	Regular verbal discipline;	Affection

Less professional	Manty (SSS)	Says he is comfortable with mathematics	Both direct and play way	Class could not be observed	Verbal discipline	Class could not be observed	Friend
	Prabin	Not good but comfortable about Mathematics	Direct	Direct	Physical punishment	Regular verbal discipline	Affection garbed in authoritarianism
	Junoka	Mathematics	Direct	Direct	Physical punishment	Regular, systematic physical punishment	Friend
	Kabir	Not good but comfortable about English	Direct	Direct	Physical punishment	Regular, systematic physical punishment	Authoritarianism
	Mahesh	Not good but comfortable about mathematics	Direct as well as play-way	Classroom teaching could not be observed	Verbal discipline	Classroom teaching could not be observed	Father-like
	Kasinath	Class was not observed	Direct	Classroom teaching could not be observed	Physical punishment	Regular physical punishment; (observed in the school and not in the classroom)	Authoritarianism
Least professional	Jyoshi	Teach lower classes where skill rather than knowledge is required	Mechanical	Mechanical	Mild physical and verbal discipline	Always mild physical and verbal discipline	Friend
	Kasla	Teach lower classes	Mechanical	Mechanical	Mild physical and verbal discipline	Always mild physical and verbal discipline	Matron-like

Least professional	Shakir	Teach lower classes	Mechanical	Mechanical	Mild physical and verbal discipline	Occasionally mild physical and verbal discipline	Friend
	Tupur	Teach lower classes	Mechanical	Mechanical	Mild physical and verbal discipline	Always mild physical and verbal discipline	Friend
	Alpana (SSS)	Teach lower classes	Mechanical	Mechanical	Mild physical and verbal discipline	Mild physical and verbal discipline; occasionally	Distance
	Magan	Teach lower classes	Mechanical	Mechanical	Mild physical and verbal discipline	Mild physical and verbal discipline	Friend
	Tejmayi	History	Direct	Question answer format	Mild verbal discipline	Mild verbal discipline	Distance
Non-professional	Aminash	Says he is comfortable with English	Direct	No teaching-proper could be observed	Mild physical and verbal discipline	No discipline measure, laissez-faire	Distance
	Pranati	Teach lower classes	Mechanical	Mechanical	No interview	No discipline measure, laissez-faire	Distance
	Meeta	Teach lower classes	Mechanical	Mechanical	No interview	Physical punishment; but not as a discipline measure, laissez-faire	Distance
	Munuaka	Hardly goes to the school					

Conclusion

An ideal typical conception of elementary teacher professionalism will include mastering content in all the subject areas at the elementary level, a competent as well as reflective approach to teaching and a preventive approach to discipline. This study shows that at present, in India, the best of teachers in rural area (categorized here as professional) have mastery mostly in first language and social studies and not in a vital subject like mathematics, follow the direct method than activity method, do not use the language of the tribal and believe in physical punishment. This is the scenario after two decades of national efforts towards teacher professionalism since the NPE 1986. That is why the parameters of *regularity* and *making an effort to teach* were considered to categorize teachers into various shades of professional and non-professional teachers in this study rather than knowledge and skills. Professional teachers in this study, irrespective of their knowledge and skills, had a *task/goal orientation* in the classroom, used affectionate *voice* in the classroom and maintained *patience* and *tenacity* while teaching children. It can be construed that these aspects emanate from commitment to teaching and children which has been emphasized by both the NCTE (1998) and NCERT (Walia, 2003). All these help in arriving at a sociological conception of elementary teacher professionalism in India.

It follows from this that teacher professionalism is dependent not only on teacher education institutions but on general education institutions like colleges/universities and on teacher themselves (to shun belief on certain aspects like direct method and physical punishment and accept activity-based teaching). According to Singh (2003), the role of universities is to strengthen subject-content knowledge while the role of teacher training institutions is to strengthen the skill aspect. The various in-service training programs of government like activity based-teaching may improve teaching style but will not be able to improve subject knowledge in a brief period. Besides, unless teachers' beliefs are directly addressed in training, removing old beliefs and inculcating new professional values like reflectivity and joyful learning will be difficult.

7

TEACHER PROFESSIONALISM IN SCHOOL AND LOCAL CONTEXTS

Introduction

Professionalism is most concerned with the quality of service. The quality of service at an empirical level is not likely to present a neat picture. A situated view of professionalism would envisage a nuanced picture of the quality of service at the local level.

> ...professional knowledge is not fixed but situated in a recurring set of unstable conditions, in a variety of localized circumstances. The creative tensions involved can not, therefore, be reduced to either/or oppositions of agency and structure but rather find expression in the multiplicity of frameworks and their consequences for professional practice (Gleeson and Knights, 2006 p 283).

A contextual view will envisage the influence of school and local contexts in shaping teacher professionalism. This can be represented by Figure 7.1.

Figure 7.1 can also be extended to include the regional and national contexts. However, this study is concerned with the interaction of teacher professionalism, the school and the local context.

Though not explicitly mentioning the name, the Government of India has adopted a three-pronged approach to improve teacher professionalism since the NPE 1986—improving the school infrastructure, improving their knowledge and skills through regular in-service training and increasing the accountability by empowering the community. From the Operation Blackboard (started in 1988) to the present Sarva Shiksha

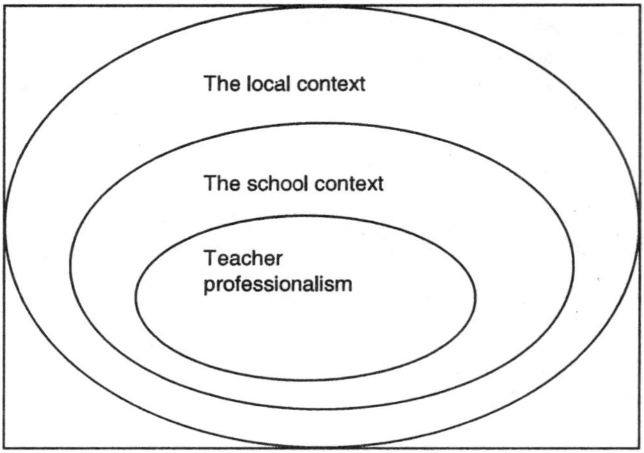

Figure 7.1 Teacher professionalism, the school and the local context

Abhiyan (started in 2000), the Government of India has been trying hard to improve the material infrastructure of the schools. Operation Blackboard was the first major national programme to improve the infrastructure of the schools. It initially mandated at least two teachers and two all-weather classrooms for every school. The next important national programme to improve the infrastructure program was District Primary Education Programme (DPEP, started in 1994). While in Operation Blackboard the infrastructure was supposed to be mobilized from other development programmes like Jawahar Rojgar Yojana (JRY—a wage employment programme), it was provided in the DPEP budget itself.

Along with the improvement of material infrastructure, the state is also trying to involve and empower the local community in education with an aim to enhance the accountability of the teachers and their performance. The major issue still seems to be not only the willingness on part of the state to give responsibility and power to the community, but the community's willingness and ability to assume responsibility (Govinda and Diwan, 2003).

Teacher Professionalism and the School Infrastructure

Children learn not only from the books but also from their surroundings. Therefore, a visually appealing classroom attracts the children and helps in their learning as well. This is very important in the Indian context. The

National Curriculum Framework, 2005 specifically mentions the physical environment and emphasizes on harnessing it for learning. A professional teacher is aware and makes use of these physical contexts, which can facilitate or hinder classroom teaching.

The infrastructures of the schools have changed greatly in the last decade. The infrastructure of the schools was acutely inadequate before Operation Blackboard. There would be at best a ramshackle wooden chair and a table in a school. Afterwards, Operation Blackboard provided for some buildings and teaching learning material (TLM). But, it was the DPEP which provisioned buildings, chairs, tables and TLM and made a perceptible change in the infrastructure of the schools.

Different schools in the study have different degrees of adequacy of infrastructure (see Appendix 7.1). But, its influence on schooling is contingent on the kinds of teachers the school has. Many teachers, who are regular and make an effort to teach, were very appreciative about the infrastructure change that DPEP has brought about.

> Before DPEP, the school was not like a school. There was not even a chair or a table. All get salary, but there is something called dignity. You came, we had no seat to offer; you would have thought what kind of job these people are doing. Children had to benefit, seeing which other children will come. The wooden chair table you had seen earlier was from Operation Blackboard. Now if a school room is opened, a 5th class student can learn a lot simply by looking at the wall (Gajendra).

This probably is the true picture. DPEP did not make a non-committed teacher into a committed teacher. However, it boosted teacher professionalism by improving the school infrastructure. It fulfilled the minimum infrastructure that is needed for schooling—building, chair and table, TLM and toilets. Observation pointed out that infrastructure is a necessary condition for education but not a sufficient one because teacher performance is necessary to utilize the infrastructure. For example, a building is meaningless if students do not come. Students may not come if no teaching happens.

The most valued infrastructure that a school can have in this tribal area is a hostel for children. The schools run by the Harijan and Tribal Welfare Department have hostels. Some Education Department schools too have hostels sponsored by the Harijan and Tribal Welfare Department. A school having a hostel has its own merit. Besides food, the children get dress, which is a luxury in this area where almost all are below poverty line. The children also stay in an environment which is focussed on education, unlike their homes. The advantage to the teachers is that they are assured of a certain number of children. They do not have to see a thin classroom, which demotivate a teacher. However, it has a latent dysfunction too. They quickly give up the struggle to enroll the local day scholars since they have the captive hostel students. The onus then is entirely on the villagers to send their children. This was observed in all the schools having hostel—Cisakh, Rupguda, Tikung. In contrast, the Baisakh School does not have an option. It neither has a hostel nor are the villagers very aware. But, the head teacher can't afford an empty classroom in the present age. Therefore, she calls the children every day while coming to the school. This happens to a lesser extent in Kesli and Raigad.

All the energy of a head teacher of the school where hostel exists goes in looking after the children, their feeding, clothing, health, etc. They are not able to teach much because of these. There is no permanent teacher in Rupguda apart from the head teacher. There are only two SSS. The head teacher is not able to mind teaching because of the burden of managing the hostel and the two SSS do not perform well as there is an expectation that the SSS need not exert themselves fully as they are only contractual teachers. Therefore, teaching does not get the attention it deserves.

Lack of infrastructure and the lack of space is affecting teaching in Cisakh. As all the children are seated in one room in this school, only one teacher teaches at any particular time. This is because the new building is under construction. On the other hand, all the classes get attention simultaneously in Bakar having more classrooms and more teachers.

Presently, most of the schools do not have any electricity connection. There was rain due to cyclone on some days during the observation period. The classrooms used to be dark and windows could not be opened. It was very cold and this hampered teaching. The lack of light might be taking some days off teaching during rainy season.

These are some examples of how infrastructure affects teaching, but infrastructure alone does not ensure higher time-on-task for teachers and children. Rupguda and Tikung are the two schools where adequate infrastructure for children in terms of space and classrooms exist. Both have hostels. Rupguda, though adequate in terms of infrastructure, is handicapped by the fact that there is no permanent teacher apart from the head teacher. There are only two SSS and they do not perform wholeheartedly. Bakar is the best in terms of average teacher performance as three out of five teachers try to teach regularly and one, who is deputed to the block, tries to teach whenever there is an opportunity. The time-on-task for teachers is highest in Upai School, which is a private school. It is not the best school in terms of the adequacy of infrastructure. Among the government schools, it is the highest in Bakar that does not have a hostel. Thus, infrastructure alone is not enough to ensure higher time-on-task for children.

Teaching learning material at present does not seem to play a major role in teacher professionalism. Baisakh and Bakar are the two schools where TLM is used adequately. The Bakar head teacher (Kosa) tries to teach with the help of TLM. But, the Baisakh head teacher (Kasla) just distributes the TLM. The use of map was observed only once where Gajendra showed the students Chilika (a lake close to the Bay of Bengal). Frequent use of TLM was observed only in two schools—Bakar and Baisakh—in spite of the provision of INR 500 per year for TLM to every teacher. One reason could be that TLM has to be taken out of the box everyday, to be distributed among the children, to be kept an eye so that children do not lose and then again put back into the box. There is considerable scope for increase of efficiency amongst teachers by more extensive and goal-oriented use of TLM.

A view prevalent in this area is that children learn actively in Upai School (the private school). Upai School does not have adequate space like Rupguda or Tikung. But, what really works is that the teachers work hard. Not a minute is wasted. The time-on-task is almost equal to the time-on-schedule. Also, the children are well supported materially and academically (through home work) by the parents. Therefore, it is not entirely the miracle of Upai School. Here, negligence is rooted out. The principal is not negligent, the teachers are not, and the parents are not. The principal has a bit of entrepreneurial spirit and a managerial approach, that is a job has to be done anyhow. That's why he has allowed a little bit of physical punishment in the school.

Such performance is quite possible in government schools too. The head teachers of government schools can benchmark students at the beginning of the year, assign classes to the teachers and could know how much the teacher has taught by the year-end. In future, duly qualified candidates can be selected, sent on probation where they will be under the watch of the head master. Only after successful probation should they be selected. They will be tied up with the panchayat. If no panchayat agrees to take them, they may be engaged in some administrative work.

Teacher Professionalism and the School Sub-culture

Teachers and students operate in the school. The school itself is located in a context of space, time, people, external relationship, ideas and value (Alexander, 2000). According to an Indian study (Sarangapani, 2003), children think that the school is a place where they learn *bol chal* (the appropriate manners for an adult), *jankari* (get information) and become eligible for a *bada admi* (desk job). In France, the school is considered as a collective venture to impart children certain values (Alexander, 2000). In the United States of America, schools can think about providing breakfast and lunch to the children, and compensate a bit for the broken families, which are beyond what is expected of them as a school (Di Giulio, 2000).

The study found that a teacher operates under the particular school context and is influenced by its culture. The surroundings and culture of each school are different. If a teacher comes to a school that is already functioning well, then it is difficult for him/her to be lackadaisical. But if a professional teacher goes to a non-functioning school, the chance is that the school may function better.

Very rarely does a school regress from a well-functioning school to a non-functioning one. Observations and interviews pointed out that a school normally transitions from a non-functioning stage to a well-functioning stage in the following way:

(a) The school is irregular.
(b) The school is regular; but teaching happens mechanically like mid-day meal (MDM).
(c) The school is regular, time-on-task is high and teaching is qualitative rather than mechanical.

Usually, the transition happens when a dedicated teacher or teachers take the initiative. Bakar transitioned to this stage (second) after Kosa took over. Presently, it is trying to go to the third stage.

> When I came (1999), there were only four Sundhi (a caste having higher ritual status than scheduled caste and tribe) and two SC children. That time there was caste feeling, probably under the concurrence of the teacher (from coastal area, Khurda). SC children were made to sit separately. For this reason, the tribal children were not coming willingly. Probably there was pressure on him (the teacher). This school site was the repository of all the garbage. People used to shit on this front road all along and sometimes in the school also. I took a shovel and started cleaning the garbage. Seeing that

> the Sundhi parents asked me why I was doing that? The children could do that as well. Later, they told the children to do. Gradually, the children did the cleaning with me. I made the SC children sit with the Sundhi children. While cleaning, I covered a handkerchief over my nose to save me from the stink. The Sundhi children saw all that and gradually the Sundhi and SC children became very close. That time two staff. The present new building was full of bamboo. Ramesh Kumar came after the other teacher took the transfer to Cuttack (Kosa).

> I came in 1982. There was no house for school. Because of some problem, the school building was left half-constructed. We did the school in some one's veranda. I used to teach children writing with charcoal on floor. The house owner objected. I showed him some paper and said that the block development officer (BDO) has ordered the class to be held on his veranda. This went on till 1992 when the present hostel building was made. Here, the parents are lackadaisical about education. I am feeling good; would have even felt better if students had improved (Gajendra).

Most schools would be in the second stage. No school has really come to the third stage because not all the teachers in a school spend their time in quality teaching. If a school is in a particular stage, then it creates a pressure on the teachers. The teacher has to live up to the reputation of the school. Neither the administrators nor the villagers will tolerate the regress of a school. For example, both Tikung and Bakar have built up a reputation as good schools. The result is that they become a sort of showcase and most officers visit these schools. That creates a constant pressure on the teachers to be dutiful. During my observation, I found that children from Monopai School go to another school, which is at a distance of 5 km, because no teaching happens in Monopai. Often, those children asked for a ride on my motorcycle while I was coming back from Tikung. That's how I came to know about it. Monopai is also located by the roadside and there is the chance of frequent visits from authorities. But, that has not created any pressure on the teachers to be good. This shows that each school is located at a particular stage of work culture and professionalism and the teachers are influenced by it.

Contrary to the evolution of schools, I did not find any evolution of teachers as such. They did not change along with time, or only regressed rather than progressed. What could be gathered from the interviews points out that the teachers who are professional had this orientation since the beginning, Virendra is an example. He said in his interview that the education of his daughter suffered because he stayed in the rural area devoid of a high school. But he performs even now, though much unhappy about this fact. Kosa at one point of time was seriously ill, but still did his duty well. He still does his duty well. Gajendra also is performing since the beginning though a lot has changed with regard to school infrastructure since then. On the other hand, Aminash could not change the Kesli School in spite of staying there for ten years. Kasla also could not change the Baisakh School and it was only after the coming of Pajhi and Manty that the school moved from first stage to the second stage of the evolution. This leads to the rather uncomfortable view that teacher dedication does not change much over the years. An interview excerpt from Mahesh says it appropriately: 'Those who are lazy and cheating mentality will not perform…cheating mentality exists from the starting point…..lazy…even if someone goes to the school every day, is he dedicated?' The implication of this is that we should put a premium on appropriate recruitment.

Teacher Professionalism and the Sub-cultures amongst the Teachers

Not only there is a school sub-culture but there are also teacher sub-cultures. Teachers in Laxmipur have their own subcultures of professionalism. There is variation in professionalism even amongst the various categories of teachers—SSS, EGS (Education Guarantee Scheme), the head teachers and the lady teachers. Thus, there are subcultures within subculture. If there are separate organizations of SSS, EGS and regular teachers, why can't there be subcultures amongst them? Teaching becomes the priority amongst EGS, SSS, head teachers and regular assistant teachers in an increasing order. Each category of teachers operates under a subculture of professionalism.

EGS teachers: EGS is needed where there may not be sufficient children to warrant the establishment of a regular school. However, it is not clear whether those children will belong to one class or multiple classes. If they belong to multiple classes, which the EGS teacher in my interview said, then the EGS teacher is not qualified to teach them. The problem does not arise practically because many EGS teachers simply do not go to the school. It was found during one of the school visits (Cisakh) that one EGS teacher had sent the performance appraisal form to the nearby head teacher through somebody else rather than himself. The head teacher of the nearby school is supposed to take the performance appraisal of the EGS teacher. If an EGS teachers cannot even go to the head teacher himself/herself for the approval of the performance appraisal form, how can one be sure if he/she goes to the school?

SSS teachers: SSS teachers are supposed to bring children to the school. But, their work varies widely. Some sort of convention has been established by which SSS usually leave the school after the MDM and come once in two-three days. Professionalism for an SSS means coming twice a week, staying half a day and teaching mechanically. Though officially they are supposed to call the children, that is exactly what they do not do. Rather they teach, though mechanically. The era of calling the children to the school is almost over. Now the teachers do not give much importance in making an effort on a day-to-day basis to bring the children to the school. I saw it only in Baisakh where the headmistress calls the children to the school. Wherever there is a hostel, the head teachers do not try hard to get the day scholars as they have the hostel students. The villagers also become indifferent to the school, as their wards can't get admission to the hostel because of the policy that children from the same village in which the hostel is located are not eligible for the hostel. Children are to be from a different village if they are to get admission to the hostel. The rationale may be rational in the sense that a hostel should benefit the children from a distance but it has this unintended consequence. Thus, SSS scheme is not very effective here. They neither teach well as it is not their principal duty nor they call the children. The SSS scheme might have very negative consequence in the future. Now, the SSS have developed a culture of absenteeism with official and public acquiescence. This may spill over even when they become regular.

The women teachers: I did not find any female teacher in my study who was committed in terms of always being regular and making the maximum effort to teach. It was found during the interviews that in most cases, the dominant theme in their life is their family. A notion probably has been built up over the years that teaching is a sort of '*engagement*' or time-pass for women. They are not able to pay full attention to teaching because they can never get rid of their household chores even if they do a paid job. There is a need to build up a subculture of professionalism amongst women teachers.

The head teachers: Observation pointed out that there are three dimensions of a head teacher's job—academic, administrative and clerical. Some are trapped in the last two, some would like to be trapped and some care none. Clerical job includes mostly filling up the information that is required under DPEP and SSA. Administration includes managing the teachers. Academic aspect is the teaching. Table 7.1 illustrates how the head teachers balance administration and academic work.

Table 7.1: Professionalism amongst head teachers

Head teachers	How they manage teaching and administration	Categorization
Tima	Devotes time equally to teaching and administration	Professional
Kosa	Devotes time equally to teaching and administration	Professional
Prabin	Devotes lot of time to administration, a little to teaching	Less professional
Kasinath	Does not give any time teaching, all time to administration; has ensured a work culture	Less professional
Kabir (Principal, Upai School)	Very little time to teaching, lot of time to administration	Less professional
Kasla	Teaching and administration, mechanically	Least professional
Magan (The only teacher in the school)	Very little time to either teaching or administration	Least professional
Aminash	Very little time to either teaching or administration; does not also care about increasing the enrollment	Non-professional

Kosa, Kasinath and Aminash present three extreme cases. Kosa does not like paper work at all, Kasinath does not like teaching at all and Aminash does not like either. Prabin and Kabir are examples of those who administer well but teach only a little. Kosa and Tima balance both well. Kasla balances both mechanically that does justice to none. Good administration means creating a work culture. Prabin and Kasinath, though they teach little, have ensured a work culture in the school. But Kosa and Tima, though they teach themselves, are not able to make the female teachers in their schools teach properly.

The head teachers have their own interpretation of duty. Prabin said that he is paid to *look after* the children. I guess this is one ethical aspect, which is still lingering in the society. The ethics of teacher as caregiver, as surrogate parent has been there for quite long. This per se is not bad. But, a latent dysfunction is that it overshadows the teaching aspect of teaching. Many head teachers predominantly focus on the care aspect than the teaching aspect in schools where a hostel is located. If they were serious enough about teaching they would have tried to do it themselves, however little. Many have not imbibed this aspect yet.

Another characteristic of the sub-culture of head teachers is the overemphasis on administration. The head teachers assume and others acquiesce that a head teacher's predominant job is administration that mostly means doing the paper work like filling up the different kinds of information required under DPEP and SSA. If the head teachers had wanted, they could have distributed the paper work or gave it to the SSS and focussed on teaching. But presently, a head teacher's supervision over assistant teachers is predominantly administrative and not academic.

The Attitude Towards the Tribals

As mentioned earlier, Laxmipur is a predominantly tribal inhabited block (68 per cent in 1991) primarily inhabited by the *Kondh* tribe. There are three principal local factors which influence education here; they are poverty, language and liquor. First, the tribals are poverty ridden which curtails their foresight and they can't think about the long-term gains of education. Second, they are addicted to liquor that further curtails their foresight. Sometimes the government is the culprit, which opens liquor shops. So, who will the people fight against for the abolition of liquor? Sometimes it is the culture where women drink. So, who will tell whom to give up liquor? The issue is complex and is not amenable to an easy solution. Third, their language is different from the mother tongue of some of the teachers and the language of all the textbooks. Teachers operate under this local context and constraints.

The teachers' attitude towards the tribals crucially impinges on their professionalism. The teachers' attitudes towards the tribals can be characterized as the following:

(a) Indifference
(b) Sympathetic: Accepting the tribals and the responsibility of teaching the tribal children who are disadvantaged.
(c) Having confidence in the tribals that they have the capacity to improve themselves and the tribal children have equal potential for learning like any other children.

The teachers who are least professional and non-professional are indifferent to the tribals. They blame the lack of awareness among the tribals as the reason for their educational backwardness. They do not exert much to teach the tribal children.

> The villagers do not bother about school. This is a *Jharia* village. Sarpanch for Laxmipur is from the village. Though VEC meeting has to be there every week, people did not come, though some of them are HM's former students. Unless children have interest they would not progress. We are revising third time. But they are not able to say. Guardians have an utter lack of interest. In this village even women drink, what they will tell to their men? (Tupur)

> Why we do job? For our children's future. That's why travelling from a suitable place is a must where education facility is there. My son is in 1st class. If he stays in an interior area, he will be dull. Only after matric, something can be done. But what till then? That is a problem. (Alpana)

Contrast this with the comment of a professional teacher who is sympathetic and accepts the responsibility of teaching the tribal children who are disadvantaged:

> I could not make my only daughter worthwhile educated enough. I stayed in interior. The children there improved but not my daughter. Never got to high school or college. I was rated good there but my daughter could not be educated. Did matric with much difficulty. After that got married. Son-in-law in Assam rifles... I am an Adivasi. I'll uplift Adivasi children. That's why I have become a teacher. Otherwise I was in weights and measures, amin (*a government job*). I left all that to teach Adivasi children. I have been 24 years. Many children I have made (Virendra).

> First posting in Laxmipur, ex-board (10 years). Next Doliamba (20 years), here 3 years…liked all places. I was teaching the right way, drawing picture on the blackboard, using aids appropriately. If not available, draw pictures on the blackboard. Children used to listen enthusiastically, used to write whichever subjects they are told. Compared to Laxmipur, SC/ST children do study in Daliamba (kond). Felt very happy seeing them writing and studying enthusiastically. More than *harijan* students. Also learned the multiplication chant. Wrote the same day whatever they were asked to write. Felt very happy. Here not like that. Probably after some time, they'll be able to do (he was telling that after he came here, more children are coming to this school). I like all schools. No school that I do not like (Pajhi).

The professional teachers are not only sympathetic but they have the confidence that the tribal children have the capacity to improve themselves and have equal potential for learning like any other children.

> One excuse is given that here the Adivasis are backward. But if the teacher try, then it is possible. SC/ST children are not radically different (Noyak).

The professional teachers and the less professional teachers are sympathetic to the tribals. They understand the poverty and the lack of awareness among the tribals. But, the less professional teachers stop at administration. They leave the onus with the tribals about how much they can use the school system. They do not take proactive steps.

The professional teachers are proactive. Lack of awareness of the tribals does not become an excuse for them. They also have confidence in the tribal children. Having confidence means the belief that tribal children also can study well albeit slowly because their language and culture are different. The non-professional teachers do not have confidence in the tribal children. Their class becomes fatalistic, i.e., children may learn by chance. But, professional teachers believe that children will certainly learn.

The challenge for a professional teacher is that sometimes, rebuke may come from the villagers rather than appreciation. They have to perform in spite of that. Students achieving higher educational qualification or getting a good job are the ultimate pride of teachers. But this requires sacrifice. Since professional teachers will try to teach and since tribal children would not progress fast, the teachers are vulnerable to a sense of frustration. People may not have patience but the teacher has to have patience. Table 7.2 summarizes the teachers' attitudes towards the tribals in the study.

Facets of Teacher Professionalism in the Locality

Various Degrees of Professionalism

There are many aspects that can be counted as professionalism in this area predominantly inhabited by the tribals. Some may be professional only in bringing the children; some may be in teaching. Some may have the language ability but not the teaching; with some, it may be the reverse. Finding a teacher who is professional in all aspects is very difficult. There are various shades of professionalism and non-professionalism amongst teachers. Following are the various shades of non-professionalism:

(a) Some do not go regularly.
(b) Some go, but they neither look after the children nor do they teach.
(c) Some go, but just look after the children.
(d) Some teach, but mechanically without any goal or objective.

On the basis of degrees of professionalism and non-professionalism, the teachers can be categorized into the following categories:

(a) Teacher: Those who only teach, and do not mind any other aspect like administration or paper work.

Table 7.2: Teachers and their attitudes towards the tribals

Categorization	Teachers	Attitude towards the tribals
Professional	Pajhi	Has confidence in the tribals.
	Kota	Accepts the tribals (considering one among them and not taking them as 'other').
	Kosa	Accepts the tribals; himself is a tribal.
	Virendra	Has concern for the tribals; himself is a tribal.
	Noyak	Has confidence in the tribals.
	Tima	Does not have complete confidence in tribal parents; but he has confidence in the learning potential of the tribal children.
	Gajendra	Believes that the tribals lack awareness, but if one keeps trying, one will succeed; accepts the tribals.
	Manty (SSS)	Accepts the tribals.
Less professional	Prabin	He feels he is defeated by failing to enlist the cooperation of the villagers with regard to the enrolling of the day scholars.
	Junoka	Encounters not the average parents but those who are constantly keeping track of the progress of their children (he is in a private school).
	Kabir	Believes in raising the awareness of the parents to improve the children.
	Mahesh	Fully accepts his responsibility towards teaching the tribal children.
	Kasinath	Negative view about the tribals.
Least professional	Magan	Indifference; has not fully accepted teaching the tribal children.
	Kasla	Does not have confidence in the tribals.
	Shakir	Does not feel anything strong about the tribals.
	Tupur	Accepts the duty to teach the tribal children.
	Alpana (SSS)	Her acceptance of the job is to a low degree.
	Tejmayi	Indifference to the tribals.

(*Continued*)

Table 7.2: *(Continued)*

Categorization	Teachers	Attitude towards the tribals
Non-professional	Aminash	Does not have confidence; does not accept the job.
	Pranati	Does not accept the job (not embracing the values and responsibilities of the job).
	Meeta	Does not accept the job.
	Munuaka	Does not accept the job.

(b) Teacher-manager: Many of the head teachers who teach a little bit and spend their major share of time in administrative work.
(c) Manager: Many head teachers who spend their entire time in administration, delegating all the teaching to the assistant teachers.
(d) The commuters: Those who just commute to the school but do not do anything.

Regularity as an End in Itself

The commuters take shelter under the claim of *regularity*. Regularity is portrayed as a virtue probably because this was the dream for administrators for decades. Regular school means where children and teacher come regularly. Regular school has come to mean a good school. 'He is regular' has come to mean as if he is professional. Teachers in Laxmipur feel good about the fact that schools in Laxmipur are regular whereas it is not so in other blocks. The predominant focus of administration is regular school and not much on the quality of teaching. Nobody asks seriously, 'regular for what'?

The Culture of Excuse

The commuters also take recourse to various excuses. The most popular excuse is the unawareness of the tribals. But the teachers do not try to impart qualitative teaching to the few children who come to the school. If they had adopted this strategy, there would have been quite a few good matriculates and graduates in tribal area. But, this did not happen because the definition of education always remained quantitative, i.e., how many children come and how often the teacher goes. The stronghold of this definition can be seen by the fact that schools and teachers are evaluated mostly by *regularity* and not *quality*.

The Issue of Local and Non-local Teachers

There seems to be a bit of subterranean tension here between the teachers from outside (coastal area) and the local teachers. While the non-local teachers accuse local teachers of disinterestedness, this is not true. For example, Kosa, Virendra Naik and Tima Garada are *professional* and they are local. But the other way round, that 'most local teachers have a commitment towards the locality' is also not true. Professional and non-professional teachers can be found amongst both the local and non-local teachers.

The Importance of Location

Staying in block head quarter is considered here almost as a reward. Surprisingly, many teachers in the study have stayed in block town for as many as 10 years. Still when they are posted at a distance from the block town, they consider that as an injustice. Nobody can remain absent in Ex-Board school (located in the block town). They will be always exposed to supervision by the authorities. Still, people prefer to come to Ex-Board. It is not without reason. Teaching in a school in the town is less onerous. Parents in town are better off and more aware. Thus, they support the students materially and encourage them to study. This is reflected from the following interview excerpt:

> 'I feel unhappy when children do not understand after repeatedly telling. In ex-board it is easy. The children understand even if you teach once. Here the children do not. I am worried for that. Sometimes I think let me try through a different method. There is a rule not to fail. First year, the child just learns the language. By the time the child learns the language he/she is in second year' (Alpana (SSS)).

Appropriate location can be an important factor for teacher motivation. Now, most of the students of the better off parents of the town go to the Upai School at the block headquarters which is a private school. Though children learn faster in Upai School, teaching is easy in Upai School because children are supported by parents; both materially and academically.

Apart from the fact that teaching is easy in the town, most teachers want to be close to their home like anybody else. Almost all teachers from the coastal area have tried to go from this area to their home district though they have to perform more strictly in the coastal area. Many say that even SSS perform very strictly in coastal area because of public pressure. But, they want to go in spite of the fact that they have to perform under stricter circumstances. Thus, one can estimate that location is a strong factor in teacher motivation.

The View about Dedication and Teaching

Teacher dedication is not easy. Both the good and bad teachers do not get salary for months. How to keep the motivation going on is indeed a matter of concern. They do not have claim to money, neither are they on a high pedestal in society like that of a professor or an administrator.

No professional teacher could really give a definite clue on how to recruit a teacher who is likely to be dedicated. While Tima said that marks could be the basis for recruitment, Kota opined that marks per se could not give a clue about dedication. Noyak opined that the local teachers are not dedicated because they were rather handed out the jobs instead of struggling for it. But, this is not the whole truth. Professional and non-professional teachers were found amongst both local and non-local teachers.

What emerged from the discussion with the teachers was that *observation* of teaching and *interview* of teachers in addition to marks are absolutely essential to assess teacher dedication and professionalism. But, they cannot be practised on a mass scale. I could not get a clue about what can be done on a mass scale to recruit the dedicated teachers. Therefore, the alternative was to find their attitude towards the tribals, Panchayati Raj and the dominant theme in their lives and whether there is any difference between professional and non-professional teachers in these respects. Dominant theme means the theme that conversation with the teachers most often led to. For example, while conversation with Pajhi most often led to discussion about corruption, conversation with many female teachers ended up talking about their children, their educational achievement, domestic problems, etc. Some teachers do not have any dominant theme as such. Some themes are manifest and some are not so obvious.

Some of the teachers could also be categorized according to the categorization of Goodson. Goodson distinguishes three kinds of teacher professionalism as follows:

Classical: The professionalism of the past, emphasizing autonomy and group control of affairs.

Practical: The professionalism of the present age, which sees the teacher as an educational worker.

Principled: It is based on morally agreed principles, desire to continuously learn, to positively care and discretionary judgment. This is the professionalism, which we should aim for (Goodson, 2000).

Table 7.3 summarizes dominant themes in teachers' lives and characterization of professionalism.

The dominant themes of teachers who are professional are some ideals like removing corruption or stopping the exploitation of the tribals. The dominant theme of teachers who are less professional is mostly administration. Family is the dominant theme in the lives of most female teachers. In one case of an unmarried elderly female teacher, the dominant concern is her brothers' children. Unlike the West where spinsters are more likely to be dedicated (Lortie, 1975), it is not so here. The reason could be cultural. The non-professional teachers are indifferent to professionalism; that is their dominant theme.

Two personality traits could be discovered about the professional teachers. They are humble and they have self-respect. Tima said that the new SSS are more qualified and have more knowledge. More qualification and wide knowledge is required in the present age. This reflects his respect for knowledge that the higher qualified SSS have, though they are temporary teachers. Kosa is down to earth. This is reflected by the fact that he himself had once cleared the garbage of the school and built it up as a well functioning school. Gajendra, though has got award, said that he has not done anything great to get an award. Both Kota and Pajhi opined that there might be more dedicated teachers who are fit for award. These opinions reflect that they have humility.

The second trait seems to be that the professional teachers can't digest insult. They have self-respect. That's why some of them left other jobs and joined teaching. Noyak left the job of Gram sevak; Virendra left the job of amin to join teaching. Kota rather faced the wrath of one dishonest head teacher than succumbing to his wrongful direction. Pajhi is angry about corruption in education. Cheating is quite burdensome for Kosa. All these can be loosely interpreted that they can not digest insult. Therefore, they will do the duty. Not doing the duty means inviting insult. The non-professional teachers probably have no problem about insult.

Conclusion

Professionalism means the quality of service. So far, there has been an attempt to define teacher professionalism in a theoretical way. But, the manifestation of teacher professionalism at the empirical level is a result of

Table 7.3: Teachers and dominant themes of their lives

Categorization	Teachers	Dominant theme
Professional	Gajendra	Keeping up to reputation (award), duty conscious since the beginning, humility, principled professionalism.
	Kosa	'Why not do the duty, why invite trouble?', principled professionalism.
	Pajhi	How corruption is ruining the society?
	Kota	Writing poetry, singing, trying to get invitation from radio or concert.
	Virendra	Exploitation of tribals; can't digest insult.
	Tima	Keeps up to reputation of himself and the school (he has got award), classical professionalism.
	Noyak	Why the locals are not performing; duty can be performed in spite of odds. Cannot digest insult, believes in a strict approach to duty.
	Manty (SSS)	Self-confidence; believes in innovative approach.
Less professional	Prabin	Believes in administration; doing the duty a little above mechanically; practical professionalism.
	Junoka	How to go up in life, this job is just the beginning; thinks he is better than other teachers; carries on guessing about the future prospect.
	Kasinath	How his service record should be perfect; believes in administration as the duty.
	Mahesh	Government is the legitimizer; do what the government says.
	Kabir (principal, Upai School)	Believes in administration; how to establish the school; not purely through teaching but by the managerial way.

(*Continued*)

Table 7.3: *(Continued)*

Least professional	Magan	How to stay in the block; predominantly administration orientation.
	Shakir	Just carry on the job mechanically; does not think about professionalism.
	Tupur (SSS)	Family; carry on the job mechanically since there is pressure from the head teacher.
	Alpana (SSS)	Family; carry on the job mechanically.
	Kasla	Just carry on the job mechanically (no interview; but what observation pointed out).
	Tejmayi (SSS)	Could not find any dominant theme; teach for some time a day and do not bother about anything else like the awareness of tribals.
	Jyoshi (SSS)	Just carry on the job mechanically (no interview; but what observation pointed out).
Non-professional	Aminash	A bit of submissive mentality; indifference to professionalism.
	Meeta	Tending to her brother's children, pay package, location; indifference to professionalism.
	Pranati	Family (what observation pointed out); indifference to professionalism.
	Munuaka (EGS)	Time pass (what observation pointed out); EGS people hardly go to the school. EGS now has only some meaning because of MDM. Indifference to professionalism.

the confluence of the school infrastructure, local culture and the teachers' worldview. Infrastructure is a minimum but not the sufficient condition for teacher professionalism. The work culture at the school and the development of teacher professionalism at the local level are other important factors that shape teacher professionalism. Teachers' worldview, which includes their orientation towards the local community like the tribals, is another important factor.

There can be a three-pronged policy towards teacher professionalism. Some who shirk duty can be monitored with administrative measures and can be employed in administrative work. Some are time-servers (neither professional nor non-professional) who can be brought in to the arena of professional teacher with professional support and administrative measures. Some are good who can be encouraged through appreciation and reward. Presently, very little gets transmitted from colleague to colleague so much so that no differentiation is made between a good and a bad teacher. Neither has a culture developed whereby colleagues inquire about the good practices of others. In this area, those who are professional would have elevated themselves to a higher level if the general professionalism level was not low.

8

THE TEACHER AND THE EXTERNAL CONTEXT

Views on Authority

Higher authorities are the principal 'critical reality definers' (Sikes, Measor and Woods, 1985). Basically, it means the message teachers get about what, how and to what extent teaching is to be done. This message has its repercussion on how much curriculum is covered, what is being stressed, how much they can shirk duty, etc. At the local level, one has to see what the negotiation is. Teachers' strategies with the higher-ups could be acceptance, bypassing, subversion and challenge (Pollard, 1987).

The higher authorities could be bureaucratic or charismatic (Sikes, Measor and Woods, 1985). While some of the supervisors do their job in a bureaucratic way trying to control the teachers relying on formal reward and punishment, some others may be trying to use symbolic reward and punishment to motivate the teachers. Supervisory behaviour can be positive or negative. Positive supervisory behaviour means the superior appreciates the work of the teacher and then suggests while negative supervising has a general tone of criticism (Bacharach, Bauer and Conley, 1986).

The nature of relation with the authorities varies according to the type of the school. In case of government schools, mostly authorities mean SI and DI as teachers mostly face them here. Others could be the Panchayati Raj Institution authorities. The principal of Upai School which is a private school does not have to deal with any authority as such. But he said that he often keeps the BDO informed about the school, though the BDO does not deal with a private school. He also has to reckon with the vigilance of the parents, some of whom are teachers in government schools. In case of

Junoka, authority means the principal as he works in a private school and he has to obey the authority completely. In case of EGS school, the authority is the BRC, but Munuaka does not seem to bother much about this authority.

Most teachers belonging to government schools who are least professional and non-professional said that their relation with authorities is good. Observation pointed out that they are either submissive, indifferent or have an attitude of fait accompli (an attitude of resignation). The principal attitude seems to be how to avoid the authorities. I think they do not want to displease the authorities because they are not so much aware of the duty of a teacher. For example, they would not mind much survey type of work. For example, I could never find Mahesh in the school as he was always deputed to the block office for office work like preparing the rolls of National Rural Employment Guarantee Scheme (NREGS). In his interview, he did not resent about this fact strongly. Probably, he believes that it is within the right of the authorities to assign teachers work that is not related to education.

Most of the professional teachers have a negative view about the authorities. The charges are that authorities give award to the undeserving, do not assign them the school of their choice and do not sanction the leave when they need and the like. Kota said that authorities speak sweetly when teachers are needed for survey type of work, but do not recognize them afterwards.

> Higher authorities (*implying SI*) when they have the work, praise us a little. When that's over they do not care. 'let you go, primary teacher. At best you will become head pundit and retire'. What's the profit or loss in this? ...If the work is there (child survey) the order would have come to him late. He will tell us to do even day and night and within time. Teachers do that even leaving teaching. When the work is over, when we need his help like when some one needs leave in a single teacher school he will tell to first arrange who will work there instead of the teacher in need of leave. Naturally, because of communication problem no one will be interested to go to a different school for the leave period (the lesson diary, etc). Now, at least the SS are there and there is some solution for the single teacher problem.

> Rather DI appreciates a bit but IAS, etc. do not appreciate our problems. They behave rudely. Here it takes even two years for children to pick up *Oriya* language. IAS people do not understand all these. 'Why you have not come up to this level?' They do not know anything about methodology, stage. They will ask about freedom struggle. Teachers are not computers. How can we teach what's not there in the books? They are IAS, OAS. They are more qualified, knowledgeable. We are HSC, CT. All those things are not in the books.

> Not to be taught at primary level. (*I think the officers may be just showing off their knowledge*). Why should we tell? Whatever is there in the books, syllabus we will teach. If we are not able to, they give some insulting remarks. (Kota; author's note in italics)

I think since he focuses on teaching, he does not like such non-academic work, which takes away energy from teaching. Pajhi has similar opinion about authorities. Observation pointed out that all these charges are not totally true. Those who complain that authorities have sent them to remote areas have already stayed in block headquarters for as many as ten years. This shows that authorities are not as biased as portrayed by some teachers. It could well be the case that they might have had bad experience with the authorities. Amongst professional teachers, only Tima who is the advisor to the teacher organization at the block level has a balanced view about authorities. He said that there are two types of authorities—some who encourage and the others who rather create fear.

> Higher authorities are of different types. Some give good advice. Some create fear. Why the children are not coming? The teacher will ring bell. Children should come. No more teachers should go door to door to collect children neither can create fear among children to come to school (Tima).

This, I think, is the real picture. Pajhi opined that award is given to the undeserving teachers. But, observation found that there was no undeserving teacher who has got an award. Kosa, Tima, and Gajendra—all have got award and they are categorized here as professional on the basis of observation and interview. Thus, the popular notion that award is given to the undeserving may not be true. What happens is that though an award is given to a sincere teacher, not all sincere teachers get an award. There can't be so many awards. Also, sincerity comes first and an award later, not the other way round. Therefore, it may so happen that though some teachers work sincerely they do not get an award for a long time.

Views on Teacher Organizations

National Commission on Teachers (NCT, 1986) pointed out that teacher organizations have predominantly concerned themselves with pay and service conditions. This can be called utilitarian or instrumental orientation of teachers. Kingdon and Muzzamil (2003) pointed out the excessive politicization that has happened with teacher organizations. While one can see lot of politicization with regard to teacher organizations at macro level, the same does not appear at the micro level. The attitude of most of the teachers in this locality towards teacher organization can be considered as indifferent or utilitarian and of a few as negative. There can also be various combinations of one's personal orientation towards teacher organization which can be either positive, negative or indifferent and one's conception of what a teacher organization's role should be. Thus, teachers have both positive as well as instrumental orientation simultaneously and negative as well as instrumental orientation towards teacher organization. Following are examples of indifferent and negative views on teacher organization:

> *Indifferent view*: I am a member of teacher organization. Yearly INR 15/- contribution. They do not send any journal. They do some official work. ...if there is some problem to the teacher they face it (Shakir).

> *Negative view:* one teacher organization. I am not in any leadership position, neither I am interested. Give contributions. Many times other teachers told me to be in some positions but not interested, avoided...lot of headache. These days I realize presenting about teachers before authorities there is not much scope... do not want to pamper the authorities, have to do while in Sangha. Powerful but those in Sangha take the first steps for their benefits, later others... I do not like that. That's why did not get into it. Annually INR 15/- not 25/- less not but number of teachers are more. 200 teachers in the block. Magazine is there. Can get if you try, do not give automatically, not all get. Annually meeting happens within the state, outside the state in Bombay, Madras, Delhi (Pajhi).

There was only one case of classical professionalism (Goodson, 2000) that involves strong belief in the organization. But, this also did not go beyond an instrumental conception of teacher organization and did not emphasize any academic role of teacher organization.

> We can't leave the class and go on Sangha works. After 4 pm or on holidays. Union is recognized in Bhubaneswar otherwise any 20 can make a Sangha. Now the main demand—pay commission...regular of SSS the amount they get is not enough to live on. About 20 states have already given the new DA merged pay. These problems, lack of house, low salary. We get 8000 while neighbouring states give 12000 (Tima).

The predominant view about teacher organization is instrumental and utilitarian across all types of teachers. Teachers expect the organization to look into their non-academic problems like pay, leave, etc. They do not expect the teacher organization to deal with academic issues.

> Sangha—work for pay in time, even if SI dilly dallies tells them to expedite, GPF to expedite (Kasinath)

Out of eight professional teachers, two have explicitly negative view about teacher organizations and five have explicitly positive view on teacher organizations. Two professional teachers who have a negative opinion about the teacher organization opine that the local branch of the teacher organization does the work of only the office bearers, their favourites and neglects the work of others. Three teachers who are professional do not hold either positive or negative view about teacher organization. Among other categories of teachers, most have not thought deeply about the role of teacher organizations. They have just an instrumental conception of a teacher organization that sees it as helping their material problems like pay, leave, transfer, etc. Nobody including the professional teachers pointed out any role of teacher organizations that can be considered as academic. There is neither much politicization bringing out any group rivalry.

What distinguishes the professional teachers from the teachers who are least professional and non-professional is that the latter are indifferent while the professional teachers are strongly concerned about teacher organizations. Though the two professional teachers gave a negative opinion but they are concerned about the role of teacher organizations, they at least defined the role in wholly instrumental terms.

Views on Awards

A system of reward is not without any shortcomings. Reward and punishment system tends to reduce risk taking and reduces intrinsic motivation (Urbanski, 1998). There are three professional teachers who have got award. Out of the three, two are very modest about it and only one feels that the award has marked him out amongst two hundred teachers in the block. He says that he has to perform to keep up to the standards of the award.

> Award—school environment and social work I have got. Though do not get any money, standing out among 200 teachers gives self-satisfaction. Also got best literacy organizer, best teacher...(Tima)

No professional teacher trivializes award per se. But, two professional teachers resent that it is not given to the right persons. They also have a negative view about the teacher organizations and authorities.

> Have not got any award, no hope to get any. One has to show that type of activities before higher authorities to get award. I am not able to show that type of activities. That's why I do not hope to get any award... There is provision to give prizes to teachers on January 26, August 15, but those teachers

> who do not go to school, drink, they get. What's the use of those prizes? One higher authority (SI) who has got governor's prize always prowls for bribe...one president awardee is saying, 'you have to spend money to get good place (block headquarter). There are around 20 interior places in this block (Pajhi).

There is some resemblance between him and Kota. Many have pessimism towards award except the few who have got it. View on award and authorities may be interrelated. Authorities give awards. If one has a negative opinion about authorities, one may also have a negative view about awards. Those who have got awards do not have a negative view about them. But, they are also intrinsically professional because the awards come later. They would have performed many years by the time the award comes. Observation pointed out that a sincere teacher has a fair chance of getting an award. But, sincerity comes first and awards later; not the other way round. *Therefore, the function of awards should be to motivate the young teachers rather than the old teachers.*

The predominant attitude of teachers who are least professional or non-professional is that they either trivialize it or are not aware about it. An award does not impress them. This shows that an award is not able to perform the function, which it should—motivate the fellow young teachers. If fellow teachers trivialize an award, then they may not try to get one.

Presently, an award comes much later. It neither drives the major part of the teaching career of the teacher who gets it nor does it drive the other teachers. There seems to be a notion that an award is given to only senior teachers and thus has relation with only seniority. Many young teachers who are in the early years of their career do not foresee an award in near future. They visualize an award as the remote reward that comes at the end of their career. The award loses its motivating potential. An award can be a motivating factor if it is given earlier and not necessarily by pure seniority. Once one gets an award, one remains award-oriented which drives oneself rather than the material benefits. Every year, some best teachers in the block may be given an award.

Views on Salary

The issue of salary sometimes looks puzzling. The popular notion, 'they pretend to teach, we pretend to pay' does not grapple with the reality. Teachers seem to get more and less salary at the same time. This is because there are two views about it—from the government and from the teachers. While demanding higher salary, the teachers project a highly idealized version of a teacher—the ideal teacher who performs his duty in a most altruistic manner. On the other hand, the government or the view from the top paints a picture of duty shirking teacher and thinks that the salary is more than appropriate for a teacher. The truth is in between. If a primary teacher performs his/her duty properly, then it is difficult to give him/her an appropriate salary. The state may not have so much resource. On the other hand, those who neglect their duty to the point of not going to the school are paid something for nothing.

Nobody except Kosa amongst the professional teachers feels that the salary has improved. Kosa feels that people no more jeer the teachers because the increase of salary has considerably improved the status of a teacher.

> Earlier the salary was low. People were telling, 'hey you master' (pejorative)! Now they call sir, they recognize. Otherwise they used to tell 'rascal teacher! Comes once in eight or 10 days, the thief! They will ask five rupees. Now all this has stopped. Teachers are getting five thousand–six thousand. This has increased their status.

On the other hand, Virendra strongly feels that a teacher should get even at par with a lecturer because he works no less. He seems to be convinced about it.

> Salary is very deficient. Seeing present situation and teacher work, the minimum should be basic of 10000/- or 8000/-. We get at best 7000–8000; 4500/- to 3700/- basic. Even B.A, B.Ed. do not get 10000. Though 8000 is class–I basic, are not the teacher working that hard? Though not in this school, there are schools where teachers work strictly from 10 am to 4 pm.

Tima is the other teacher who seems to be convinced that primary is the foundation.

> In foreign, good students are recruited for teacher. Here the opposite. How difficult to build the children. Who is not fit for anything else are made teachers. third class, skill, qualification, people just see the post, not the job.

Probably he does not know that it is not true that good students are recruited for teachers in foreign countries, especially the West. Most other teachers' opinion is centred on comparison with either Andhra Pradesh or the pay scale of the central government. When professional teachers give opinion on salary, they always compare it with the job while the non-professional teachers do not. Virendra almost challenges and asks in what way a primary teacher works less than a lecturer that he is paid considerably less than a lecturer! Tima, advisor to the teacher organization at the local level, reflects on all the material problems encountered by the teachers like housing, medical, etc. On the other hand, the non-professional teachers compare salary with the cost of living. This probably is the difference in the attitude between the professional teachers and the non-professional teachers.

The teachers who are SSS (contract teachers) feel very strongly that the salary is extremely low.

> I'll tell about SSS how much problem. Teaching like regular, if the work is in the same village then could have punctual work at low salary. Also timely salary matters. Salary is main. Still we do to some extent. But salary is the main problem. Will the teacher be interested? who'll do at low salary? They are involved in all voter list, etc., any job. They do not have any facility though government job. If government holds adamant that do at such low salary or quit, no body will be interested. If they get higher salary then will think – I am getting such salary, must do something. Still SSS do. Some schools do not have any other teacher except SSS. They teach. Do other works. They are like regular teacher in that case. I can not say what was happening earlier, but now people are aware. Panchayati Raj people do not think/know SSS get low salary. They think that why SSS would not come? (Alpana)

But most teachers project a sort of fait accompli attitude regarding salary. They have to take it or leave it whatever salary government pays them.

> ...salary is 1500. Scheme is good; but will they work faithfully? But forcing them to work at 1500/- also is not right. But we can not tell to government. Only we can tell it to ourselves. Government will tell, 'do the duty or we'll appoint some one else.' No way not to do. 1500 or 1000 (Mosa)

On balance, it seems that permanent teachers are rather contented with the salary as they would have protested vehemently if they considered it as very low. The fait accompli attitude towards government has one latent dysfunction. Teachers have lost initiative because of this attitude. Now whatever has to be done has to be done by the government. There is no grass root movement towards professionalism. Table 8.1 summarizes the views on salary, authority, teacher organization and awards of all the teachers studied.

Table 8.1: Teachers' views on salary, authority, teacher organization and award

Categorization	Teachers	View on salary	View on authority	View on teacher organization	View on award
Professional	Pajhi	Payment is less compared to the job; attitude of resignation	Negative; they are corrupt	Negative	Says it is not given to the right people
	Kota	Payment is less compared to the job; fait accompli	Negative	Negative; instrumental	Good work is not the way to it
	Kosa	Much better than earlier; status has improved	Fait accompli	Positive; instrumental	He has got it; but indifferent
	Virendra	In what way a teacher works less than a lecturer that he/she will be paid less?	Negative	Positive; instrumental	Not aware but says that it is good if it exists
	Noyak	Does not have complaints about the salary	Fait accompli	Positive; instrumental	Positive; but considers block level award as fake
	Tima	Aware of all the material deficiencies of teachers; compares with Andhra Pradesh	Differentiated, i.e., some encourage some create fear	Very positive but instrumental; advisor of block level teacher organization	Very positive; values the award which he has got though it does not bring money
	Gajendra	Compares with Andhra Pradesh but not much concerned	Believes that there should be positive supervision	Positive and instrumental	Modest about the award he has got and thinks that one should work whether award comes or not
	Manty (SSS)	Thinks that he gets very less compared to what he is capable of	Positive	Concerned about the possible division of teacher organization into junior and regular	Does not approve the way it is given now; debunks it

Less professional	Prabin	Compares with central scale	Believes that authorities are apathetic	He was president at subdivision level	Believes award to be fake
	Junoka	Believes that it is low	Principal is the authority	Not thought about it	Has not yet thought about it; just starting the career
	Kabir	Projects that he is not concerned about money	Keeps relation with local authorities like BDO for smooth running of the school; instrumental, pro-establishment	Very negative view on organization	Has got award; positive view
	Kasinath	Salary is low but does not complain	Believes in strict supervision	Narrow utilitarian attitude towards organization	Modest about award; so far he has got a certificate by the BDO that he is regular. A clean service record that does not create any problem for pension is considered by him as the award
	Mahesh	Says that if we compare the prices, it is low; attitude of resignation	Positive; does not grudge inspection	Believes in teacher organization but instrumental attitude	Considers the cancel of transfer by villagers as something akin to award

(*Continued*)

Table 8.1: *(Continued)*

Least professional	Jyoshi	No interview			
	Kasla	No interview			
	Shakir	Fait accompli	Submissive	Not much concerned	Not concerned
	Tupur	Thinks that SSS salary is extremely low; but also not much concerned	Negative; thinks that they are all corrupt and merciless	Narrow utilitarian	Is not aware
	Alpana (SSS)	Miserable	Fait accompli	Positive view about SSS organization	Says that award will induce teachers to perform well
	Magan	Fait accompli	Fait accompli to government; good relation with block level; pro-establishment	Not much concerned and would not like to work in official capacity; instrumental	Says that award is given to senior teachers; does not aim for award as of now
	Tejmayi	Salary should be at least 5000	Has not thought much about higher authority	Not thought about it	Not thought about it
Non-professional	Aminash	Feels it is low	Submissive	Instrumental; also not much concerned	Not concerned
	Pranati	No interview			
	Meeta	No interview	Though no interview could be taken because of their unwillingness, observation in the school pointed out that they are indifferent to all these		
	Munuaka	Extremely low	BRC is their authority; Indifference	EGS does not have organization	

9

CONCLUSION

Emerging Contours

The concern about teacher professionalism is of recent origin as compared to profession and professionalization. This has a political dimension too, apart from the educational dimension. Governments around the world want to make their school education of high quality. There is a global concern about moving the twenty-first century with the right knowledge, skills and values. Teacher professionalism is situated in the struggle between the market and the community (Touraine, 2000, as cited in Bates, 2007). One can say that teacher professionalism is situated in the pull and push of the state, market and the community. Therefore, "there is a struggle among different stakeholders over the definition of teacher professionalism and professionality for the twenty-first century (Whitty et al., 1998, as cited in Day, 2007, p. 597). In this context, the victim probably is teacher autonomy.

Increasingly, the teachers are feeling the pressure of achievement scores in the USA and UK. Chance is that the Indian teacher will feel the same in near future rather than far. The state intervention in teacher professionalism has taken the shape of prescribing standards for teacher professionalism. Most of the scholars in the West are unanimous in their opinion that these state interventions in the form of standards will reduce teacher autonomy and, therefore, may be detrimental to teacher professionalism in the long term (Hinai and Ahmed, 2007). Teachers' professional and personal identities are important for job fulfilment, commitment and self-efficiency (Day, 2007). The state prescriptions usually run contrary to this important aspect. But it may also be the case that teachers' perception of what is considered as teacher professionalism itself is undergoing a transition. The new teachers, whose professional lives do not extend beyond the last decade, view the teaching profession in more instrumental terms. Therefore, there may be an evolving transition in teacher professionalism towards the more instrumental, and technical aspect (as cited in Day, 2007, p. 607). The classical notion of autonomy as an essential part of professionalism may be losing its grip among the new breed of teachers.

Building teacher professionalism is now a concern around the world, and also in India. The usual state measures have been to prescribe standards of teacher professionalism that are applicable to all teachers. India too is now on the way to prescribe standards for the teachers (see ADEPTS [Advancement of Educational Performance through Teacher Support]), an MHRD-UNICEF Initiative, June 2006–January 2007). There may not be any respite for the Indian government in the near future with regard to teacher professionalism. There may be another massive orientation of teachers required for ICT (Information and Communication Technology) in education.

Professionalism emphasizes knowledge, skills and ethics. There have been attempts to visualize the knowledge base of primary teaching through the concepts like 'pedagogical content knowledge' (Shulman, 2004). But the present challenge is more than just mastering textbook knowledge. Knowledge is now more fluid than it was ever before. It is so fluid that it cannot be imparted by a few days in-service training in a year. Knowledge as information is obsolete now. Information is changing very fast. Teachers now need to be adept in locating various sources of knowledge rather than knowledge per se. These various sources of knowledge can be other people, other books and the internet. For example, teachers can improve their knowledge of mathematics, English or computer by searching concerned persons locally and getting the knowledge from them. A primary teacher can contact a high school teacher of the locality or a person from the local cyber café to improve his/her knowledge of English or the computer. If a teacher has to know anything about human anatomy or health, he/she can talk to the local doctor and know it. Waiting for the in-service training for such things may prove elusive. Imparting such creative way of acquiring knowledge to the children is the challenge for teacher professionalism rather than knowledge.

In this context, teacher professionalism should be viewed as a continuous process. To some extent, it should be a constituent of their lives.

'Teachers' professional and personal identities are important for job fulfilment, commitment and self-efficiency' (Day, 2007, p. 597). Professionalism is best manifest in a way of life. It does not emphasize only knowledge and skills. The level of knowledge and skills required for being considered as professional will vary from country to country. But what is required is a way of life that has its dominant theme—honing of knowledge and skills constantly. Along with this, professionalism also means 'commitment', 'dedication' and such values which are considered as constituents of teacher professionalism (see NCTE, 1998, in the Indian context). So long professionalism does not become the dominant theme in teachers' lives, teacher professionalism has no meaning. Teacher professionalism can be defined as 'a way of life having its dominant theme curiosity for knowledge and skills, care and concern for children and based on an ethical premise that values teaching in itself'.

Apart from knowledge and skills, two ethical issues have to be dealt with in the present age to have a clear picture of teacher professionalism in India; these are the notions of guru and the extent of altruism necessary for professionalism. Primary teaching has both a special and shadowed relationship with society (Lortie, 1975). This seems to be true in case of India too. On some occasions, teachers are revered as guru and on some other occasions they are lampooned. The notion of guru has been mentioned in many books and commission reports probably to boost the status of present day teachers. The notion of guru might have propelled many teachers towards dedication to their jobs, but the notion is not without limitations. The notion of guru contains historical as well as mythological baggage. The present day teachers are not comparable to the notion of guru of either mythology or history. The present day teacher is a British creation for the purpose of mass education. So, they cannot be compared with the ancient gurus who always hobnobbed with the powers. The present day teacher is a successor of the teacher as a paid employee of the British period. The present day teacher operates under a framework decided by the state while it was not so with the guru. The present day teacher lives fully in the society and society demands accountability from the teacher. It is not clear whether the guru was demanded accountability like the present day teacher. The guru was almost infallible. But, the present teacher is not considered infallible. She/he is rather considered as a facilitator of learning.

While the guru–pupil relation might have been hierarchical, the present age emphasizes democratic relation in the classroom. Therefore, teacher professionalism has to partially detach itself from the notion of guru.

Another notion which always worries a teacher is altruism—that the teacher should be a sacrificer. Movies about teachers portray an extreme degree of dedication and sacrifice, which an average teacher is hardly likely to attain. The teaching methods in these movies are also not likely to be approved by any board of education. But, the question of altruism always remains live for the teaching profession. Professionalism requires altruism but that need not be unlimited to the point of sacrificing one's life. Professionals also command remuneration or compensation from the society for doing some important service. This compensation need not necessarily be entirely symbolic. It is also material, like money.

Therefore, teachers' demand for better material conditions is not an act of unprofessionalism. According to Behar (1996), teaching need not bother too much on altruism, as other established professions themselves do not practice much altruism these days. Therefore, it is legitimate on the part of teachers to be concerned about their material positions. But while the material benefits are the concern of teacher organizations universally, including India, teacher organizations in other countries also do a lot more related to the profession—inquiring the state of the teaching profession, its relative status in the society and training of the members of the profession.

If one includes both the teachers who are least professional and clearly non-professional in this study, then there is quite a crisis as they outnumber the teachers who are professional and less professional. But this study also shows that there is a great deal of scope to raise professionalism as the number of outright non-professional teachers who can't be changed is less. Most of the teachers have potential to be professional.

APPENDICES

Chapter 3

Appendix 3.1: Development of teacher education institutions in India

India	Total normal schools	Enrollment	Training colleges	Enrollment
1881–82	106	3,886	2	
1893	131		3	
1913	500	11,000	15	1,400

Source: Devi, 1968; collated from different pages.

Appendix 3.1.1

States/UT	Upto 1940	1941 –50	1951 –55	1956 –60	1961 –65	1966 –70
Assam	5	19				
Gujarat	6	7	8	14	10	2
Himachal Pradesh	1		1	1	1	
Jammu and Kashmir	1		6	2	1	5
Karnataka	8	14	10	10	16	16
Madhya Pradesh	4	6	6	23	1	
Maharashtra	19	27	20	30	16	7
Orissa	7	3	8	15	5	16
Uttar Pradesh	10	33	11	43	54	11
Andaman & Nicobar Islands				1		
Delhi	1	1				
Goa, Daman and Diu					1	1
Nagaland			1	1	1	
Pondicherry				1	1	
Tripura			1	2	1	
Total	72	110	72	143	108	58

Source: NCERT, 1977.

Appendix 3.2: Comparison of salary in different countries

Countries	Average annual salary	
	Teachers	**Other public servants**
Australia	3 years trained Aus$ 33,472 4 years trained Aus$ 34,654	Administrative Officer class 1 Aus$ 24,805 Administrative Officer class 2 Aus$ 28,191
Hong Kong	HK$ 3,09,972- linked to points 17–44 of the civil service masters pay scale, but in real terms lower as most teachers do not receive all civil service benefits—especially housing	Point 26 of the master pay scale HK$ 3,57,960
Japan	25% more pay than other graduate civil servants since 1974	
People's Republic of China	Average teachers' income (1991): 2,257 Yuan per annum	Average salary of state employees: 2,563 Yuan per annum
Singapore	Sing$ 25,920	Sing$ 25,350
Taiwan	81 units	61 units
USA	US$ 20,649	US$ 27,525

Source: Morris and Williamson, 1998.

Appendix 3.2.1: Teachers' salaries in US dollars (PPP) at starting salary, after 15 years of experience and at the top of the salary scale, with minimum level of training, by level of education

		Primary education		
Country	**Year**	**Starting salary (1)**	**Salary after 15 years of experience (2)**	**Salary at top of scale (3)**
WEI countries				
Argentina	2003	6,459	8,997	10,771
Brazil	2003	...	...	...
Chile	2004	10,922	12,976	17,500
Egypt	2002–03	1,029	2,148	...
India	2002–03	11,547	18,927	...

(*Continued*)

Appendix 3.2.1: *(Continued)*

Indonesia	2003–04	800	1,266	2,412
Jamaica	2002–03	11,200	13,854	13,854
Jordan	2002–03	8,537	11,846	29,813
Malaysia	2003	14,604	14,604	19,751
Paraguay	2003	6,804	6,804	6,804
Peru	2004	7,302	7,302	7,302
The Philippines	2003–04	9,314	10,281	11,072
Sri Lanka	2004	2,903	3,694	3,694
Thailand	2004–05	5,922	14,554	27,757
Tunisia	2002–03	12,969	13,109	14,893
Uruguay	2003	4,023	4,315	5,042
WEI mean	**2004**	**7,622**	**9,645**	**13,128**
OECD countries				
Australia	2004	29,712	43,991	43,991
Austria	2003–04	25,446	33,644	50,782
Belgium (Fl.)	2003–04	28,168	39,050	47,279
Belgium (Fr.)	2003–04	26,335	36,643	44,500
Czech Republic	2003–04	15,222	19,994	25,291
Denmark	2003–04	33,693	37,925	37,925
England	2003–04	28,769	42,046	42,046
Finland	2003–04	27,922	32,541	32,541
France	2003–04	23,112	31,090	45,872
Germany	2003–04	37,718	46,935	48,938
Greece	2003–04	23,700	28,646	34,540
Hungary	2003–04	11,340	14,512	19,348
Iceland	2003–04	19,350	22,396	24,948
Ireland	2003–04	26,674	44,185	50,071
Italy	2003–04	23,753	28,731	34,951
Japan	2003-04	24,469	45,753	58,373
Luxembourg	2003–04	46,306	63,769	94,380
Mexico	2003–04	12,665	16,669	27,606
The Netherlands	2003–04	31,235	40,588	45,341
New Zealand	2004	18,641	36,063	36,063
Norway	2003–04	29,618	35,420	36,679
Poland	2003–04	6,394	10,263	10,652
Portugal	2003–04	19,189	31,635	49,644

(Continued)

Appendix 3.2.1: *(Continued)*

Republic of Korea	2004–05	28,569	48,875	78,472
Scotland	2003–04	28,603	45,616	45,616
Spain	2003–04	31,381	36,342	45,334
Sweden	2003–04	25,152	29,522	33,849
Switzerland	2003–04	39,285	51,956	62,260
Turkey	2003–04	16,678	18,416	20,768
United States	2003–04	32,703	39,740	...
OECD average	**2004**	**25,727**	**35,099**	**42,347**

Source: Adapted from UNESCO, 2006, Table 5.h.i

Appendix 3.2.2: Teachers' salaries in relative terms/Teachers' salaries in US dollars (PPP) as a percentage of GDP per capita, at starting salary, after 15 years of experience and at the top of the salary scale, with minimum level of training, by level of education

		Primary education		
Country	**Year**	**Starting salary (1)**	**Salary after 15 years of experience (2)**	**Salary at top of scale (3)**
WEI countries				
Argentina	2003	56	78	94
Brazil	2003	...	...	...
Chile	2004	96	114	154
Egypt	2002–03	27	57	...
India	2002–03	402	658	...
Indonesia	2003–04	23	36	68
Jamaica	2002–03	294	364	364
Jordan	2002–03	201	279	702
Malaysia	2003	151	151	205
Paraguay	2003	149	149	149
Peru	2004	130	130	130
Philippines	2003–04	201	222	239
Sri Lanka	2004	74	94	94
Tunisia	2002–03	181	183	208
Uruguay	2003	49	52	61
WEI mean	**2004**	**145**	**183**	**206**

(Continued)

Appendix 3.2.2: *(Continued)*

OECD countries[1]				
Australia	2004	92	136	136
Austria	2003–04	78	103	156
Belgium (Fl.)	2003–04	90	124	151
Belgium (Fr.)	2003–04	84	117	142
Czech Republic	2003–04	82	107	136
Denmark	2003–04	105	118	118
England	2003–04	93	136	136
Finland	2003–04	94	109	109
France	2003–04	80	107	158
Germany	2003–04	131	163	170
Greece	2003–04	110	133	160
Hungary	2003–04	71	91	121
Iceland	2003–04	60	69	77
Ireland	2003–04	73	122	138
Italy	2003–04	87	105	128
Japan	2003–04	83	155	197
Luxembourg	2003–04	77	106	157
Mexico	2003–04	125	164	272
Netherlands	2003–04	95	123	137
New Zealand	2004	76	147	147
Norway	2003–04	73	87	90
Poland	2003–04	52	83	86
Portugal	2003–04	106	175	274
Republic of Korea	2004–05	138	237	380
Scotland	2003–04	93	148	148
Slovakia	2003–04	...	...	...
Spain	2003–04	121	140	175
Sweden	2003–04	81	95	109
Switzerland	2003–04	113	150	179
Turkey	2003–04	221	244	275
United States	2003–04	82	100	...
OECD average	**2004**	**95**	**130**	**157**

[1]Calculated by UNESCO Institute for Statistics.

Source: Adapted from UNESCO, 2006, Table 5.h.ii

Appendix 3.3: Pre-service teacher education requirements for primary education, 2001

Countries	Duration of initial education programme in years	Consecutive programme(*) or Concurrent programme(!)	Mandatory teaching experience as licensing requirement	Post-degree examination for teacher employment
Australia	4	!	a	No
	4	*	a	No
Austria	3	!	a	No
Belgium (Fl)	3	!	a	No
Belgium (Fr)	3	!	a	No
Canada (Quebec)	4	*	a	No
Chile	m	m	a	No
Czech Republic	4	*	a	No
Denmark	4	!	a	No
Finland	5	!	a	No
France	5	*	a	Yes
Germany	5.5	!	a	Yes
	5.5–6.5	!	a	Yes
Greece	4	!	a	Yes
Hungary	4	!	a	No
Iceland	3	*	m	No
	4	!	m	No
Ireland	3	*	1	No
	4.5	!	a	No
Israel	4	!	1	No
Italy	4	!	1	Yes
Japan	2	!	a	Yes
	4	!	a	Yes
	6	!	a	Yes
Korea	4	!	a	Yes
Mexico	4	!	a	Yes/No
Netherlands	4	!	a	No
New Zealand	3	!	2	No
	4	*	2	No
Norway	4	!	a	No

(Continued)

Appendix 3.3: *(Continued)*

Portugal	3	!	a	No
	4	!	1	No
	6	*	1	No
Slovak	4	!	a	No
Republic	7	*	a	No
Spain	3	!	1	Yes
Sweden	3.5	!	a	No
Switzerland	3–4	!	a	No
Turkey	4	!	1	No
United King-	3–4	!	1	No
dom (Eng-land)	4	*	1	No
United	4	!	1	No
Kingdom (N. Ireland)	4	*	1	No
United King-	3.75–4.75	*	1	No
dom (Scot-land)	4	!	1	No
United King-	3–4	!	1	No
dom (Wales)	4	*	1	No
United States	4	!	3	No

Notes: a: Data not applicable because the category does not apply; m: Data not available

Source: Adapted from OECD, 2005: 106, Table 4.1.

Appendix 3.4: Professional development for teachers, public schools – 2004

Countries	What is the minimum professional development requirement for teachers in a school year?	Who decides the professional development activities an individual teacher undertakes?	Are professional development activities planned in a context of individual school development priorities?	Are schools allocated a budget to determine their involvement in professional development?	Is the completion of professional development activities required for the promotion or recertification of teachers?	Can teachers get a leave of absence and/or a research grant to undertake study/research activities?	Do teachers generally make a financial contribution to cover the costs of professional development activities (e.g. transport, course fees and course materials)?
Australia	Generally none, 5 days in two states, 37.5 hours per year in another state	Generally teacher and school management, often in line with system priorities	Yes, but not exclusively	Generally yes	It varies; e.g., in one jurisdiction, teachers must undertake professional development for promotion to senior teacher classification	It varies but usually a leave of absence, sometimes research grants or scholarships are available	It varies, if training is personally initiated the teacher will pay (e.g., a national or international conference)
Austria	15 hours	Primarily teacher, School management and inspectorate if performance is poor	Yes, but not exclusively	Yes	No	Leave of absence	Sometimes
Belgium (Fl)	None	Teacher, School management	Yes, but not exclusively	Yes	No	None	Often

(*Continued*)

Appendix 3.4: *(Continued)*

Belgium (Fr)	6 half-days	Teacher	Yes, but not exclusively	No	No	None	Sometimes
Canada (Quebec)	None	Teacher, School management	Yes, but not exclusively	Yes	No	Leave of absence	Sometimes
Chile	None	Teacher, School authority	No	No	No	Both leave of absence and research grant	Never
Denmark	None	Teacher, School management, Local educational authority	Yes, but not exclusively	Yes	No	Both leave of absence and research grant	Sometimes
Finland		Teacher, School management, Local educational authority	Yes, but not exclusively	No	No	Leave of absence	Sometimes
France	None	Teacher, Inspectorate	No	No	No	Leave of absence	Generally no, except if training is personally initiated
Germany	None	Teacher, Local educational authority	Yes, but not exclusively	Sometimes	No	Leave of absence	Sometimes
Greece	None	Teacher, Central/regional/local educational authority	No	No	No, but used as a selection criterion to become principal or school advisor	Both leave of absence and research grant	Sometimes

(Continued)

Appendix 3.4: *(Continued)*

Hungary	120 hours over a period of 7 years	School management taking teachers' preferences into consideration, Teacher alone if activity is not funded by school	Yes, but not exclusively	Yes	No, but can result in exceptional career advancement	Both leave of absence and research grant if the board of teachers in schools agrees and funding is found in school. Possible also if school authorizes it as a professional development mandatory activity	Often, if the teacher undertakes programmes other than once officially provided; For programmes officially provided, teachers cover about 20% of the costs
Ireland	None[1]	Teacher, except for activities organized to implement reforms	Yes, but not exclusively	No[2]	No	Leave of absence with pay is available for certain relevant courses	Sometimes, if teacher personally initiates a programme
Israel	None	Teacher, School management	Yes, but not exclusively	Only for schools under self- management	Yes, for recertification, Yes, unofficially for promotion	None, but teacher can get a sabbatical year	Often, when not undertaken during sabbatical year
Italy	None	Teacher	Yes, but not exclusively	Yes	No	Leave of absence	Often

(Continued)

Appendix 3.4: *(Continued)*

Japan	None		No	No	No	Both leave of absence and research grant	Always
Korea	None	Teacher	No	Yes	Yes, for promotion	Both leave of absence and research grant	Often
Netherlands	169 hours (10% of total workload)	Teacher, School management	Yes, but not exclusively	Yes	No	None, but teacher can get a sabbatical year	Sometimes
Sweden	104 hours	Teacher, School management	Yes, but not exclusively	Yes	No	Both leave of absence and research grant	Never
Switzerland	Generally 5 to 10 days[3]	Primary teachers; Regional education authority for activities related to implementation of reforms	Yes, but not exclusively	Yes	Yes, non- fulfillment of professional development requirement might imply promotion deferral	None (generally)	Often
United Kingdom (Eng)	None	Teacher, School management	Yes, but not exclusively	Yes, but if not earmarked	Yes, for promotion to principal	Yes, but at the discretion of the school	Sometimes
United Kingdom (N.Irl)	None	Teacher, School management; Local educational authority	Yes, but not exclusively	Yes	Yes, for promotion	Yes, but at the discretion of the employer	Never

(Continued)

Appendix 3.4: *(Continued)*

United Kingdom (Scot)	1 week	Teacher, School management	Yes, but not exclusively	Yes	No	None	Varies according nature of training
United Kingdom (Wal)	None	Teacher, School management	Yes, but not exclusively	Funding available from within the school's overall budget and through optional additional funding	Yes, for promotion to principal	Yes, but at the discretion of the school	Sometimes
United States[4]	Varies by school district; often about 30 credit hours in first two to five years of teaching	Teacher, School management; Local educational authority	Yes	No, with few exceptions[5]	Yes	Yet, but infrequently	No, except for university courses

[1] Except for primary school teachers to attend a professional development programme designed to support the implementation of *the primary school curriculum* (1999), currently averaging 6 days per annum.

[2]An exception for primary and lower secondary education is the *school development planning initiative,* which allocates a small budget to schools.

[3]Regulated in some cantons but not in others. No national regulation exists.

[4]Local educational authorities are typically allocated a budget for professional development activities.

The table should be interpreted as broad indications only and not strict comparability across countries.

Source: OECD, 2005 p 124.

Definition: Professional development refers to in-service training which seeks to update, develop and broaden the knowledge teachers acquired during initial education and provide them with new skills and professional understanding. Professional development may also be provided to accompany the implementation of educational reforms. It is distinct from further 'qualifying training' which normally enables teachers to teach another subject or at another educational level (additional qualification).

Appendix 3.5: Pupil–teacher ratio/pupils to teaching staff ratios by level of education, calculations based on full time equivalents

Country	Year	Pre-primary (1)	Primary (2)
WEI countries			
Argentina[1]	2002	22.6	19.1
Brazil	2003	18.3	23.5
Chile	2004	21.4	27.1
Egypt	2003–04	24.2	21.9
India	2002–03	40.5	39.9
Indonesia	2003–04	15.9	23.1
Jamaica	2003–04	22.1	27.5
Jordan	2003–04	20.4	19.4
Malaysia[2]	2003	19.8	17.4
Paraguay	2003	18.5	17.0
Peru	2004	23.5	22.5
Philippines	2003–04	31.4	34.5
Russian Federation	2003–04	...	17.0
Sri Lanka	2004	...	22.5
Tunisia	2003–04	19.4	20.6
Uruguay	2003	27.7	20.8
Zimbabwe	2003	...	38.6
WEI mean	**2004**	**23.3**	**24.3**
OECD countries			
Australia[3]	2004	...	16.4
Austria	2003–04	17.4	15.1
Belgium	2003–04	15.6	12.9
Czech Republic	2003–04	13.4	17.9
Denmark	2003–04	6.9	x(4)
Finland	2003–04	12.7	16.3
France	2003–04	18.8	19.4
Germany	2003–04	13.9	18.8
Greece	2003–04	12.7	11.3
Hungary	2003–04	10.5	10.7
Iceland	2003–04	7.3	x(4)
Ireland	2003–04	14.0	18.3
Italy	2003–04	12.5	10.7

(*Continued*)

Appendix 3.5: *(Continued)*

Japan	2003–04	17.7	19.6
Luxembourg[4]	2003–04	...	...
Mexico	2003–04	28.3	28.5
Netherlands	2003–04	x(2)	15.9
New Zealand	2004	9.4	16.7
Norway[4]	2003–04	...	11.9
Poland	2003–04	...	...
Portugal	2003–04	16.5	11.1
Republic of Korea	2004–05	20.8	29.1
Slovakia	2003–04	12.5	18.9
Spain	2003–04	13.9	14.3
Sweden	2003–04	11.2	12.1
Switzerland[4]	2003–04	18.2	14.3
Turkey	2003–04	18.7	26.5
United Kingdom[3,5]	2003–04	17.6	21.1
United States	2003–04	14.5	15.0
OECD mean	**2004**	**14.8**	**16.9**
Other UOE countries			
Croatia	2003–04	...	...
Cyprus	2003–04	18.7	17.8
Estonia	2003–04	7.3	...
Israel	2003–04	30.2	16.9
Latvia	2003–04	13.9	14.9
Liechtenstein	2003–04	15.5	10.3
Lithuania	2003–04	8.2	11.0
Malta	2003–04	68.2	19.0
Romania	2003–04	18.4	17.8
Slovenia	2003–04	16.3	15.2
The FYR of Macedonia	2003–04	11.3	...

[1]Tertiary (type A) education includes public institutions only.
[2]Tertiary (type B) education includes public institutions only.
[3]Includes only general programmes in upper secondary education.
[4]Public institutions only.
[5]The ratio of students to contact staff refers to public institutions only.
a: Data not applicable because the category does not apply; n: magnitude is nil; ...: Data not available; x(y): Data are included in another category/column (y) of the table.

Source: Adapted from UNESCO, 2006, Table 5.c

Appendix 3.6: Average class size in primary education by type of institutions

		Primary education			
Country	**Year**	**Public institutions**	**Government-dependent private institutions**	**Independent private institutions**	**Total public and private institutions**
WEI countries					
Argentina	2003	25.3	26.9	26.6	25.6
Brazil	2003	26.4	a	18.5	25.4
Chile	2004	30.6	34.0	23.5	31.2
China	2003–04	34.7	a	36.1	34.7
Egypt	2003–04	42.7	37.0	34.2	42.5
India	2002–03	39.9	...	...	...
Jamaica	2002–03	42.0	a	...	42.0
Jordan	2003–04	28.7	a	27.8	28.4
Malaysia	2003	30.5	a	...	...
Paraguay	2003	17.6	21.0	15.9	17.8
Peru	2004	17.0	27.0	14.0	16.8
Philippines	2003–04	39.6	a	33.6	39.1
Russian Federation	2003–04	15.6	a	9.7	15.6
Sri Lanka	2004	25.3	...	a	...
Thailand	2004–05	22.3	36.4	a	23.8
Tunisia	2003–04	25.6	a	23.2	25.6
Uruguay	2003	19.5	a	...	...
WEI Mean	**2004**	**28.4**	...	**23.9**	**28.3**
OECD countries					
Australia	2004	24.2	24.5	a	24.3
Austria	2003–04	20.1	20.7	x(2)	20.1
Belgium (Fr.)	2003–04	20.3	21.1	a	20.6
Czech Republic	2003–04	20.6	16.9	a	20.6
Denmark	2003–04	19.8	17.3	a	19.5
France	2003–04	...	...	...	...
Germany	2003–04	22.0	23.0	x(2)	22.1
Greece	2003–04	18.1	a	21.7	18.3
Hungary	2003–04	20.3	18.9	a	20.2

(Continued)

Appendix 3.6: *(Continued)*

Iceland	2003–04	17.1	14.3	n	17.1
Ireland	2003–04	23.9	a	...	...
Italy	2003–04	18.3	a	19.7	18.4
Japan	2003–04	28.5	a	33.9	28.6
Luxembourg	2003–04	15.6	20.5	21.0	15.8
Mexico	2003–04	19.9	a	22.7	20.1
Netherlands	2003–04	x(4)	x(4)	a	22.2
Norway	2003–04	a	a	a	a
Poland	2003–04	20.6	11.3	11.9	20.4
Portugal	2003–04	16.0	25.0	19.9	16.4
Republic of Korea	2004–05	33.6	a	33.4	33.6
Slovakia	2003–04	19.9	19.6	n	19.9
Spain	2003–04	19.3	24.6	22.0	20.7
Switzerland	2003–04	19.3	14.1	16.3	19.2
Turkey	2003–04	26.7	a	14.8	26.4
United Kingdom	2003–04	26.0	a	10.7	24.3
United States	2003–04	23.6	a	19.4	23.1
OECD mean	**2004**	**21.5**	**19.3**	**20.6**	**21.4**
Other UOE countries					
Albania	2002–03	24.9	a	14.3	24.4
Bulgaria	2002–03	20.3	n	9.2	20.2
Cyprus	2003–04	21.3	a	17.0	21.0
Estonia	2003–04	20.5	a	14.0	20.3
Israel	2003–04	26.5	a	a	26.5
Liechtenstein	2002–03	15.3	n	12.7	15.2
Lithuania	2003–04	15.0	a	11.7	14.9
Malta	2003–04	20.3	27.4	20.2	21.7
Romania	2003–04	18.6	a	14.3	18.6
Slovenia	2003–04	18.3	21.0	n	18.3
The FYR of Macedonia	2003–04	21.3	a	a	21.3

Source: Adapted from UNESCO, 2006, Table 5.d.
a: Data not applicable because the category does not apply; n: magnitude is nil; ...: Data not available; x(y): Data are included in another category/column (y) of the table.

Appendix 3.7: Workload of teachers in primary education

Country	Year	Teaching hours per year Primary education	Teaching weeks per year Primary education
WEI countries			
Argentina	2003	810	38
Brazil	2003	860	40
Chile	2004	873	40
Egypt	2003–04	812	38
India	2002–03	1,013	52
Indonesia	2003–04	1,260	44
Jamaica	2003–04	950	38
Jordan	2003–04	810	36
Malaysia	2003	761	42
Paraguay	2003	752	39
Peru	2004	810	38
Philippines	2003–04	1,182	40
Russian Federation	2003–04	656	34
Sri Lanka	2004	987	42
Thailand	2004–05	800–1,000	40
Tunisia	2003–04	735	32
Uruguay	2003	660	37
WEI Mean	**2004**	**872**	**39**
OECD countries			
Australia	2004	874	40
Austria	2003–04	792	38
Belgium (Fl.)	2003–04	803	37
Belgium (Fr.)	2003–04	722	37
Canada	2003–04	809	40
Czech Republic	2003–04	640	42
Denmark	2003–04	...	38
Finland	2003–04	680	38
France	2003–04	918	35
Germany	2003–04	793	40

(*Continued*)

Appendix 3.7: *(Continued)*

Greece	2003–04	780	40
Hungary	2003–04	777	37
Iceland	2003–04	653	36
Ireland	2003–04	946	37
Italy	2003–04	726	33
Japan	2003–04	648	35
Luxembourg	2003–04	774	36
Mexico	2003–04	800	41
Netherlands	2003–04	930	40
New Zealand	2004	985	39
Norway	2003–04	741	38
Poland	2003–04	677	39
Portugal	2003–04	880	36
Republic of Korea	2004–05	828	37
Scotland	2003–04	950	38
Spain	2003–04	880	37
Turkey	2003–04	639	38
United States	2003–04	1080	36
OECD mean	**2004**	**805**	**38**

Source: Adapted from UNESCO, 2006, Table 5.f

Appendix 3.8: Age distribution of teachers

		Primary education					
		< 30	30–39	40–49	50–59	> 60	Unknown
Country	**Year**	**(1)**	**(2)**	**(3)**	**(4)**	**(5)**	**(6)**
WEI countries							
Argentina	2002	30.5	31.4	27.2	10.0	0.9	n
Brazil	2003	29.3	34.7	25.2	9.7	1.2	n
Chile	2004	10.7	22.1	28.4	29.9	8.9	n
Indonesia	2003–04	51.6	34.9	9.8	3.7	a	n
Jamaica	2003–04	26.1	21.5	27.2	23.8	1.4	n
Jordan	2003–04	35.9	38.2	19.9	6.0	n	n
Malaysia	2003	26.1	42.2	23.4	8.3	n	n

(Continued)

Appendix 3.8: *(Continued)*

Paraguay	2003	42.5	37.7	14.4	4.3	1.0	n
Sri Lanka	2004	8.4	37.8	35.2	18.5	n	n
WEI mean	**2004**	**29.0**	**33.4**	**23.4**	**12.7**	**1.5**	**n**
OECD countries1							
Austria	2003–04	12.7	26.8	38.7	21.3	0.6	n
Belgium	2003–04	23.0	26.5	30.1	19.1	1.3	n
Denmark	2003–04	...	...	...	...	...	n
Finland	2003–04	14.0	32.2	29.4	23.3	1.1	n
France	2003–04	15.9	28.8	32.5	22.5	0.3	n
Germany	2003–04	6.8	18.5	23.7	43.0	8.0	n
Greece	2003–04	12.4	45.6	28.3	13.4	0.4	n
Hungary	2003–04	15.9	31.8	35.0	14.8	1.4	1.0
Iceland	2003–04	13.4	29.7	28.6	22.0	6.3	n
Ireland	2003–04	23.1	19.8	28.6	23.3	5.1	a
Italy	2003–04	0.9	15.9	32.4	34.4	4.9	11.5
Luxembourg	2003–04	28.2	23.9	22.8	24.1	1.0	n
Netherlands	2003–04	20.2	20.1	32.5	24.9	2.3	n
New Zealand	2004	14.2	20.2	29.5	26.3	6.4	3.4
Norway	2003–04	10.8	28.0	23.5	29.4	8.2	n
Portugal	2003–04	16.5	24.8	32.9	23.4	2.3	n
Republic of Korea	2004–05	26.7	29.6	24.1	18.4	1.2	n
Slovakia	2003–04	22.1	24.9	24.8	22.6	5.7	n
Spain	2003–04	12.7	22.2	32.1	28.4	4.5	n
Sweden	2003–04	9.4	20.8	23.6	36.0	10.1	n
Switzerland	2003–04	21.1	22.3	30.7	23.0	2.5	0.4
United Kingdom	2003–04	22.5	23.8	23.9	28.9	0.9	n
OECD mean	**2004**	**16.3**	**25.5**	**28.9**	**24.9**	**3.6**	**0.7**
Other UOE countries							
Cyprus	2003–04	45.7	46.3	5.7	1.9	0.3	n
Israel	2003–04	20.6	33.0	28.9	16.4	1.1	n
Latvia	2003–04	16.5	31.3	29.9	15.9	6.4	a
Liechtenstein	2003–04	20.8	25.4	34.6	16.9	2.3	n
Lithuania	2003–04	12.0	34.0	31.8	17.6	4.6	n

(Continued)

Appendix 3.8: *(Continued)*

Malta	2003–04	36.4	20.0	14.3	26.4	2.9	n
Romania	2003–04	30.7	22.9	26.4	19.4	0.6	a
Slovenia	2003–04	15.7	33.7	36.9	12.6	0.5	0.5
The FYR of Macedonia	2003–04	10.5	30.7	30.2	25.4	3.2	n

[1]Calculated by UNESCO Institute for Statistics.
a: Data not applicable because the category does not apply; n: magnitude is nil; …: Data not available; x(y): Data are included in another category/column (y) of the table.

Source: Adapted from UNESCO, 2006, Table 5.g.

Appendix 3.9: Percentage of women among teachers in public and private institutions, by level of education (based on headcounts)

Country	Year	Pre-primary education (1)	Primary education (2)
WEI countries			
Argentina	2002	97	86
Brazil	2003	94	90
Chile	2004	98	78
Indonesia	2003–04	98	52
Jamaica	2003–04	98	89
Jordan	2003–04	41	64
Malaysia	2003	99	66
Paraguay	2003	88	72
Sri Lanka	2003	…	79
WEI mean	**2004**	**89**	**75**
OECD countries[1]			
Austria	2003–04	99	91
Belgium	2003–04	98	78
Finland	2003–04	97	76
France	2003–04	81	81
Germany	2003–04	97	83
Greece	2003–04	99	62
Hungary	2003–04	100	96
Iceland	2003–04	97	x(3)
Ireland	2003–04	92	84

(Continued)

Appendix 3.9: *(Continued)*

Italy	2003–04	100	95
Luxembourg	2003–04	98	71
Netherlands	2003–04	x(2)	82
New Zealand	2004	99	83
Norway	2003–04	...	73
Portugal	2003–04	98	82
Republic of Korea	2004–05	99	74
Slovakia	2003–04	100	92
Spain	2003–04	91	69
Sweden	2003–04	96	81
Switzerland	2003–04	98	78
United Kingdom	2003–04	97	81
OECD mean	**2004**	96	**80**
Other UOE countries			
Cyprus	2003–04	99	83
Israel	2003–04	99	85
Latvia	2003–04	100	97
Liechtenstein	2003–04	100	74
Lithuania	2003–04	100	98
Malta	2003–04	99	87
Romania	2003–04	100	87
Slovenia	2003–04	100	97
The FYR of Macedonia	2003–04	99	69

[1]Calculated by UNESCO Institute for Statistics.

a: Data not applicable because the category does not apply; n: magnitude is nil; ...: Data not available; x(y): Data are included in another category/column (y) of the table.

Source: Adapted from UNESCO, 2006, Table 5.g.w.

Chapter 4

Appendix 4.1: The structure of administration of education in Orissa in 1872

D.P.I. Calcutta

↓

Vardhaman South West School inspector

↓

2 Deputy inspectors (Orissa)

Appendix 4.2: The structure of administration of education in Orissa in 1875

Inspector (all boys) Inspectoress (girls)

↓

Assistant inspector

↓

Deputy inspector (District)

↓

Sub inspector (primary)

Appendix 4.3: Number of new primary schools and EGS centres opened and enrolment in DPEP Phase I and II

District	NPS opened	NPS enrolment	EGSC opened	EGSC enrolment	AIE (EGS UP) centres opened	AIW enrolment
Bargarh	99	2,175	315	5,910	153	3,519
Bolangir	51	2,212	387	11,267	239	5,497
Boudh	72		62	1,751	10	230
Dhenkanal	92	3,628	264	9,354	03	69
Gajapati	116	4,044	395	11,187	28	644
Kalahandi	31	1,650	1,285	51,790	128	2,944
Kandhmal	57	1,739	336	13,236	89	2,047
Keonjhar	166	6,188	82	2,514	01	23
Koraput	226	6,780	214	6,541	01	23
Malkangiri	81		155	5,018		
Mayurbhanj	200	3,150				
Nawarangpur	95	3,088	448	14,604	66	1,518
Nuapda	44	1,408	181	5,430	19	437
Rayagada	78	2,989	656	20,096	00	00
Sambalpur	01	4,586	476	13,380	97	2,231
Sonpur	55	1,705	106	3,598	43	989

Note: NPS: New Primary School, EGSC: Education Guarantee Scheme Centre, AIE: Alternative and Innovative Education.

Source: OPEPA, 2002, as cited in Government of Orissa, 2003a, pp. 32–33.

Appendix 4.4: Ratio of upper primary schools to primary schools and primary and upper primary schools (Schools per DI)

District	Ratio of upper primary schools to primary school (1)	Primary and upper primary schools (Schools per DI) (2)
Angul	3.82	389.50
Balasore	1.98	546.40
Bargarh	3.54	926.50
Bhadrak	2.02	880.50
Bolangir	4.97	774.00
Boudh	5.32	702.00
Cuttack	3.26	568.80
Deogarh	3.54	534.00
Dhenkanal	2.96	497.30
Gajapati	8.68	1,045.00
Ganjam	4.22	907.75
Jagatsinghpur	2.80	800
Jajpur	2.23	1,097
Jharsuguda	3.70	776
Kalahandi	4.67	1,035
Kandhmal	6.23	
Kendrpada	2.45	934
Keonjhar	2.86	487.60
Khurda	3.04	838.50
Koraput	7.85	1,044.50
Malkangiri	8.72	510.50
Mayurbhanj	3.70	747.20
Nawarangpur	6.06	727.50
Nayagarh	3.01	1,100
Nuapda	4.40	847
Phulbani		587.70
Puri	2.99	637
Rayagada	7.98	384.40
Sambalpur	4.23	414.70
Sonpur	4.32	468.50
Sundergarh	3.94	863.70

Source: Col. 1: Directorate of Elementary Education, Orissa 2001–02; Col. 2: Directorate of Elementary Education, Orissa 2002, as cited in Government of Orissa, 2003a, pp. 62–63.

Appendix 4.5: SSS (Swechchasevi Siksa Sahayaka) position as on 20-03-2002

District	Target	Engaged
Angul	284	218
Balasore	841	646
Bargarh	346	326
Bhadrak	511	351
Bolangir	351	327
Boudh	103	83
Cuttack	595	450
Deogarh	105	76
Dhenkanal	324	253
Gajapati	93	39
Ganjam	575	391
Jagatsinghpur	389	275
Jajpur	607	450
Jharsuguda	150	108
Kalahandi	311	277
Kandhmal	196	158
Kendrpada	504	337
Keonjhar	495	369
Khurda	360	277
Koraput	183	127
Malkangiri	71	56
Mayurbhanj	721	649
Nawarangpur	159	132
Nayagarh	250	202
Nuapda	139	100
Puri	423	326
Rayagada	143	108
Sambalpur	204	169
Sonpur	159	159
Sundergarh	431	353
Total	10,023	7,792 (77.74%)

Source: Directorate of Elementary Education, 2002 as cited in Government of Orissa, 2003a, pp. 47–48.

Appendix 4.6: Number of teachers according to educational qualification

District	No. of sample schools	Gender	No. of teachers: Below class X	Class X	10 +2	Graduates	PG
Boudh	50	Male	7	45	12	22	1
		Female	1	21	12	16	3
		Total	8	66	24	38	4
Kandhma	50	Male	4	30	21	24	2
		Female	1	30	23	13	5
		Total	5	60	44	37	7
Koraput	50	Male	3	27	26	20	2
		Female	1	12	18	17	6
		Total	4	39	44	37	8
Malkangiri	50	Male	0	30	26	27	1
		Female	0	17	17	18	1
		Total	0	47	43	45	2
Mayurbhanj	50	Male	4	36	20	26	0
		Female	2	19	14	24	4
		Total	6	55	34	50	4
Nawarangapur	50	Male	4	44	16	19	2
		Female	1	40	14	21	2
		Total	5	84	30	40	4
Nuapada	50	Male	8	49	21	7	2
		Female	2	25	8	6	1
		Total	10	74	29	13	3
Sonepur	50	Male	8	52	24	17	4
		Female	0	16	22	6	2
		Total	8	68	46	23	6

Source: Baseline Assessment Study (2001), TE and SCERT, Bhubaneswar, as cited in Government of Orissa, 2003a, p. 83.

Appendix 4.7: Achievement of primary school teachers in language

District	80% and above	60–79%	50–59%	30–49%	29% and less	Total teachers	Mean (%)
Balasore	11	12	37	12	00	72	57.19
Kendrapada	10	24	20	22	04	80	57.75
Nuapada	00	04	30	22	09	65	41.30
Sonepur	02	08	21	13	01	45	47.33

(*Continued*)

Appendix 4.7: *(Continued)*

Koraput	00	04	16	28	12	60	39.00
Rayagada	01	03	24	24	08	60	43.23
Kandhamal	00	02	19	17	02	40	38.78
Mayurbhanja	03	04	23	32	08	70	44.69
Nawarangapur	01	02	18	30	14	65	37.14
Malkangiri	00	01	16	33	05	55	33.57

Source: Government of Orissa, 2003a, p 84.

Appendix 4.8: Achievement of primary school teachers in mathematics

District	80% and above	60–79%	50–59%	30–49%	29% and less	Total teachers	Mean (%)
Balasore	08	07	35	20	02	72	56.40
Kendrapada	10	06	39	22	03	80	56.71
Nuapada	02	03	25	24	11	65	46.75
Sonepur	01	04	23	15	02	45	45.36
Koraput	01	06	18	20	15	60	41.17
Rayagada	01	05	20	21	13	60	42.96
Kandhamal	01	03	15	11	10	40	40.75
Mayurbhanja	04	07	18	31	10	70	46.29
Nawarangapur	02	05	26	23	09	65	43.87
Malkangiri	00	04	17	22	12	55	40.83

Source: Government of Orissa, 2003a, p 84.

Appendix 4.9: Regionwise and social groupwise incidence of poverty, rural Orissa, 1999–2000

Region	Social groups			All
	ST	SC	Others	
Coastal	66.63	42.18	24.32	31.74
Southern	92.42	88.90	77.65	87.05
Northern	61.69	57.22	34.67	49.81
Orissa	73.08	52.30	33.29	48.01

Source: Haan De Arjan and Amresh Dubey, 2003 as cited in Government of Orissa, 2004, p 24.

Appendix 4.10: NSS regionwise trend in poverty ratio, rural Orissa

	Year			
Region	**1983–84**	**1987–88**	**1993–94**	**1999–2000**
Coastal	57.90	48.40	45.30	31.80
Southern	80.80	83	68.80	87.20
Northern	75.20	61	45.80	49.90
Orissa	65.29	55.58	48.56	48.01

Source: Haan De Arjan and Amresh Dubey, 2003 as cited in Government of Orissa, 2004, p 24.

Appendix 4.11: Districtwise poverty ratio

District	**1983**	**1987–88**	**1993–94**	**1999–2000**
Balangir	79.83	57.91	42.43	48.79
Balasore	72.15	50.88	33.37	41.39
Cuttack	56.71	43.74	48.96	27.98
Dhenkanal	81.45	54.39	34.68	47.53
Ganjam	56.34	45.22	29.57	18.18
Kalahandi	85.9	84.99	68.19	83.76
Keonjhar	78.27	65.66	62.99	61.92
Koraput	78.2	76.54	57.82	78.62
Mayurbhanj	83.45	64.44	48.19	68.42
Kandhamal	74.57	71.92	75.59	75.42
Puri	49.47	54.99	67.66	45.21
Sambalpur	58.43	54.5	37.78	42.02
Sundergarh	78.31	53.56	45.15	36.48
Mean	71.78	59.90	50.18	51.98
SD	11.67	11.74	14.39	19.39

Source: Haan De Arjan and Amresh Dubey, 2003, as cited in Government of Orissa, 2004, p 25.

Appendix 4.12: Development ranking of districts in Orissa in 1990

District	Agriculture	Industry	Basic infrastructure	Total development
Sundergarh	7	1	1	1
Puri	2	2	2	2
Sambalpur	4	3	3	3
Cuttack	1	5	4	4
Dhenkanal	8	4	5	5
Keonjhar	11	6	6	6
Ganjam	5	10	8	7
Balangir	3	9	12	8
Balasore	6	10	10	9
Mayurbhanj	9	8	9	10
Koraput	12	7	11	11
Phulbani	13	12	7	12
Kalahandi	10	11	13	13

Source: Meher and Pasayat, 2004, p 40.

Appendix 4.13: Poverty in Orissa, 1999–2000, NSSO 55th round

Social group	HCR	Contribution to poverty	Monthly per capita consumption expenditure	No. of sample households
ST	73.10	41.01	284.55	861
SC	52.30	22.74	351.10	747
OBC	39.70	26.02	394.96	1067
Others	24.01	10.23	477.80	800
Total	48.14	100	372.95	3477
Coastal region	31.81	31.44	425.18	1795
Southern region	87.14	33.40	246.29	575
Northern region	49.84	35.15	368.59	1107

Source: Haan De Arjan and Amresh Dubey, 2003, Extreme Deprivation in Remote Areas of India: Social Exclusion as Explanatory Concept, paper for Manchester Conference on Chronic Poverty, as cited in Panda Manoj, 2004, p 177.

Appendix 4.14: Growth of literacy in Orissa

Year	Literacy rate
1951	15.80
1961	21.66
1971	26.18
1981	33.62
1991	49.09
2001	63.61

Source: Government of Orissa, 2003a.

Appendix 4.15: Natural calamities in Orissa

	1961–70	1971–80	1981–90	1991–2000
Normal years	2	0	4	3
Droughts	4	2	2	4
Whirlwinds, tornados, cyclones	4	5	2	2
Floods and droughts	0	3	2	1

Source: Government of Orissa, 1996, DBS, 2002, as cited in Nayak, 2004, p 210.

Appendix 4.16: Growth of education in Orissa

Item	1947–48	1950–51	1960–61	1969–70	1978–79	1988–89
Primary schools	6,814	9,801	21,858	26,554	34,593	39,293
Enrolment (lakh)	2.55	3.15	14.29	18.26	26.12	35.02
Middle schools	286	501	1,307	4,047	7,150	9,125
Enrolment (lakh)	0.32	0.40	1.07	3.18	5.01	9.70
Secondary schools	106	172	452	1543	2167	4239
Enrolment (lakh)	0.15	0.16	0.44	1.71	2.63	7.66
College	12	14	29	77	106	433
Enrolment (lakh)	0.4	0.6	0.11	0.42	0.88	2.6

Source: Education in Orissa 1988–89, Directorate of Elementary Education (Statistics Cell), Bhubaneswar, Orissa.

Appendix 4.17: Growth of education in Orissa, 1991–92 to 1997–98

Item	1991–92	1992–93	1993–94	1994–95	1995–96	1996–97	1997–98 (p)
Primary schools	54,595	54,652	55,052	56,156	56,656	65,552	65,552
Formal	41,204	41,204	41,604	41,604	42,104	42,104	42,104
Non-formal	13,391	13,448	13,448	14,552	14,552	23,448	23,448
Enrolment (000s)	3,989	4,042	4,,097	4,179	4,265	4,531	4,591
Formal	3,654	3,706	3761	3,815	3,887	3,945	4,005
Non-formal	335	336	336	364	378	386	586
Teachers	1,11,499	1,15,460	1,18,788	1,20,392	1,25,092	1,34,488	1,34,488
Formal	98,108	1,02,012	1,05,340	1,05,840	1,10,540	1,11,040	1,11,040
Non-formal	13,391	13,448	13,448	14,552	14,552	23,448	23,448
Upper primary school	10,941	11,308	11,816	12,256	12,406	12,406	12,406
Enrolment (000s)	1,076	1,113	1,166	1,207	1,292	1,318	1,384
Teachers	39,955	39,751	39,951	39,993	40,206	40,706	40,706

Source: Economic Survey 1998–99, Government of Orissa.

Appendix 4.18: Compound rate of growth (%)

Year	Primary schools	Upper primary schools
2001/1947	3.43	7.08
1986/1947	4.39	8.86
1990/1986	1.63	2.30
2001/1986	0.68	2.02
2001/1990	0.20	1.70

Source: Tilak J.B.G., 2003, Education in Orissa, as cited in Government of Orissa, 2003a, p 26.

Appendix 4.19: Distribution of primary school by management

	Number	Percentage
Government primary school	35,339	85.45
Primary section in upper primary school (I–VIII)	4,683	11.32
Primary section in high school (I–X)	244	0.59
Primary section in higher secondary school (I–XII)	27	0.07
Primary schools under SC/ST Development Department	1,062	2.57
Total government schools	41,355	100
Schools under private sector		
Minority managed and aided primary schools	273	36.45
Others (English medium, Saraswati Sishu Mandir, etc.) without recieving grant-in-aid from government	476	63.55
Total	749 (01.78)	100
Grand Total	**42,104**	**100**

Source: Directorate of Elementary Education, Orissa, 2002–03, as cited in Government of Orissa, 2003a, p 27.

Appendix 4.20: Access of schooling facilities in Orissa

District	Habitations	Unserved habitations for primary school	% SC population	% ST population	Out of school aged disabled children 6–14 years
1	2	3	4	5	6
Angul	2,396	527	16.82	11.68	6,340
Balasore	3,816	465	18.57	10.57	7,917
Bargarh	1,712	123	18.44	19.56	3,894
Bhadrak	2,341	238	21.71	01.69	5,736
Bolangir	2,328	148	15.39	22.06	5,668
Boudh	1,329	307	19.64	12.92	1,293
Cuttack	2,788	194	18.19	03.49	10,108
Deogarh	865	249	14.60	33.31	1,883
Dhenkanal	1,841	306	16.03	12.69	5,763
Gajapati	1,817	564	08.77	47.88	1,757
Ganjam	3,680	501	17.91	02.93	12,353
Jagatsinghpur	1,962	136	21.72	00.61	6,210
Jajpur	2,408	152	22.87	07.40	8,338
Jharsuguda	903	186	17.15	31.88	1,997
Kalahandi	3,465	798	17.01	28.88	3,854
Kandhmal	1,792	100	18.21	51.51	2,090
Kendrpada	3,238	541	19.83	00.40	7,094
Keonjhar	1,730	116	11.49	44.52	11,643
Khurda	3,788	1,169	13.62	05.14	5,202
Koraput	1,768	560	13.41	50.67	2,897
Malkangiri	5,430	752	19.96	52.36	2,717
Mayurbhanj	2,110	405	06.99	57.87	8,580
Nawarangpur	1,823	471	15.09	55.27	5,160
Nayagarh	1,176	150	13.78	05.96	5,257
Nuapda	3,156	738	13.09	35.95	2,085
Puri	2,974	401	18.56	00.27	7,883
Rayagada	2,963	1,049	14.07	56.04	5,763
Sambalpur	1,968	1,049	17.07	35.08	2,099
Sonpur	870	78	22.11	09.50	1,511
Sundergarh	4,711	911	08.78	50.74	7,249
Total	73,148	12,839			

Source: Col. 3: Directorate of Elementary Education, 2002, as cited in Government of Orissa, 2003a, pp. 35–36; Col. 6: OPEPA, 2002, as cited in Government of Orissa, 2003a, pp. 35–36.

Appendix 4.21: Financial support to primary education in Orissa (in crore)

Year	Total receipt (current price)	Total revenue expenditure	Revenue expenditure (RE) on education	RE on education as % of total revenue expenditure	Total capital expenditure	Capital expenditure (CE) on education	CE on education as % of total capital expenditure	Plan expenditure on education	Non-Plan Expenditure on Education	Total Expenditure on Education
1950–51	53.97	12.0	1.380	11.50	5.9				1.370	1.370
1951–52	57.37	10.9	1.260	11.56	9.1				1.520	1.520
1952–53	50.5	11.6	1.476	12.72	7.7				1.480	1.480
1953–54	60.6	13.2	1.766	13.38	10.1				1.740	1.740
1954–55	56.1	15.5	1.903	12.28	13.9				1.900	1.900
1955–56	73.9	24.2	2.509	10.37	15.7				2.510	2.510
1956–57	72.8	22.8	2.798	12.27	15.5				2.800	2.800
1957–58	79.8	23.5	3.118	13.27	20.4				3.120	3.120
1958–59	92.5	25.9	3.355	12.95	11.6				3.350	3.350
1959–60	115.3	24.7	4.072	16.49	14.8			1.600	2.410	4.070
1960–61	119.7	35.5	4.330	12.20	11.8			1.770	2.560	4.350
1961–62	161.6	52.6	6.725	12.79	14.2			1.080	5.640	6.720
1962–63	214.2	65.9	7.681	11.66	26.9			2.210	5.470	7.680
1963–64	247.9	71.1	7.896	11.11	30.5			2.270	5.630	7.900
1964–65	333.7	79.2	9.650	12.18	41.7			3.600	6.050	9.650
1965–66	333.9	91.3	10.517	11.52	32.6			4.060	6.460	10.520
1966–67	353.3	104.4	12.623	12.09	34.3			1.090	11.530	11.620
1967–68	362.5	113.2	15.984	14.12	17.8			2.220	13.760	15.980

(*Continued*)

Appendix 4.21: *(Continued)*

1968–69	423.8	131.8	18.790	14.26	24.8			2.430	16.360	18.790
1969–70	432.5	131.9	20.400	15.47	22.1			0.900	19.490	20.390
1970–71	434.4	139.9	23.480	16.78	25.0			1.820	21.820	23.640
1971–72	513.9	165.6	27.220	16.44	29.9			3.300	23.970	27.360
1972–73	591.4	192.8	29.630	15.37	32.4			4.880	25.680	30.560
1973–74	568.9	212.5	34.760	16.36	38.7			4.880	28.650	33.530
1974–75	605.9	223.6	46.800	20.93	47.4	0.398	0.84	2.380	44.410	46.790
1975–76	756.9	276.4	58.810	21.29	57.7	1.334	2.31	4.900	53.900	58.800
1976–77	894.1	308.2	64.940	21.07	55.7	1.197	2.15	7.420	57.120	64.520
1977–78	1003.2	340.2	70.830	20.82	82.5	0.932	1.13	9.940	60.340	70.240
1978–79	1095.3	412.7	80.690	19.55	111.5	1.000	0.90	12.460	63.560	76.020
1979–80	1180.3	459.6	86.650	18.85	146.7	1.594	1.09	14.980	66.780	81.760
1980–81	1257.3	540.5	106.100	19.63	187.8	1.738	0.93	17.500	70.000	87.500
1981–82	1715.1	573.6	131.500	22.93	167.9	1.748	1.04	20.020	76.220	93.240
1982–83	2375.3	824.6	136.040	16.50	182.4	1.961	1.08	22.540	76.460	99.000
1983–84	2778.6	782.7	153.040	19.55	184.5	2.227	1.21	25.060	79.660	104.720
1984–85	2730.2	896.8	175.100	19.52	235.8	3.440	1.46	27.580	115.710	143.290
1985–86	3085.4	1000.9	168.560	16.84	257.2	8.500	3.30	25.930	166.070	192.000
1986–87	3412.3	1248	251.310	20.14	323	14.338	4.44	25.070	216.430	241.530
1987–88	3980.7	1407.6	279.990	19.89	390.2	3.616	0.93	31.970	243.530	275.500
1988–89	4632.2	1693.4	329.480	19.46	463.3	14.793	3.19	56.280	267.220	323.500
1989–90	4832.2	2003.2	407.940	20.36	452.8	17.099	3.78	119.890	315.870	435.760
1990–91	6097	2190.5	444.550	20.29	651.1	9.588	1.47	98.630	326.090	424.720

(Continued)

Appendix 4.21: *(Continued)*

1991–92	6877.2	2635	538.300	20.43	655.7	4.658	0.71	65.920	452.280	518.200
1992–93	8003.9	3048.9	698.070	22.90	579.9	9.160	1.58	57.950	530.350	588.300
1993–94	8831.3	3482.2	718.260	20.63	563.3	5.117	0.91	110.750	545.960	656.710
1994–95	9228.1	4035.5	858.000	21.26	546.7	1.318	0.24	168.280	678.340	846.620
1995–96	10866.7	4697.9	953.000	20.29	439.3	4.200	0.96	199.650	746.700	946.350
1996–97	12017	5117.2	1024.000	20.01	864.5	12.560	1.45	231.020	815.000	1046.020
1997–98	14035.7	5536.5	1166.000	21.06	846.3	2.600	0.31	262.390	883.300	1145.690
1998–99	15379.9	7318.3	1431.000	19.55	962.3	3.700	0.38	293.760	951.600	1245.360
1999–2000	15716.6	8061.9	1720.000	21.33	1073.2	9.060	0.84	325.130	1019.900	1345.030

Source: Mishra Prahalad, 2002, Study on State Finance of Elementary Education (Sponsored by The Orissa Primary Education Programme Authority), Xavier Institute of Management, Bhubaneswar.

Appendix 4.22: Financial support to primary education in Orissa (in crore)

Year	Total receipt	Total revenue expenditure	Revenue expenditure (RE) on education, sports, art and culture	RE on education as % of total RE	Total capital expenditure	Capital expenditure (CE) on education, sports, art and culture	CE on education, sports, art and culture as % of total capital expenditure	Total expenditure on education, sports, art, culture as % of total expenditure
2000–01 (A)	15,726.97	8,828.79	1,741.58	19.73	7,378.35	18.90	0.26	10.86
2001–02 (RE)	19,202.16	10,224.1	1,762.28	17.24	9,851.35	10.32	0.10	8.83
2002–03 (RE)	20,398.95	10,896.31	1,880.39	17.26	9,648.65	22.95	0.24	9.26
2003–04 (BE)	16,354.74	12,520.76	1,923.60	15.36	4,342.57	71.69	1.65	11.83

Note: Expenditure on general education averages a little more than 97% out of the total revenue expenditure on general education, sports, art and culture. 'RE' denotes revised estimate and 'BE' denotes budget estimate. RE-Revised Estimate reflects the real situation than the 'BE'

Source: CYSD, 2003, A Critical Reflection on Education Budget: Orissa, Centre for Youth and Social Development, Bhubaneswar.

Appendix 4.23: Financial support to primary education in Orissa (in crore)

	Total non-plan expenditure	Total plan expenditure	State plan expenditure	Central plan expenditure	Centrally sponsored plan expenditure	Total expenditure
2000–01(A)	Ele 929.06	Ele 97.47	Ele 90.03	Ele 0	Ele 7.44	Ele 1,026.54
	Sec 111.52	Sec 329.27	Sec 307.67	Sec 21.60	Sec 0	Sec 440.80
2001–02 (RE)	Ele 940.39	Ele 136.86	Ele 58.69	Ele 42.15	Ele 36.02	Ele 1,077.26
	Sec 115.30	Sec 186.56	Sec 171.46	Sec 15.10	Sec 0	Sec 301.86
2002–03 (RE)	Ele 1,053.80	Ele 75.07	Ele 19.99	Ele 18.04	Ele 37.04	Ele 1,128.87
	Sec 440.96	Sec 29.8	Sec 16.30	Sec 13.50	Sec 0	Sec 470.76
2003–04 (BE)	Ele 987.95	Ele 152.31	Ele 83.31	Ele 0	Ele 69.00	Ele 1,140.26
	Sec 417.57	Sec 42.59	Sec 42.59	Sec .02	Sec 0	Sec 460.06
2004–05 (RE)						Ele 1,121.59
2005–06 (BE)						Ele 1,256.15
2006–07 (BE)						Ele 1,321.66

Note: 'A' denotes actual, 'Ele' denotes elementary and 'Sec' denotes secondary education. 'RE' denotes revised estimate and 'BE' denotes budget estimate. 'RE' reflects the real situation than the 'BE'.

Source: CYSD, 2003; CYSD, 2006.

Chapter 7

Appendix 7.1: Infrastructure of schools

Raigad
Three pucca buildings; enough rooms; more than sufficient for children. The school has a boundary wall with iron gates, tubewell and a big garden. There is a hostel.
Classroom: Very simple; nothing else is there in the classroom except some homilies and directions (east, west, north, south).
TLM use was not observed.

Tikung
School by the roadside; there is a hostel.
Two asbestos buildings sufficient for children.
Big garden, swing, seesaw, tubewell, boundary wall with iron gates,
Veranda wall – Drawings of Laxman Nayak (freedom fighter from Koraput), Gapabandhu Das (freedom fighter from Puri); use of TLM was not observed.

Bakar
One two-storied pucca building and one asbestos building sufficient for children, tubewell, toilet, boundary walls.
The classroom walls: One big blackboard, maps (India, Orissa, Koraput, tree and its parts, solar and lunar eclipse, words).
TLM is adequate and use of TLM was frequent.

Cisakh
Two asbestos buildings. Pucca building under construction. There is a hostel.
School has a tubewell, toilet, boundary wall with iron gates and a nice small garden.
Classroom: Asbestos classroom about 20 × 15 feet; it is not sufficient for children; other rooms are used for hostel purpose. One blackboard, one iron coat, two plastic chairs and one wooden table in the classroom.
Maps: Great men, Koraput, Orissa, birds, Azadi Ke Senani, fruits, flowers, domestic animals, vegetables, pollution, environment.
East, West, North, South is written on the walls. Wall clock; pictures related to letters, body parts, great men, fruits, one letter and different formation in a circle.
I saw that all the children's uniforms here were much cleaner and healthier. There are two cycles for girls.

Baisakh
One pucca building, not fully sufficient for children, one class is seated on the veranda; toilet, drinking water from a spring very nearby, one swing, one seesaw.
Classroom: There is provision for temporary partitioning so that one hall can be converted into two rooms. I did not see this anywhere else. The wall is made into blackboard up to a height of one meter from the floor so that children can write freely.
TLM: One globe, numbers, ludo, letter boards, cards with pictures, drawing aids, letter writing aids, badminton racket, maps, a board where one can fix letters and draw by fixing different strings. Wall clock came as a free gift when all these supplies were bought. All these were brought of the INR 500 annual TLM grant per teacher. SSS Manty showed me the TLM. Extensive TLM use was observed.

Upai Public School (Private)
Rental pucca building, not sufficient for children; benches for sitting; Maruti van for commuting.
TLM: TLM use was not observed in standard 3.

Kesli
One asbestos building and that is not sufficient for children.
Classroom walls: States and their capitals, four directions, national anthem, districts of Orissa, days of week in English and Oriya, months, numbers, seasons; all these in Oriya: maps of animals, human skeleton, vegetables.
TLM: Its use was not observed.

Raigad
One asbestos house; it is sufficient for the handful children who come now.

Daliamb EGS
No building

BIBLIOGRAPHY

Agar, Michael H., 1986, *Speaking of Ethnography*, New Delhi: Sage Publications.

Aggarwal, J. C., 1984, *Landmarks in the History of Modern Indian education*, Delhi: Vikas Publishing House (Pvt.) Ltd.

Akai, Hisako, 1999, *The Relevance and Effectiveness of Elementary Teacher Education Programs in DIET*, New Delhi: Department of Teacher Education and Extension, NCERT.

Alexander, Robin, 2000, *Culture and Pedagogy: International Comparisons in Primary Education*, Oxford, UK: Blackwell Publishers.

All India Federation of Education Association, 1966, *Handbook on Teachers Organizations in India*, New Delhi: All India Federation of Education Association.

Althusser, L., 1972, 'Ideology and Ideological State Apparatus' In: Cosin B. R. (Ed.), *Education, Structure and Society*, pp. 242–280, Harmondsworth: Penguin.

Anand, S. P., 1996, *Development of a Motivational Package to Promote Teacher Effectiveness*, Bhubaneswar: Regional Institute of Education.

Anderson, Lorin W., 2004, *Increasing Teacher Effectiveness*, Paris: UNESCO and International Institute of Educational Planning retrieved from http://unesdoc.unesco.org/images/0013/001376/137629e.pdf on October 10.

Anitha, B. K., 2005, 'Quality and the Social Context of Rural Schools', *Contemporary Education Dialogue*, 3(1): 28–60.

Apple, Michael W., 2001, Markets, Standards, Teaching and Teacher Education, *Journal of Teacher Education*, 52(3): 182–196 retrieved from http://jte.sagepub.com on April 22, 2008.

Apple, Michael W., 1995, *Education and Power*, London: Routledge.

Archer, M., 1984, *Social Origins of Educational Systems*, London: Sage Publications.

Arora, G. L., 2002, *Teachers and Their Teaching: Need for New Perspective*, New Delhi: Ravi Books.

Atkinson, P. A. and Delamont, S., 1980, The Two Traditions in Educational Ethnography, *British Journal of Sociology of Education,* 1(2): 139–152.

Atkinson, P. A., Delamont, S. and M. Hammersley, 1988, Qualitative Research Traditions, *Review of Educational Research,* 38(2): 231–250.

Bacharach, Samuel B., Scott C. Bauer and Sharon Conley, 1986, Organizational Analysis of Stress: The Case of Elementary and Secondary Schools, *Work and Occupations,* 13: 7–32, accessed on July 1, 2008.

Barber, Bernard, 1963, Some Problems in the Sociology of Profession, *Daedalus,* Fall: 669–688.

Barnard, H. (Ed.), 1861, *The American Journal of Education,* 10(25): New York: Johnson Reprint Corporation.

Barnard, H. (Ed.), 1863, *The American Journal of Education,* 13(33): (New Series No. 8), New York: Johnson Reprint Corporation.

Barnard, H. (Ed.), 1868, *The American Journal of Education,* 17(4): New York: Johnson Reprint Corporation.

Bate, Tony, Bob Gough and Peter Stammers, 1999, The Role of Central Government and its Agencies in the Continuing Professional Development of Teachers: An Evaluation of Recent Changes in its Financing in England, *Journal of in-Service Education,* 25(2): 321–335.

Bates, Richard and Tony Townsend, 2007, 'The Future of Teacher Education: Challenges and Opportunities' In: Townsend and Bates, (Eds.) *Handbook of Teacher Education, Globalisation, Standards and Professionalism in Times of Change,* pp. 727–734, Dordrecht, Netherlands: Springer.

Bates, Richard, 2007, 'Regulation and Autonomy in Teacher Education: System or Democracy' In: Townsend and Bates (Eds.), *Handbook of Teacher Education, Globalisation, Standards and Professionalism in Times of Change,* pp. 127–140, Dordrecht, Netherlands: Springer.

Batra, Poonam, 2005, Voice and Agency of Teachers: Missing Link in National Curriculum Framework 2005, *Economic and Political Weekly,* XL(40): 4347–4356.

Beer, John J. and W. David Lewis, 1963, Aspects of The Professionalisation of Science, *Daedalus,* Fall: 764–784.

Behar, S. C., 'Teachers' Search for an Identity' In: Dhar T. N. (Ed.), 1996, *Professional Status of Teachers,* pp. 59–73, New Delhi: National Council for Teacher Education.

Ben-Peretz, Miriam, 2001, The Impossible Role of Teacher Educators in a Changing World, *Journal of Teacher Education*, 52(1): 48–56.

Bernard, H. Russel, 1995, *Research Methods in Anthropology*, New Delhi: Altamira Press.

Bernstein, B., 1997, 'Class and Pedagogies: Visible and Invisible' In: Halsey A. H., et al (Ed.), pp. 59–79.

Biddle, Bruce J., Thomas L. Good and Ivor F. Goodson, (Eds.), 1997, *International Handbook of Teachers and Teaching*, London: Kluwer Academic Press.

Bottery, Mike and Nigel Wright, 1997, Impoverishing a Sense of Professionalism: Who's to Blame?, *Educational Management Administration Leadership*, 25(1): 7–24 retrieved from http://ema.sagepub.com on April 13, 2008.

Boucher, Leon, 1985, 'Teachers Unions: Some Swedish Perspectives' In: Lawn Martin, (Ed.) pp. 141–157.

Bourdieu, Pierre, 1997, 'The Forms of Capital' In: Halsey A. H., et al (Eds.), pp. 46–58.

Bourdieu, Pierre, 1977, 'Cultural Reproduction and Social Reproduction' In: Karabel J. and Halsey A.H. (Eds.), pp. 487–511.

Bourdieu, P. and J. Passeron, 1977, *Reproduction in Education, Society and Culture*, London: Sage Publications.

Boyd, W., 1950, *The History of Western Education*, London: A and C Black.

Broudy, H. S., 1962, *Building a Philosophy of Education*, Englewood Cliffs, New Jersey: Prentice Hall.

Brubacher, J. S., 1947, *A History of the Problems of Education*, New York: McGraw Hill.

Brubacher, J. S., 1950, *Modern Philosophies of Education*, New York: McGraw Hill Book Company.

Burbules, Nicholas C. and Kathleen Densmore, 1991, The Limits of Making Teaching a Profession, *Educational Policy*, 5(1): 44–63 retrieved from http://epx.sagepub.com on April 23, 2008.

Burke, Andrew, 1998, 'Teacher Professionalisation and Teacher Empowerment' In: NCERT, *Teacher Empowerment and School Effectiveness at Primary Stage*—A Compendium of Studies Presented in the International Seminar on Teacher Empowerment and School Effectiveness at Primary Stage Organized by NCERT in New Delhi on 23–25 July 1997.

Caldwell, Brian J., 2000, Strategic Intentions for Professionals in World Class Schools, *Prospects*, 30(2): 189–200.

Cambourne, Brian, 2001, Conditions for Literacy, *Learning*, 55(4): 414–429.

Carr, David, 2000, *Professionalism and Ethics in Teaching*, London: Routledge.

CYSD, 1990, *Evaluation of Adult Education Program*, Bhubaneswar: Centre for Youth and Social Development.

CYSD, 2003, *A Critical Reflection on Education Budget*, Bhubaneswar: Centre for Youth and Social Development.

CYSD, 2006, *Budget Watch 2: Pattern of State Spending in Orissa: A Summary Report*, Bhubaneswar: Centre for Youth and Social Development.

Chambliss, J. J. (Ed.), 1996, *Philosophy of Education: An Encyclopedia*, New York and London: Garland Publishing Inc

Chapman, M., 1995, Designing Literacy Learning Experiences in a Multiage Classroom, *Language Arts*, 72: 416–428.

Charney, R. S., 1992, *Teaching Children to Care: Management in the Responsive Classroom*, Greenfield, MA: Northeast Foundation for Children.

Cheng, Yin Cheong, Magdalen Mo Ching and Kwok Tung Tsui, 2001, *Teaching Effectiveness and Teacher Development: Towards a New Knowledge*, Hong Kong: Kluwer Academic Press.

Chopra, R. K., 1993. *Status of Teachers in India*, New Delhi: National Council of Educational Research and Training.

Clarke, Prema, 2001, *Teaching and Learning: The Culture of Pedagogy*, New Delhi: Sage Publications.

Collins, R., 1977, Functional and Conflict Theories of Educational Stratification, *American Sociological Review*, 36(6): 1002–1019.

Collins, Randall, 1979, *The Credential Society*, New York: Academic Press.

Cosin, B. R., 1972, *Education, Structure and Society: Selected Readings*, London: Open University Press.

Curtis, S. J. and M. E. A. Boultwood, 1953, *A Short History of Educational Ideas*, London: University Tutorial Press Ltd.

Darling, Hammmond Linda and Gary Sykes (Eds.), 1999, *Teaching as the Learning Profession: Handbook of Policy and Practice*, San Fransisco: Jossey-Bass.

Das, D. P., 1970, Odisare Annunta Shrenira Bikasa (Development of Underdeveloped Sections in Orissa), *Utkal Prasanga*, August: 6–48.

Das, Amulya, 2003, 'Community Participation and School Management' In: Government of Orissa, 2003a, 264–296.

Das, N. D. and Tripathi P. B., 2003, 'Strengthening Teaching of Science in Schools' In: Government of Orissa, 2003a, 332–348.

Day, Christopher, 2007, 'School, Reform and Transitions in Teacher Professionalism and Identity' In: Townsend and Bates (Eds.), *Handbook of Teacher Education, Globalisation, Standards and Professionalism in Times of Change*, Dordrecht, Netherlands: Springer, 597–612.

Delamont, S. (Ed.), 1987, *The Primary School Teacher*, London: The Falmer Press.

Demaine, J., 1981, (Reprinted in 1982, 1983), *Contemporary Theories in the Sociology of Education*, London: The MacMillan Press Ltd.

Denzin, N. and Lincoln, Y. (Eds.), 1994, *Handbook of Qualitative Research*, Thousand Oaks, Caliofrnia: Sage Publications.

Department of Education, Office of Postsecondary Education, US, 2002, *Meeting the Highly Qualified Teachers Challenge: The Secretary's Annual Report on Teacher Quality*, Washington DC.

Devi, R. S., 1968, 'Origin and Development of Teacher Education in India' In: S. N. Mukherji (Ed.), 1–40.

Dewey, J., 1916, *Democracy and Education*, New York: The Macmillan Company.

Dhal, Prafulla Kumar and Brahmotri Biswal, 'Out of School Children in Orissa' In: Government of Orissa, 2003a, 380–383.

Dhar, T. N. (Ed.), 1996, *Professional Status of Teachers*, New Delhi: National Council for Teacher Education.

Di, Giulio R.C., 2000, *Positive Classroom Management: A Step-By-Step Guide To Helping Students Succeed*, Thousand Oaks: Corwin Press.

Dombey, Henrietta, 2003, Interactions between Teachers, Children and Texts in Three Primary Classrooms in England, *Journal of Early Childhood Literacy*, 3(1): 37–58 retrieved from http://ecl.sagepub.com on April 19, 2008.

Doyle, W., 1986, 'Classroom Organisation and Management' In: M. Wittrock (Ed.), *Handbook of Research on Teaching* (3rd ed.), pp. 392–431, New York: Macmillan.

Dreben, R., 1977, 'The Contribution of Schooling to the Learning of Norms' In: Karabel J. and Halsey A. H., *Power and Ideology in Education*, pp. 544–550, Oxford: Oxford University Press.

Dreikurs, R., Grunwald, B. G. and F. C. Pepper, 1998 (2nd ed.), *Maintaining Sanity in the Classroom: Classroom Management Techniques*, Washington, D.C.: Taylor & Francis.

Duke, D. (Ed.), 1979, *Classroom Management: The 78th Yearbook of the National Society for the Study of Education, Part II*, Chicago: University of Chicago Press.

Dwibedi, Jugala Kishore, 1968, Odisare Ingrajanka Prathamika Siksaniti (Policy on Primary Education of the English in Orissa, *Siksaloka,* No. 2, June: 21–24.

Dyer, Caroline, 1996, *The Improvement of Primary School Quality in India: Successes and Failures of Operation Blackboard*, Edinburgh Papers in South Asian Studies, Number 4 retrieved from http://www.csas.ed.ac.uk/fichiers/DYER.pdf on October 10, 2008.

Emmer, E. T., 1994, Towards an Understanding of the Primacy of Classroom Management and Discipline, *Teaching Education*, 6(1): 65–69 accessed on October 15, 2008 from http://pdfserve.informaworld.com/375584_758077589_757655329.pdf

Emmer, Edmund T., 2001, Classroom Management: A Critical Part of Educational Psychology, With Implications for Teacher Education, *Educational Psychologist,* 36(3): 103–112.

Englert, C. S., 1984, Measuring Teacher Effectiveness from the Teacher's Point of View, *Focus on Exceptional Children,* 17(2): 1–14.

Evetts, Julia, 2003, The Sociological Analysis of Professionalism: Occupational Change in the Modern World, *International Sociology,* 18(2): 395–415 retrieved from http://iss.sagepub.com on July 1, 2008.

Fenn, Richard K., 2003, 'Religion and the Secular: The Sacred and the Profane: The Scope of the Argument' In: Fenn Richard K. (Ed.), *The Blackwell Companion to Sociology of Religion*, pp. 3–22, London: Wiley-Blackwell.

Fessler, Ralph and Judith C. Christensen, *The Teacher Career Cycle: Understanding and Guiding The Professional Development of Teachers,* New York: Allyn and Bacon.

Fields, Marjorie V., 1988, Talking and Writing: Explaining the Whole Language Approach to Parents, *The Reading Teacher,* 41(9): 896–908.

Fields, Marjorie V., Katherine L. Spengler and M. Lee Dorris, 1991, *Let's Begin Reading Right: Developmentally Appropriate Beginning Literacy*, New York: MacMillan Publishing Company.

Freire, P., 1972, *Pedagogy of the Oppressed*, London, Harmondsworth, Middlesex: Penguin Books Ltd.

Freire, P., 1973, *Education: The Practice of Freedom*, London: Writers and Readers Publishing Co-operative.

Frost, J. L. (Ed.), 1968, *Early Childhood Education Rediscovered: Readings*, New York: Holt, Rienhart and Winston, Inc.

Fwu, Bih-Jen and Hsiou-Huai Wang, 2002, The Social Status of Teachers in Taiwan, *Comparative Education Review*, 38(2): 211–224.

Gandhi, M. K., 1962, *True Education*, Ahmedabad: Navjivan Publishing House.

Geer, B., 1966, Occupational Commitment and the Teaching Profession, *School Review*, 77(1): 31–47.

Ghadei, P. C., 1993, Bidyalaya o Ganasiksa bibhagara Safalya (Success of the School and Mass Education Department), *Utkal Prasanga*, March: 35–37.

Gideonse, Hendrik D., 1993, The Governance of Teacher Education and Systemic Reform, *Educational Policy*, 7(4): 395–426 retrieved from http://epx.sagepub.com on April 22, 2008.

Gilroy, Peter, 1998, New Labor and Teacher Education in England and Wales: The First 500 Days, *Journal of Education for Teaching*, 24(3): 221–230.

Ginsberg, Mark and Lindsay Beverly (Eds.), 1995, *The Political Dimension in Teacher Education: Comparative Perspectives on Policy Formation, Socialization and Society*, London: The Falmer Press.

Giroux, H., 1983, *Theory and Resistance in Education*, London: Bergin & Garvey.

Gleeson, Denis and David Knights, 2006, Challenging Dualism: Public Professionalism in 'Troubled' Times, *Sociology*, 40(2): 277–295 retrieved from http://soc.sagepub.com on July 1, 2008.

Goatley, Virginia J., 2000, Exploring School Learning Communities: Students' Early Literacy Transformations, *Reading & Writing Quarterly*, 16 (4):337-360.

Goodson, Ivor, 2000, The Principled Professional, *Prospects*, 30(2): 181–188.

Gordon, June A., 2005, The Crumbling Pedestal: Changing Images of Japanese Teachers, *Journal of Teacher Education*, 56(5): 459–470.

Government of India, 1972, *The Report of the Secondary Education Commission, 1972*, http://www.education.nic.in/cd50years/q/3C/3U/Toc.htm, accessed on March 29, 2008.

Government of Orissa, 1989, *Education in Orissa, 1988–89*, Bhubaneswar: Directorate of Elementary Education, Statistics Cell.

—, 1993, *Education for All by 2000 AD: Orissa State Plan of Action, Report of The Task Force: A Draft*, Bhubaneswar: Department of School and Mass Education.

—, 1996, *Education in Orissa, 1995–96 (Manuscript)*, Bhubaneswar: Directorate of Mass Education, Statistics Cell.

—, 2001, *White Paper on Orissa State Finances*, Bhubaneswar: Department of Finance.

—, 2003, *Review of Primary Education in Orissa: A Draft Paper for Discussion*, Bhubaneswar: Department of School and Mass Education.

—, 2003a, *Vision 2020: An Agenda for School and Mass Education – Report of the Task Force*, Bhubaneswar: Department of School and Mass Education.

—, 2004, *Human Development Report 2004*.

Govinda, R. and Josephine Y., 2004, *Para Teachers in India: A Review*, Paris: UNESCO.

Govinda, R. and Rashmi Diwan (Eds.), 2003, *Community Participation and Empowerment in Primary Education*, New Delhi: Sage Publications.

Goyal, U. C. and R. K. Chopra, 1990, *Elementary School Teachers: A Profile*, New Delhi: NCERT.

Griffith, Francis, 1973, *A Handbook for the Observation of Teaching and Learning*, Michigan, Midland: Pendell Publishing Company.

Haan, De Arjan and Amresh Dubey, 2003, *Poverty in Orissa: Divergent Trends: With Some Thoughts on Measurement Issues*, Mimeo, Paper Presented at the Workshop on Monitoring of Poverty in Orissa, 26–27 February, Bhubaneswar.

Hall, Roland, 1967, 'Dialectic' In: Paul Edwards (Editor in Chief), *The Encyclopedia of Philosophy*, pp. 385–389, New York: The Macmillan Company and The Free Press.

Hallack, Jacques and Muriel Poisson, 2007, *Corrupt Schools, Corrupt Universities What Can Be Done*, Paris: UNESCO and International Institute of Educational Planning retrieved from http://unesdoc.unesco.org/images/0015/001502/150259e.pdf on October 10.

Halliday, M. A. K., 1975, *Learning How to Mean: Explorations in The Development of Language*, London: Edward Arnold.

Hallinan, Maureen T. and Vladimir T. Khmelkov, 2001, Recent Developments in Teacher Education in The United States of America, *Journal of Education for Teaching*, 27(2): 175–158.

Halsey, A. H., Hugh Lauder, Phiilip Brown and Amy Stuart Wells, 1997, *Education, Culture, Economy and Society*, Oxford: Oxford University Press.

Hammersley, Martin and Paul Atkinson, 1983, *Ethnography: Principles in Practice*, London and New York: Tavistock Publications.

Hammmond, Darling Linda and Gary Sykes (Eds.), 1999, *Teaching As the Learning Profession: Handbook of Policy and Practice*, San Fransisco: Jossey-Bass.

Hansen, J. Merrell, 1979, Discipline and Classroom Management: Different Strokes for Different Folks, *NASSP Bulletin*, 63: 40–47 retrieved from http://bul.sagepub.com on April 18, 2008.

Hansen, J. F., 1979, *Sociocultural Perspectives on Human Learning: An Introduction to Educational Anthropology*. Englewood Cliffs, New Jersey: Prentice Hall.

Hargreaves, Andy and Leslie N. K. Lo, 2000, The Paradoxical Profession: Teaching at the Turn of the Century, *Prospects*, 30(2): 167–180.

Hargreaves, Andy, 2000, Four Ages of Professionalism and Professional Learning, *Teachers and Teaching*, 6(2): 151–182.

Havighurst, Robert J., 1983, 'Teaching Profession' In: *The New Encyclopedia Britannica*, pp. 9–16, Chicago: Helen Hemingway Publisher.

Hawley, Willis D. and Linda Valli, 1999, 'The Essentials of Effective Professional Development: A New Consensus' In: Darling Hammmond Linda and Gary Sykes (Eds.), 127–150.

Henson, John, 1987, An Evaluation of Aspects of Teacher Professionalism, as Evidenced by Salary and Structure Proposals, *Educational Management Administration Leadership*, 15: 165–170 retrieved from http://ema.sagepub.com on April 13, 2008.

Hergenhahn, B. R., 1988, *An Introduction to Theories of Learning*, New Jersey: Prentice Hall Inc.

Hinai, Al and Ahmed M., 2007, 'The Interplay Between Culture, Teacher Professionalism and Teacher Professional Development at Times of Change' In: Townsend and Bates, (Eds.) *Handbook of Teacher Education, Globalisation, Standards and Professionalism in Times of Change*, pp. 41–52, Dordrecht, Netherlands: Springer.

Hoffman, Jo, 2002, Flexible Grouping Strategies in the Multiage Classroom, *Theory into Practice*, 41(1): 41–47.

Howard, Means James, 1963, Homo Medicus Americanus, *Daedalus*, Fall, 701–724.

Hoyle, Eric, 2001, Teaching: Prestige, Status and Esteem, *Educational Management Administration Leadership*, 29(2): 139–52 retrieved from http://ema.sagepub.com on April 13, 2008.

Hugen, T., Neville T. and Postlethwaite (Eds.), 1985, *The International Encyclopaedia of Education*, New York: Pergamon Press.

Hughes, Everett Cherrington, 1959, Prestige, *The Annals of the American Academy of Political and Social Science*, 325: 45–49.

Hughes, Everett C., 1963, Professions, *Daedalus*, Fall, 655–668.

Illich, Ivan, 1971, *Deschooling Society*, New York: Harper and Row.

Ivie, Stanley D., Roebuck F. and Short R. 2001, Experienced Teachers Insist That Effective Teaching is Primarily a Science, *Education*, 121(3): 519–534.

Jena, S. L. and Damodar Mahaptra, 2003, 'Elementary Education and Early Childhood Care and Education in Orissa' In: Government of Orissa, 2003a, II: 1–106.

Jenny, Lewis M., Timothy Marjoribanks and Marie Pirotta, 2003, Changing Professions—General Practitioners' Perceptions of autonomy on the Frontline, *Journal of Sociology*, 39(1): 44–61, retrieved from http://jos.sagepub.com on July 1, 2008.

Joint World Bank/DFID PSAL Preparation Mission, 2003, *Aide-memoire*, Orissa, February.

Jones, V. and Jones L., 1990, *Comprehensive Classroom Management*, Boston: Allyn & Bacon.

Kabi, T., 1985, Odisare Prathamika Siksara Agragati (Development of Primary Education in Orissa), *Utkal Prasanga*, October: 79–80.

Kabir, H., 1961, *Indian Philosophy of Education*, Bombay: Asia Publishing House.

Kanungo, Trilochan, 2004, 'Agony of Orissa' In: Panda (Ed.), 99–116.

Kaushik, V. K. and Ravi Prakash, 1999, *Sociology of Teaching and Curriculum*, New Delhi: Kanishka.

Khora, Sthabir, 2005, Continuing Low Literacy: The Case of Orissa, *Economic and Political Weekly*, 40(10): 928–930.

Khora, Sthabir, 2008, Teacher Motivation: An Exploration into the Role of Values and Social Support, *Indian Journal of Social Work*, 69(1): 33–44.

Kingdon, Geeta Gandhi and Mohammad Muzammil, 2001, A Political Economy of Education in India-1, The Case of UP, *Economic and Political Weekly*, 36(32), 3052–63.

Kingdon, Geeta Gandhi and Mohammad Muzammil, 2001a, A Political Economy of Education in India-II, The Case of UP, *Economic and Political Weekly*, 36(32), 3178–85.

Kingdon, Geeta Gandhi and Mohammad Muzzamil, 2003, *The Political Economy of Education in India: Teacher Politics in Uttar Pradesh*, New Delhi: Oxford University Press.

Klegon, Douglas, 1978, The Sociology of Professions: An Emerging Perspective, *Work and Occupations*, 5(3): 259–283.

Klette, Kirsti, 2002, Reform Policy and Teacher Professionalism in Four Nordic Countries, *Journal of Educational Change*, 3: 265–282 retrieved from http://ema.sagepub.com on July 1, 2008.

Knight, Christopher, 1984, Teacher Professionalism: Views and Comments, *Educational Management Administration Leadership*, 12: 164–166 retrieved from http://ema.sagepub.com on April 13, 2008.

Korthagen, Fred A. J. and Kessels Jos P. A. M., 1999, Linking Theory and Practice: Changing the Pedagogy of Teacher Education, *Educational Researcher*, 28(4): 4–17, retrieved from http://ema.sagepub.com on July 6, 2008.

Kothari, Brij, P. G. Vijay Sherry Chand and Rajeev Sharma, 2000, *A Review of Primary Education Packages in M.P.*, Ahmedabad: Indian Institute of Management.

Kreidler, W. J., 1984, *Creative Conflict Resolution*, Glenview: Ill Scott Foresman.

Krishnamurti, J., 1978, *Beginnings of Learning*, Middlesex, Harmondsworth, England: Penguin Books.

Larson, M. S., 1977, *The Rise of Professionalism: A Sociological Analysis*, London: University of California Press.

Lee, Jaekyung, 2001, School Reform Initiatives as Balancing Acts: Policy Variation and Educational Convergence among Japan, Korea, England and the United States, *Education Policy Analysis Archives*, 9(13): 14-19 retrieved from http://www.eric.ed.gov/PDFS/ED460966.pdf on March 3, 2011.

Lindgren, H. C., 1976 (5th ed.), *Educational Psychology in the Classroom*, New York: John Wiley & Sons.

Lindsay, Margaret (Ed.), 1961, *New Horizons for the Teaching Profession*, Washington D.C.: National Commission on Teacher Education and Professional Standards.

Lortie, Dan C., 1975, *The School Teacher: A Sociological Study*, Chicago: University of Chicago Press.

Maanen, John Van (Ed.), 1995, *Representation in Ethnography*, New Delhi: Sage Publications.

Maanen, John Van, 1995, 'An End to Innocence: The Ethnography of Ethnography' In: Maanen John Van (Ed.), 1–35.

Mahanti, K. K. and M. N. Kundu, 2003, 'Education of Scheduled Tribe Children' In: Government of Orissa, 2003a: 297–324.

Mahanty, Debasish and Trilochan Tripathy, 2005, Socioeconomic Implications of Gender Earning Differentials: Education Sector in Orissa, *Economic and Political Weekly*, 40(21): 2190.

Mahanty, Manoranjan and Bijoy Kumar Bahidar, 1993, *Orissa Daridra Kanhiki (Why Orissa is poor)*, Cuttack: Orissa Book Store.

Mahanty, J., 1977, Siksara Bigata Pragatisila Dasandhi (The Last Progressive Decade of Education), *Utkal Prasanga*, January: 67–72.

Mahapatra, Bharati, 2003, Going to the School in the Raj: Primary Education in India (1805–1903) With Focus on Orissa, Bhubaneswar: Published By Dr V.B. Shastry, I.R.C. Village.

Mahapatra, J. D., 1988, Odisare Narisiksara Prasara (Development of Education of Women in Orissa), *Utkal Prasanga,* June: 9–10.

Mahapatra, K., 1978, Odisara Punarjanma (Rebirth of Orissa), *Utkal Prasanga,* March/April: 3–7.

Mahapatra, M. C., 1977, *Adhunika Siksa O Odissa (Modern Education and Orissa),* Berhampur: Grantha Mandir.

Mahapatra, P. C., 2003, 'Universal Literacy and Empowerment' In: Government of Orissa, 2003a: 107–126.

Mahanty, K. K. and M. N. Kundu, 2003, 'Education of Scheduled Tribe Children' In: Government of Orissa, 2003a: 297–324.

Majhi, Jadav, 1991, 8th Five-Year Plan, *Utkal Prasanga,* January: 22–24.

Mani, R. S., 1965, *Educational Ideas and Ideals of Eminent Indians,* New Delhi: New Book Society of India.

Manzer, Ronald A., 1970, *Teachers and Politics: The Role of The National Union of Teachers in the Making of Educational Policy in England and Wales since 1944,* Manchester: Manchester University Press.

Marchisan, Marti L., 2001, 'The Write Way', *Intervention in School & Clinic,* 36(3): 154–162.

Maria, Ines Marcondes, 1999, Teacher Education in Brazil, *Journal of Education for Teaching,* 25(3): 203–213.

Martin, Lawn, (Ed.), 1985, *The Politics of Teacher Unionism: International Perspectives,* London: Croom Helm.

Mcclure, Maureen W., 1999, Teaching—the Peculiar Profession: A Review Essay, *Educational Administration Quarterly,* 35: 562–572.

Meher, Rajkishore, 1999, *Development Disparities in a Backward Region (A District Level Analysis),* New Delhi: APH Publishing Corporation.

Meher, Rajkishore and Pasayat Chitrasen, 2004, 'Development Scenario of Orissa Districts – A Temporal Analysis' In: Pasayat, 1–43.

Mehta, Arun C., 2004, *Elementary Education in India: Analytical Report,* NIEPA and Department of Elementary Education and Literacy, Ministry of Human Resource Development, Government of India.

Metzger, Walter P., 1987 A Spectre is Haunting American Scholars: The Spectre of "Professionism", *Educational Researcher,* 16(6): 10–19.

MHRD, 1990, *Report of the Committee on Minimum Levels of Learning* accessed from http://education.nic.in/cd50years/r/2S/99/2S990101.htm on October 10.

—, 1996, *Development of Education in India 1995–96 with Special Reference to Teacher Education*, New Delhi: Ministry of Human Resource Development.

—, 2006, *ADEPTS (Advancement of Educational Performance through Teacher Support)*, an MHRD-UNICEF Initiative, June 2006–January 2007.

Mishra, Baidyanath et al., 1991, *Economic Development of Orissa*, Cuttack: Vidyapuri.

Mishra, Baidyanath, 1990, *Agricultural Development: Problems and Prospects*, New Delhi: Ashish Publication.

Mishra, C., 1980, Adivasi Samasya Upare Mora Nijaswa Matamata (My Opinion on the Problem of the Tribes), *Utkal Prasanga*, September: 31–35.

Mishra, J. K. and Sivamurthy M., 1963, Primary and Secondary Educational Prospects in Orissa, *Asian Economic Review*, 5(2): 180–186.

Mishra, P., 2002, *Study on State Finance of Elementary Education (Sponsored by The Orissa Primary Education Programme Authority)*, Bhubaneswar: Xavier Institute of Management.

Mishra, Surendra Nath, 2003, 'Nutritional Support to Primary Education (Mid Day Meal Programme) in Orissa' In: Government of Orissa, 2003a: 362–379.

—, 2004, *Child Nutrition and Primary Education*, New Delhi: Anmol Publication.

Misra, B. B., 1961, *Indian Middle Classes: Their Growth in Modern Times*, London: Oxford University Press.

Miyan, Mahammad, 2004, *Professionalisation of Teacher Education*, New Delhi: Mittal Publications.

Mohanty, Bimal, 2004, 'Fiscal Situation in Orissa: A Review' In: Panda Rajkishore (Ed.), 117–150.

Mohanty, Mohit Mohan, 2003, 'Mathematics Education in the Schools of Orissa' In: Government of Orissa, 2003a: 349–361.

Montessori, M., 1984, *The Absorbent Mind*, New York: Dell Publishing Company Inc.

Moore, Alex, 2004, *The Good Teacher: Dominant Discourses in Teaching and Teacher Education*, London: Routledge Falmer.

Morris, P. and J. Williamson, 1998, Teacher Education in the Asia-Pacific Region: A Comparative Analysis, *Asia-Pacific Journal of Teacher Education and Development*, 1: 17–27.

Mukherjee, H. M., 1962, *Education for Fullness*, Bombay: Asia Publishing House.

Mukherji, S. N. (Ed.), 1968, *Education of Teachers in India,* (Vol.1), New Delhi: S. Chand & Co.

NCERT, 1977, *Survey of Teacher Education at Elementary Level,* New Delhi: National Council of Educational Research and Training.

—, 1990, *Fifth All India Educational Survey,* New Delhi: National Institute of Educational Research and Training.

—, 1998, *Sixth All India Educational Survey,* New Delhi: National Institute of Educational Research and Training.

—, 2000, *The National Curriculum Framework,* New Delhi: National Council of Educational Research and Training.

—, 2005, *National Curriculum Framework,* Accessed from http://www.ncert.nic.in/html/pdf/schoolcurriculum/framework on October 10.

Nair, V. S., 1987, *Swami Vivekananda—the Educator,* New Delhi: Sterling Publishing Pvt. Ltd.

Nash, P., Kazamias A and H. Perkonson, 1965, *The Educated Man: Studies in the History of Educational Thought,* London: John Wiley & Sons Inc.

National Council of Teachers of Mathematics (NCTM), 1989, *Curriculum and Evaluation Standards for School Mathematics,* Reston, VA: NCTM.

National Writing Project 1990, *Perceptions of Writing,* Edinburgh: Nelson.

Nayak, Bibhudatta, 2004, 'Reviewing Orissa Economy: The Areas for Structural Change' In: Panda Rajkishore (Ed.), 209–228.

NCT, 1986, *The Teacher and Society—Report of The National Commission on Teachers- 1,* New Delhi: Controller of Publications, Government of India.

NCTE, 1998, *Competency Based and Commitment Oriented Teacher Education for Quality School Education (Pre-Service Education),* New Delhi: National Council of Teacher Education.

—, 1999, *Profile of Teacher Educators,* New Delhi: National Council of Teacher Education.

NCTE, UNESCO, 1999, *Education of Teachers: The SAARC Experience,* New Delhi: National Council of Teacher Education.

Neave, Guy, 1992, *The Teaching Nation: Prospects for Teachers in the European Community,* Oxford: Pergamon Press.

Nelson, Howard F, 1994, *International Comparison of Teacher Salaries and Conditions of Employment,* Washington DC: National Centre for Education Statistics.

Nias, Jennifer, 1999, 'Primary Teaching as a Culture of Care' In: Prosser (Ed.), 66–81.

Nunes, Terezinha and Peter Bryant, 1996, *Children Doing Mathematics*, Oxford, UK: Blackwell.

Noordegraaf, Mirko, 2007, From "Pure" to "Hybrid" Professionalism: Present-day Professionalism in Ambiguous Public Domains, *Administration & Society*, 39: 761–785.

Nurullah, S. and J. P. Naik, 1943, *History of Education in India during the British Period*, Bombay: Macmillan and Co.

OECD, 2005, *Teachers Matter: Attracting, Developing and Retaining Effective Teachers*, Paris: Organization for Economic Co-operation and Development.

OPEPA, 2001, *DPEP Annual Report 2000-01, 16th Joint Review Mission (14 Nov–2 Dec 2001) Part II State Reports*, Bhubaneswar: Orissa Primary Education Program Authority.

Paine, S. *et al.*, 1983, *Structuring Your Classroom for Academic Success*, Champaign, Illinois: Research Press.

Palmer, Jesse, 2001, Conflict Resolution: Strategies for the Elementary Classroom, *Social Studies*, 92(2): 65–69.

Panda, K. C., 2003, 'Secondary and Vocational Education' In: Government of Orissa, 2003a: 127–239.

Panda, Manoj, 2004, 'Economic Growth and Poverty during the 1990s: Did Orissa Benefit from the Reforms?' In: Panda Rajkishore (Ed.), 167–182.

Panda, Rajkishore (Ed.), 2004, *Reviewing Orissa Economy: Opportunities and Areas of Action*, New Delhi: A.P.H. Publishing Corporation.

Pareek, Ramesh, 1996, *Role of Teaching Profession*, Jaipur: Printwell (in association with Rupa).

Parkay, Forrest W. and Beverly Hardcastle Stanford, 1992, *Becoming a Teacher: Accepting the Challenge of a Profession*, London: Allyn & Bacon.

Pasayat, Chitrasen, 2004, *Rural Development of Orissa: Problems and Potentials*, New Delhi: Mohit Publication.

Pathak, Avijit, 2002, *Social Implications of Schooling*, Delhi: Rainbow Publishers.

Pattnaik, D. P., 2003, 'Enhancing Language Abilities and Competencies' In: Government of Orissa, 2003a: 325–331.

Patnaik, P. K., 'Promoting Core Compentence, Capacity Building of Teachers, Staff Development and Good Governance' In: Government of Orissa, 2003a: 240–263.

Petress, Ken, 2001, The Ethics of Student Classroom Silence, *Journal of Instructional Psychology*, 28(2): 104–107.

Pfadenhauer, Michaela, 2006, Crisis or Decline? Problems of Legitimation and Loss of Trust in Modern Professionalism, *Current Sociology*, 54(4): 565–578.

Pollard, Andrew, 1987, 'Primary School Teachers and Their Colleagues' In: Delamont S. (Ed.): 100–119.

Porter, A. C., Brophy, J., 1988, Synthesis of Research on Good Teaching: Insights from the Work of the Institute for Research on Teaching, *Educational Leadership*, 45(4): 74–85.

Pratte, Richard and John L. Rury, 1988, Professionalism, Autonomy and Teachers *Educational Policy*, 2(1): 71–89 retrieved from http://epx.sagepub.com on April 22, 2008.

Preissle, Judith, Grant, Linda, 1998, Exploring The Ethnography of Education, *Journal of Contemporary Ethnography*, 27(1): 3–9.

Prosser, Jon (Ed.), 1999, *School Culture*, London: Paul Chapman Publishing Ltd.

Rajput, J. S. and K. Walia, 2002, *Teacher Education in India*, New Delhi: Sterling Publishers Pvt. Ltd.

Rao, K. Sudha (Ed.), 2002, *Educational Policies in India: Analysis and Review of Promise and Performance*, Delhi: National Institute of Educational Planning and Administration.

Rath, S. N., 1977, *The Development of the Welfare State in Orissa (1950–60)*, Cuttack: S. Chand & Company Ltd.

Reddy, K. Narasimha, 1984, *Students, Teachers and Parents: Interactions in Educational Settings*, Delhi: Ajanta Publications.

Richardson, Robert G., 1983, 'History of Medicine' In: *The New Encyclopedia Britannica*, pp. 823–841, Chicago: Helen Hemingway Publisher.

Rowan, Brian, 1994, Comparing Teachers' Work with Work in other Occupations: Notes on the Professional Status of Teaching, *Educational Researcher*, 23(6): 4–17 retrieved from http://ema.sagepub.com on April 21, 2008.

Rubin, L. J., 1985, *Artistry in Teaching*, New York: Random House.

Sabharwal, Virinder K., 2002, 'Staff Development: Teacher Training' In: Rao (Ed.): 235–260.

Samal, J. K., 1984, *History of Education in Orissa: 1905–1936*, Calcutta: Punthi Pustak.

Samantaray, N., 1975, Swatantra Odissa Pradesa Gathanara Sankhipta Parichaya (A Brief Introduction of Establishment of Separate Orissa Province), *Utkal Prasanga*, April: 3–12.

Sarangapani, Padma, 2003, *Constructing School Knowledge: An Ethnography of Learning in an Indian Village*, New Delhi: Sage Publications.

Sawyer, Geoffrey, 1983, 'Legal Profession' In: *The New Encyclopedia Britannica*, pp. 779–784, Chicago: Helen Hemingway Publisher.

Sciulli, David, 2005, Continental Sociology of Professions Today: Conceptual Contributions, *Current Sociology*, 53(6): 915–942 retrieved from http://csi.sagepub.com on July 1, 2008.

Senapati, R., 1996, *Odissa Sasana O Pragati (Orissa Administration and Progress)*, Binod Bihari, Cuttack: Friends Publishers.

Seshadri, C., 2000, *Year 2000 Assessment: Education for All-Primary Teacher Training in EFA Decade*, New Delhi: National Institute of Educational Planning and Administration.

Shah, Beena, 1995, *Determinants of Teacher Effectiveness*, Ambala Cantt: The Indian Publication.

Shanker, Albert, 1985, In Support of Teachers: The Making of a Profession, *NASSP Bulletin*, 69: 93–99 retrieved from http://bul.sagepub.com on April 22, 2008.

Sharma, Rashmi, 2000, Decentralization, Professionalism and the School System in India, *Economic and Political Weekly*, 35(42): 3765–3774.

Sharma, Ramnath and Rajendra Kumar Sharma, 2004, *History of Education in India*, Delhi: Atlantic Publishers.

Shen, Anping, 1994, Teacher Education and National Development in China, *Journal of Education*, 176(2): 57–71.

Shores, R. E., et al., 1993, Classroom Influences on Aggressive and Disruptive Behaviors of Students With Emotional and Behavioral Disorders, *Focus on Exceptional Children*, 26(2): 1–10.

Shulman, Lee S., 2004, *The Wisdom of Practice: Essays on Teaching, Learning, and Learning to Teach*, San Francisco: Jossey-Bass.

Siegrist, Hannes, 2002, Professionalization/Professions in History, *International Encyclopedia of the Social and Behavioral Sciences*, Amsterdam: Elsevier Science.

Sikes, J Patricia, Lynda Measor and Peter Woods, 1985, *Teacher Careers: Crises and Continuities*, London: The Falmer Press.

Singh, B., 1979, *Adivasi Pilankapain Vikasa Jojana* (Development Plan for Tribal Children), *Utkal Prasanga*, April: 9–11.

Singh, L. C. and P. C. Sharma, 1995, *Teacher Education and the Teacher*, New Delhi: Vikas Publications.

Singh, R. P., 1984, *The Teachers in India*, New Delhi: National Publishing House.

Singh, R. P., 2003, 'Toward a New Look at Teacher Education in India' In: Tilak J. B. G., (Ed.), *Education, Society and Development: National and International Perspectives*, 367–384, Delhi: APH Publishing Corporation.

Siniscalco, Maria Teresa, 2002, *A Statistical Profile of the Teaching Profession*, Paris: ILO and UNESCO.

Smith, Ralph J., 1983, 'Engineering' In: *The New Encyclopedia Britannica*, pp. 860–862, Chicago: Helen Hemingway Publisher.

Sockett, Hugh T., 1996, Teachers for the 21st Century: Redefining Professionalism, *NASSP Bulletin*, 80, 22–29 retrieved from http://bul.sagepub.com on April 13, 2008.

Spackman, Frances, 1991, *Teachers' Professional Responsibilities*, London: David Fulton.

Sparks and Loucks-Horsley S., 1995, 'Five Models of Staff Development' In: Ornstein A. C. and L. S. Behar (Eds.), 1995, *Contemporary Issues in Curriculum*, pp. 293–318, Needham Heights, Mass: Allyn & Bacon.

Spindler, George and Louise (Eds.), 1987, *Interpretative Ethnography of Education: At Home and Abroad*, London: Lawrence Erlbaum Associates Publishers.

Spindler, George and Louise, 1987, 'Teaching and Learning How to Do the Ethnography of Education' In: Spindler, George and Louise (Eds.), pp. 17–36.

Sprick, R. and L. M. Howard, 1995, *The Teacher's Encyclopedia of Behaviour Management: 100 Problems/500 Plans*, Sopris West: Longwont, CO.

Sri Aurobindo International Institute of Educational Research, 1988, *The Good Teacher and the Pupil*, Auroville: Sri Aurobindo International Institute of Educational Research.

Srivastava, G. N. Prakash, 2004, *Perspectives in Teacher Education*, New Delhi: Concept Publishing.

Srivastava, R. S., 1984, *Contemporary Indian Philosophy*, Ranchi: Sharad Publications.

Stefanich, Gregory P. and Bell Louise C., 1985, A Dynamic Model for Classroom Discipline, *NASSP Bulletin*; 69: 19–25 retrieved from http://bul.sagepub.com on April 19, 2008.

Stewart, Susan C. and William H. Evans, 1997, Setting the Stage for Success: Assessing the Instructional Environment, *Preventing School Failure*, 41(2): 53–56.

Stinnett, T. M., 1968, *Professional Problems of Teachers*, London: The Macmillan Company.

Strauss, Gerge, 1963, Professionalism and Occupational Associations, *Industrial Relations,* 3: 8–9.

Swami, S. Sreedhar, 1980, *Teacher Organization in India*, Delhi and Kanpur: All India Federation of Education Association.

Sykes, Gary, 1991, In Defense of Teacher Professionalism as a Policy Choice, *Educational Policy*, 5(2): 137–149 retrieved from http://epx.sagepub.com on April 13, 2008.

Tankersley, Melody, 1995, A Group-Oriented Contingency Management Program, *Preventing School Failure,* 40(1): 19–24.

Thapan, M., 1991, *Life at School: An Ethnographic Study*. Delhi: Oxford University Press.

The American Academy of Arts and Sciences, 1963, The Professions, *Daedalus,* Fall.

Thomas, Elwyn, 1993, 'The Professional Development and Training of Teacher Educators' In: Thomas Elwyn *et al.*, 1–19.

Thomas, Elwyn et al., 1993, *Professional Development of Teachers: Policy, and Practice in Initial Teacher Training,* London: Commonwealth Secretariat.

Tilak, J. B. G., 2003, *Globalisation and Challenge for Education,* New Delhi: SHIPRA, National Institute of Educational Planning and Administration.

Tilak, J. B. G. (Ed.), 2003a, *Education, Society and Development: National and International Perspectives,* Delhi: APH Publishing Corporation.

Townsend, Tony and Richard Bates (Eds.), 2007, *Handbook of Teacher Education, Globalisation, Standards and Professionalism in Times of Change,* Dordrecht, Netherlands: Springer.

Travens, R. 1968, 'Analysis of the Characteristics of Children in the Montessori Method' In: Frost (Ed.), 25–63.

Tripathi, P., 1977, Praudhasiksara Nabadigaanta (New Vistas in Adult Education), *Utkal Prasanga,* February: 15–21.

Tyagi, R. S. and P. C. Mahapatra, 2000, *Educational Administration in Orissa – Structure, Processes and Future,* New Delhi: National Institute of Educational Planning and Administration,.

Umar, Sahid, 2006, *Orissa Prasanga,* Bhubaneswar: Ayan Prakasan.

UNESCO, 2000, Professionalism in Teaching, *Prospects* (114), 30(2): June.

UNESCO, 2006, Education Counts: Benchmarking Progress in 19 WEI Countries, *World Education Indicators, 2006.*

Urbanski, Adam, 1998, Teacher Professionalism and Teacher Accountability: Toward a more Genuine Teaching Profession, *Educational Policy,* 12(4): 449–457 retrieved from http://epx.sagepub.com on April 22, 2008.

U.S. Department of Education, Office of Postsecondary Education, 2002, *Meeting the Highly Qualified Teachers Challenge: The Secretary's Annual Report on Teacher Quality*, Washington DC.

Verderber, Kathleen S. and Rudolph F. Verderber, 1986, *Interact: Using Interpersonal Communication Skills. Belmont*, CA: Wadsworth.

Villa, Paula R. (Ed.), 2006, *Teacher, Change and Development*, New York: Nava Science Publishers.

Villegas-Reimers Eleanora, 2003, *Teacher Professional Development: An International Review of Literature*, Paris: International Institute for Educational Planning.

Vollmer, Howard M. and Donald L. Mills, 1966, *Professionalizaiton*, New Jersey: Prentice Hall Inc.

Walia, K. (Ed.), 2003, *Teacher Commitment*, New Delhi: National Council of Educational Research and Training.

Waller, W., 1932, *The Sociology of Teaching*, New York: Wiley.

Weber, C., 1960, *Basic Philosophies of Education*, New York: Reinhardt & Co.

Weber, Max, 1994, 'Class, Status, Party' In: Grusky David, *Social Stratification in Sociological Perspectives*, pp. 113–121, Oxford: Westview Press.

Weber, Sandra and Claudia Mitchell, 1999, 'Teacher Identity in Popular Culture' In: Prosser Jon (Ed.), pp. 161–178.

Weinert, Franz E., Friedrich-W. Schrader and Andreas Helmke, 1990, Educational Expertise: Closing the Gap between Educational Research and Classroom Practice, *School Psychology International*, 11: 163–180 retrieved from http://spi.sagepub.com on April 19, 2008.

Willis, Paul, 1977, *Learning to Labor: How Working Class Kids Get Working Class Jobs*, Columbia University Press.

Wolcott, Harry F., 1995, 'Making a Study More Ethnographic' In: Maanen (Ed.), 79–111.

Working Group Report on Elementary and Adult Education, 2001, *Tenth Five Year Plan, 2002–07*, Department of Elementary Education and Literacy, Ministry of Human Resource Development, Government of India.

World Bank, 1997, *Primary Education in India*, Delhi: World Bank and Allied Publishers.

—, 2003, *A Review of Educational Progress and Reform in the District Primary Education Program (Phases I and II)*, The World Bank, accessed from http://www-wds.worldbank.org/external/ on October 10, 2008.

Wueste, Daniel E. (Ed.), 1991, *Professional Ethics and Social Responsibility*, Lanham Maryland: Rowman and Littlefield Publishers Inc.

Yang, Daping and Jianqiang Wu, 1999, Some Issues in the Reform and Development of Teacher Education and Training in China, *Teacher Development*, 3(2): 157–172.

Ziv, Avner, 1979, The Teacher's Sense of Humor and the Atmosphere in the Classroom, *School Psychology International*, 1: 21–23 retrieved from http://spi.sagepub.com on April 19, 2008.

INDEX

adult education
  in Orissa, 100–3
Akai, Hisako, 55
Alexander, Robin, 68, 114, 117, 150
Althusser, L., 16
Anand, S.P., 126
Anderson, Lorin W., 43, 125, 127
Anitha, B.K., 126
Apple, Michael W., 18, 19, 23, 24, 43, 44
Archer, M., 18

Bacharach, Samuel B., Scott C. Bauer and Sharon Conley, 166
Barber, Bernard, 31
Barnard, H., 47, 48, 49, 50
Bate, Tony, Bob Gough and Peter Stammers, 67
Bates, Richard, 41, 177
Batra, Poonam, 69
Behar, S.C., 36, 180
Ben-Peretz, Miriam, 39
Bernstein, B., 22
Bottery Mike and Nigel Wright, 43
Bourdieu, Pierre, 14
Burbules, Nicholas C. and Kathleen Densmore, 39, 43
Burke, Andrew, 23

Caldwell, Brian J., 42, 114
Carr, David, 26, 31, 36, 40, 43
Chambliss, J.J., 2, 10, 12
Chopra, R.K., 114
Clarke, Prema, 114, 116
Collins, Randall, 34
Curtis, S.J. and M. E.A. Boultwood, 2, 3, 6, 12, 22

Das, D.P., 91
Day, Christopher, 43, 44, 177, 178, 179
Demaine, J., 14, 22
Devi, R.S., 50, 51
Dewey, J., 3, 8, 11
Dhar, T.N., 36
Di Giulio, R.C., 43, 150
Dreben, R., 14, 22
Dwibedi, Jugala Kishore, 88

education person, 4
  qualifications of an, 4
education, 1
  aims of, 1
  and environment, 6–8
  and experience, 10–11
  definition of, 21–24
  goals of, 4
  in Orissa, development of, 86–113
  theoretical perspectives on, 1: philosophical, 1–13; sociological, 13–20
educative work, 12
  stages of, 12
environment, 8
  importance of, in education, 6–8
Evetts, Julia, 26, 33, 36, 40, 42

Fenn, Richard K., 32
freedom in education, 9
Freire, P., 24
Fwu, Bih-Jen and Hsiou-Huai Wang, 67–68

Gandhi, M.K., 2
Ghadei, P.C., 93, 107
Gideonse, Hendrik D., 43
Giroux, Henry, 19, 24
Gleeson, Denis and David Knights, 38, 145
good teacher, 42
Goodson, Ivor, 40, 169
Gordon, June A., 75

Govinda, R. and Rashmi Diwan, 146
Goyal, U.C. and R. K. Chopra, 70, 114

Hall, Roland, 22
Hallack, Jacques and Muriel Poisson, 43, 126
Hammmond, Darling Linda and Gary Sykes, 43
Hansen, J. Merrell, 133, 139
Hargreaves, Andy and Leslie N. K. Lo, 44
Hargreaves, Andy, 37, 41
Hawley, Willis D. and Linda Valli, 66
Henson, John, 43
Hinai, A.L. and Ahmed M., 40, 41, 44, 177
Hoyle, Eric, 37, 42, 43, 74
Hugen, T., Neville T. and Postlethwaite, 10
Hughes, Everett Cherrington, 28, 75
humanism
as the aim of education, 3
hybrid professionalism, 34
ingredients of, 35

Illich, Ivan, 17
Ivie, Stanley D., Roebuck F. and R. Short, 133

Jenny, Lewis M., T. Marjoribants and Marie Pirotta, 34

Kingdon, Geeta Gandhi and Mohammad Muzammil, 44, 81, 168
Klegon, Douglas, 32, 38, 39
Klette, Kirsti, 43
Knight, Christopher, 43
Korthagen, Fred A. J. and P.A.M. Kessels Jos, 135
Krishnamurti, J., 8

Larson, M.S., 30, 31, 36, 37, 40
learning
stages in, 12
liberal education, 2
Lortie, Dan C., 179

Mahanty, J., 105
Mahapatra, M.C., 87, 88
Mani, R.S., 3, 4, 5, 9, 12, 23
Manzer, Ronald A., 76
Mcclure, Maureen W., 36
Mehta, Arun C., 57
Metzger, Walter P., 32, 40
Misra, B.B., 38
Montessori, M., 7, 10, 22, 23
Moore, Alex, 45
Morris, P. and J. Williamson, 61, 71
Mukherjee, H.M., 2, 5, 11, 22

Nash, P., Kazamias, A and H. Perkonson, 23
National Council for Teacher Education, 56
National Policy on Education, 1986, 54
components of, 54
Nelson, Howard F., 61, 68
Nias, Jennifer, 37
Noordegraaf, Mirko, 34, 36
Nunes, Terezinha and Peter Bryant, 44
Nurullah, S. and J.P. Naik, 51, 53

occupational esteem, 73
occupational prestige, 73
occupational status, 73
Orissa, 86
education of SCs/STs in, 98–100
elementary education in, 96–98
school education in, growth in, 87–96

Pfadenhauer, Michaela, 32, 34
politicization of teachers, 81
in India, 81
Pollard, Andrew, 166
Pratte, Richard and John L. Rury, 39, 43
profession, 26, 40, 46
characteristics of, 26–32
concept of, 26, taxonomic approach to understand the, 26; origin of, 46
constituents of, 40
professional teacher(s), 41, 124
facets of: subject knowledge, 130–33; teaching skills, 133–39; discipline, 139–40
imperatives for a, 41–42
perspectives of, on authority, 166–68; on teacher organizations, 168–70; on awards, 170–71; on salary, 171–73

professionalism, 26, 40, 42, 46, 85, 145, 178
and the contemporary society, 34
as an ideology, 40
aspects, 40, 41
concept of, 26, origin of, 46
constituents of, 40
in teaching, 46
professionalization, 40, 42
professionism, 40

Rath, S. N., 91, 92
Rowan, Brian, 36, 43
Rubin, L.J., 133

Sabharwal, Virinder K., 63
Samal, J.K., 88, 89, 90
Sarangapani, Padma, 114
school education
in Orissa, 87: in pre-independence period, 87–90; in post-independence period, 90-96
school system, 47
Sciulli, David, 26, 33, 38, 42
Senapati, R., 88, 92
Seshadri, C., 71
Shanker, Albert, 43
Sharma, Rashmi, 37
Shen, Anping, 68
Shulman, Lee S., 114, 130, 178
Sikes J Patricia, Lynda Measor and Peter Woods, 166
Singh, R.P., 27, 130, 144
Siniscalco, Maria Teresa, 67, 70, 71, 72
Sockett, Hugh T., 43, 45
Spackman, Frances, 36, 41, 77
Sparks and Loucks-Horsley S., 63
status
concept of, 72
of teacher, 74–76
Stinnett, T.M., 36, 42, 76, 77
Strauss, Gerge, 41, 104
Swami, S. Sreedhar, 44, 78, 80, 81, 82, 83
Sykes, Gary, 36, 43

teacher absenteeism, 126
in India, 126–27

teacher education
history of, 47–50, in India, 50–60
in India, 50: before independence, 50–52; after independence, 52–60
in Orissa, 103–8
in Western countries, role of state in, 60–76
teacher professionalism, 40, 85, 114, 177
ages of, 41
and school infrastructure, 146–52
and the school sub-culture, 150–52
and the teacher sub-culture, 152–55
facets of: subject knowledge, 130–33;
teaching skills, 133–39; discipline style, 139–40
in rural areas, 125–29
in the Indian context, 43–45
in the Western context, 42–43
phases of, 40–41
state and, relationship between, 47
teachers' organizations, 76
in India, 77, evolution of, 77–80; and strikes, 81–83
in the West, 76–77, 83–84
teaching standards
in India, 69
in the West, 68–69
teaching
and other professions, difference between, 37–38
as a profession, 36–37
method of, 12
Thapan, M., 114, 115
Tripathi, P., 101

Urbanski, Adam, 43, 170

Villegas-Reimers, Eleanora, 62, 64, 65, 66
Vollmer, Howard M. and Donald L. Mills, 32, 40

Walia, K., 60, 127, 144
Weber, Max, 72, 76
Weinert, Franz E., Friedrich-W. Schrader and Andreas Helmke, 114
Willis, Paul, 19
Wueste, Daniel E., 26